The Sexual Imperative in the Novels of Sir Henry Rider Haggard

The Sexual Imperative in the Novels of Sir Henry Rider Haggard

Richard Reeve

ANTHEM PRESS

Anthem Press
An imprint of Wimbledon Publishing Company
www.anthempress.com

This edition first published in UK and USA 2020
by ANTHEM PRESS
75–76 Blackfriars Road, London SE1 8HA, UK
or PO Box 9779, London SW19 7ZG, UK
and
244 Madison Ave #116, New York, NY 10016, USA

First published in the UK and USA by Anthem Press 2018

Copyright © Richard Reeve 2020

The moral right of the authors has been asserted.

All rights reserved. Without limiting the rights under copyright reserved above,
no part of this publication may be reproduced, stored or introduced into
a retrieval system, or transmitted, in any form or by any means
(electronic, mechanical, photocopying, recording or otherwise),
without the prior written permission of both the copyright
owner and the above publisher of this book.

British Library Cataloguing-in-Publication Data
A catalogue record for this book is available from the British Library.

Library of Congress Cataloging-in-Publication Data
Library of Congress Control Number: 2019954190

ISBN-13: 978-1-78527-255-4 (Pbk)
ISBN-10: 1-78527-255-1 (Pbk)

This title is also available as an e-book.

FOR MONIQUE

CONTENTS

Acknowledgements		ix
	Introduction	1
Chapter One	The Sexual Imperative	5
Chapter Two	The Origins of Haggard's Fictional Writing	11
Chapter Three	The Early Novels (1884–95): Youthful Anger	41
Chapter Four	The New Woman, Female Self-Sacrifice and Spirituality (1887–1901)	77
Chapter Five	Spiritual Love and Sexual Renunciation (1899–1908)	99
Chapter Six	The Final Fiction: Spiritual Consolation and the Dictates of the Sexual Imperative (1909–30)	125
Chapter Seven	Summation: A Personal Odyssey	155
Appendix: Plot Summaries		165
Notes		173
Bibliography		189
Index		195

ACKNOWLEDGEMENTS

I would like to record my sincere thanks to John Holmes and Andrew Nash for their unfailing encouragement and advice during the conception and gestation of this book; to Stephen Coan for his kind suggestions on some South African aspects of my research; and to Adrian Poole for his advice on initiating the doctorate that spawned the book. I am grateful also to Nada Cheyne for kindly agreeing that I might use quotations from Haggard's letters and his Rough Diary; to Robert Langenfeld for allowing me to draw, in Chapter Four, on material from my article 'H. Rider Haggard and the New Woman: A Difference in the Genre in *Jess* and *Beatrice*', published in *English Literature in Transition 1880–1920*, 59.2 (2016): 153–74, and to Oxford University Press for their permission to draw, in Chapter Two, on material from my article 'Henry Rider Haggard's Debt to Anthony Trollope: Dr Therne and Dr Thorne', published in *Notes and Queries*, 261.2 (June 2016): 274–78.

Finally, I acknowledge with affection the encouragement, practical advice and forbearance of my family as the book gradually took shape.

INTRODUCTION

Criticism of Rider Haggard's fiction has traditionally tended to focus heavily upon his early romances published between 1885 and 1892, especially *King Solomon's Mines* (1885) and *She* (1887) and, at least in recent years, to centre on their political and psychological resonances. Very little critical attention has been given to those eleven of his fictional works which are defined as novels, as opposed to romances, in the frontispiece of his books of fiction published after 1904. For the purposes of this book I shall adhere to this categorisation. In the last twenty years, very few books dedicated solely to Haggard have been produced, criticism of his work being vested mainly in chapters in wider books and in journal articles. Commentators, including Sigmund Freud, have recognized the psychosexual aspects of some of the earlier romances and have observed particularly that *She* derives in part from its author's personal emotional geography. Wendy Katz has proposed that Haggard's works 'are in fact a giant repository of his own attitudes'.[1] These convincing readings of a pervasive but, at least sometimes, unconscious outworking of personal issues, often sexual ones, in the plots, settings and imagery of some of Haggard's romances are well argued. However, there has been no detailed exploration of the more obvious, and plainly conscious, treatment in virtually all his novels of emotional and sexual relationships that have their origin in his own experiences – and the connection in this respect between Haggard's novels and his romances.

While Haggard himself makes no direct reference to any link between his personal experiences and his fiction, he does acknowledge that his most familiar romance hero Allan Quatermain is 'only myself set in a variety of imagined situations, thinking my thoughts and looking at life through my eyes'.[2] And, in a passage in *She*, Haggard makes some significant observations on the relationship between the imagination, or fiction, and fact. The explorer Holly has just described seeing the tomb of two young lovers, with its carved epitaph, 'Wedded in Death', and has imagined for them a background suggestive of that of Haggard and his first love, Lilly Jackson. Haggard continues:

> Let him who reads forgive the intrusion of a dream into a history of fact […] besides who shall say what proportion of fact, past, present, or to come, may lie in the imagination? What is imagination? Perhaps it is the shadow of the intangible truth, perhaps it is the soul's thought.[3]

Holly's apology for the intrusion of dream upon fact is of course a clever inversion by Haggard of the point he really wants to make – that in his fiction he sometimes represents personal fact. And in his novels, where the focus on the theme of the sexual imperative is at its most unrelieved, the frequent intervention of the narrator, whose views seem to embody those of Haggard towards his personal experiences, passing moral judgement on the characters, is a clear indication of a deep personal interest on the part of the author in the issues his books present. Lilias Haggard, in her biography of her father, does not directly consider the relationship between his life and his fiction, but she does comment that 'the deep emotional experiences, his loves and his tragedies [...] remained active, insistent, his daily companions, until the hour of his death'.[4] Haggard's nephew Godfrey, in the foreword to Lilias's book, records of his uncle that 'his novels were his principal outlet. He gave expression in his writing to the thoughts that overflowed his mind'.[5] By 'novels', Godfrey here is almost certainly referring to all of Haggard's fictional work. And, writing in this family biography, Godfrey is in all probability giving voice to a view that was generally held by the family. There is little doubt that both Haggard and his close relatives were very well aware of the connection between his fiction and what he had experienced personally. Although, perhaps more exactly, the connection was between Haggard's fiction and his recollection and interpretation of what he had experienced. Sir John Kotze, a judge for whom Haggard worked in the Transvaal and with whom he maintained a long friendship, writes of Haggard in his autobiography:

> His was an extraordinary mind. He was emotional and much given to romancing. His imagination impelled him into a world of fancy which for the time had complete hold of his sense, and hence he described as fact what was mere fiction.[6]

Kotze's fascinating side-lighting of Haggard's deeply emotional nature further reinforces the argument that he tended to fictionalize his personal experiences.

Haggard's novels have received comparatively little attention, certainly not over the last thirty years. In 1960 Morton Cohen observed the personal elements in *Dawn* and *The Witch's Head*, claiming that Haggard used the latter as 'a device by which he can compensate psychologically for the blows he had to suffer in earlier years'.[7] Some twenty years later D. S. Higgins covered the novels chronologically in his biography of Haggard[8] but, while he acknowledges the autobiographical resonances in some of them, he does not consider in any detail the relationship between them. More recently, Lindy Stiebel has noted, without further exploration and without differentiating between the novels and romances, that many of Haggard's male protagonists 'yearn eternally after their irrevocably lost first love', and she has connected this observation with Haggard's lifelong love for Lilly Jackson.[9] Norman Etherington writes that Haggard used his novels 'to relive vicariously the sufferings of his early disappointments in love' but considers that 'when he dealt with problems special to himself [...] his books were pedestrian'.[10] And in an earlier article, Etherington contends that Haggard's first five novels are interesting primarily 'because of their suppression of the elemental themes unleashed in [his] romances'.[11] Although Etherington observes that 'there was a gradual convergence between the themes of the later romances and the obsessive concerns of Haggard's realistic novels', he considers that these themes render these romances inferior to the early romances in which 'Haggard marches virtuous men into the wilderness where they reveal hidden impulses and confront the awesome mysteries of their deepest inner selves'.[12] While, then, Etherington identifies the personal element in some of Haggard's novels, he considers only seven of them in total, and these briefly, and he does not pursue and document the detail of the connection between the fact of Haggard's own experiences and the fictional representations in his books. And while he notes a thematic similarity between the novels and some of Haggard's later romances, he fails to observe an identical likeness in the early romances. Moreover, he judges that his entertainment of issues deeply personal to himself vitiates Haggard's fiction. No systematic attempt exists at detailed textual exegesis of Haggard's novels in order to document the regularity with which he creates fictional representations of the same themes concerning the sexual imperative, how his consideration of these themes develops throughout these books and the extent to which they connect with Haggard's profound personal concerns. Neither, crucially, has there been any appreciation of the way in which such a consideration of his novels illuminates his romances, revealing an identical concern in them with the key themes of the novels. The objective of the present book, then, is to explore these neglected questions and in doing so to consider whether they have anything to contribute to the literary assessment of Haggard's fiction.

The book accumulates its argument through a comparative reading of Haggard's early novels – *Dawn* (1884), *The Witch's Head* (1884), *Colonel Quaritch V. C.* (1888) and *Joan Haste* (1895) – which deal with the damaging capacity of the sexual imperative and the impact of sexual betrayal, but which also depict the inspiring, quasi-divine and eternal nature of genuine love; of *Jess* (1887) and *Beatrice* (1890), which explore the subject of sexual relations outside marriage and illustrate the spiritual aspects of genuine love; of *Stella Fregelius* (1904) and *The Way of the Spirit* (1906), which explore the relationship between the sexual and spiritual aspects of love and consider the feasibility of a renunciation of sexual love in favour of a purely spiritual one and the reunion of lovers in an afterlife; and of *Love Eternal* (1918) and *Mary of Marion Isle* (1929), which reiterate the themes of the preceding novels but, crucially, recognize the inevitability of the pull of the sexual imperative in the human predicament. This book examines the evolution of Haggard's treatment of various aspects of the sexual imperative throughout these novels and documents a corresponding evolution in his contemporary romances. It considers Haggard's personal emotional history – in particular regarding his relationships with key women in his life – drawing upon his autobiography, his diaries, his correspondence – especially letters to family and close friends – and also upon several biographies. And it explores ways in which Haggard related these significant aspects of his autobiography to his fictional renditions. Throughout the book I shall consider the sexual imperative in the terms in which Haggard repeatedly represents it; that is as the involuntary and life-changing impact upon the male of the sexual allure of the female.

Chapter One

THE SEXUAL IMPERATIVE

Ten of Haggard's eleven novels consider the impact of potentially destructive sexual and emotional urges, primarily upon the male. Haggard expresses these urges in terms of a conscious but wholly irresistible psychological imperative, a fundamental part of human existence, offering the possibility of ultimate happiness but capable also of causing emotional chaos and sometimes accompanied by an unshakeable undertow of guilt. These ten novels also consider related aspects of the same subject, including the divine, spiritual and elevating qualities of genuine love, the validity of sexual union outside the marriage contract, the possibility of a renunciation of the sexual aspects of love in favour of the spiritual and the reunion of lovers in an afterlife. It is not Haggard's novels alone that maintain a constant focus on these themes. They feature in all but two of his forty-four full-length romances. As a measure of this concentration, five out of the ten novels that deal with the sexual imperative have women's names as their respective titles (and Haggard originally entitled his first novel *Angela* until it was discovered that the title had been used previously), and twenty-three of his romances have as their titles either a woman's name or a sobriquet. This focus on women occurs from the very start of Haggard's romance writing, despite his reference to his intention in writing *King Solomon's Mines* to produce 'a book for boys',[1] and the claim of the book by its narrator, Allan Quatermain, that 'there is no woman in it – except Foulata'.[2] In reality both Foulata, the faithful native lover of one of the explorers, and the evil witch Gagool, are central to the action and can be seen as representing the duality of woman. Haggard sheds a little light on this concentration in an article he wrote about his first book, *Dawn* (1884), in *The Idler* in 1893. Of Angela, the book's heroine, he writes: 'before I had done with her, I became so deeply attached to my heroine that, in a literary sense, I have never quite got over it'.[3] Later in the same article he proposes that 'women are so much easier and more interesting to write about, for whereas no two of them are alike, in modern men [...] there is a paralysing sameness'.[4]

Haggard may be referring to the perceived feminine challenge to traditional institutions and, implicitly, to the male in the 1880s, of which Elaine Showalter has observed: 'Feminism, the women's movement, and what was called "the Woman Question" challenged the traditional institutions of marriage, work and the family.'[5] Peter Gay notes that in the 1880s feminist reform legislation 'began to dismantle England's time-honoured patriarchal system'.[6] But it is difficult to believe that Haggard's interest in writing about women, which primarily took the form of their emotional impact on males, did not also derive from what Michael Mason has pointed out was a tendency in the 1880s 'to decouple a woman's sexuality from her reproductive capacities',[7] and that the 'paralysing sameness' he observes about men reflects the conservative male response to contemporary discussions of female sexuality. As Sally Ledger has proposed, 'the figure of the New Woman was utterly central to the literary culture of the fin-de-siecle years'.[8]

Mason contends that Victorian society 'had a widespread and principled belief that there should be discipline and unobtrusiveness in all sexual activity'.[9] Nevertheless, to quote Roy Porter and Leslie Hall, 'sex was a recurrent topic of debate during the Victorian era [...]. The dangerousness of sex was the unavoidable theme [...]. If sex was not concealed, there were strong feelings that its manifestations ought to be'. At the same time, as Porter and Hall contend, it was plain that 'unrespectable sex was highly visible'. It was equally plain that the moral and legal balance in respect of sexual activity favoured the male. In the context of this double standard, Porter and Hall refer to the Divorce Law of 1857, which ruled that 'Mere adultery in a man as opposed to a wife, was no matrimonial crime', and to the contagious diseases acts of 1864, 1866 and 1869, which aimed to solve the problems of venereal disease in the forces 'by policing female prostitutes'.[10]

John Holmes notes that 'For the mid-Victorians sex was a private matter, and the role of sexuality in their self-perceptions [...] was between themselves'. He argues that D. G. Rossetti and his followers 'challenged the mid-Victorian masculine order by exposing this private sphere to public scrutiny', and that Wilfred Blunt later, internalizing 'both the sexuality voiced by Rossetti and the values of its mid-Victorian opponents' articulated a compromise in which 'the grown man remains a public figure with responsible concerns and no hint of his sexuality is allowed to move beyond the strictly private sphere'.[11] This appears to be the male whom Haggard finds uniform and uninteresting. But, while his concentration upon women is undeniable, his main focus is upon the frequently destructive impact they have on men rather than on any character analysis of the women themselves. Shannon Young has observed that Ayesha in *She* 'reflects the narcissistic fears and desires of the men who encounter her and therefore her characterization reveals more about them than about the nature of the feminine'.[12] The same may be said of the female protagonists in the whole of Haggard's fiction.

There was certainly nothing unique about an author in the latter half of the nineteenth century writing fiction that centrally concerned the sexual imperative. The writers of the sensation novels in the 1860s had represented female sexuality and challenging and dissatisfied women like Estella in Charles Dickens's *Great Expectations* (1861), Isabel Carlyle in Ellen Wood's *East Lynne* (1861), Lucy Graham in Mary Braddon's *Lady Audley's Secret* (1862), Aurora Floyd in Braddon's eponymous novel of 1863, and Nell Lestrange in Rhoda Broughton's *Cometh Up As A Flower* (1867). Showalter has observed, of the 1880s, that 'The crisis in race and class relations [...] had a parallel in the crisis of gender' and that there was at this period 'a fascination with the figure of the sexually voracious *femme fatale*'.[13] She appears to be making reference to a growing tide of feminism, reflected in a literary sense by the New Women writers, who themselves were concerned with female sexuality and sexual behaviour, and whose heroines were regarded, as Ledger has pointed out, as 'sexually transgressive'[14] and also to fictional representations of irresistible but destructive women like Lizzie Greystock in Trollope's *The Eustace Diamonds* (1873). Carolyn Dever has observed: 'Women offer a formidable, and frequently insurmountable, challenge to heterosexual male figures in Victorian fiction.'[15] These challenges were levelled in a number of arenas; in respect of class by Estella, the legal by Lizzie and the psychosexual by heroines like Lucy and Aurora. In the mid-1870s Hardy had begun to write about failed relationships and sexually charged but socially constrained young women and went on to develop the theme in his subsequent novels, culminating in a controversial examination of marriage in *Jude the Obscure* (1895). In 1897 Bram Stoker offered in his portrayal of Lucy Westenra in *Dracula* a strikingly frank depiction of female sexuality. The revival of interest in the works of the spiritualist philosopher Emanuel Swedenborg in the late nineteenth century prompted writing on the subjects of a love that was both sexual and spiritual and of the reunion of lovers in an afterlife by spiritualists like Laurence Oliphant and George Barlow, and novels focussing on the same topics such as Barlow's *Woman Regained* (1895), Theodore Watts-Dunton's *Aylwin* (1898) and, later, Marie Corelli's *The Life Everlasting* (1911).

In 1910 Sigmund Freud's *Three Essays on the Theory of Sexuality* was published in America, the first of his works to be translated into English, as Peter Keating points out, adding that 'a general awareness of Freud and Freudianism only developed in Britain in the few years before the First World War'.[16] There is no evidence that Haggard read Freud or owed any conscious debt to his writings. But Norman Etherington's assertion that 'Haggard's early romances expounded and dramatized a theory of the psyche that bore a close resemblance to Freud's conception'[17] is hard to refute. Etherington bases his argument primarily upon readings of *King Solomon's Mines*, *She* and *Allan Quatermain* and the way in which their themes of journeys into the unknown can be held to equate to the search for self-identity. Of course these early romances (and indeed the majority of Haggard's fiction) were written before Freud's works became available in English. Indeed it is Freud who refers to *She* and to *Heart of the World* (1896) in *The Interpretation of Dreams* (1899) in which he relates a dream whose origin he attributes to having read these two romances. Freud believes that *She* is 'full of hidden meaning […] the eternal feminine, the immortality of our emotions',[18] acknowledging Haggard's dramatic consideration of ideas he himself had yet to write about. Young observes that *She* 'laid out the psychosexual territory that resonated with Freud'.[19] Similarly, Etherington proposes that 'Freud and Jung […] took a particular interest in Haggard because they saw in his novels an implicit model of the self which corresponded closely to their own explicit models'.[20] In evidence he refers to the words of the eponymous narrator in *Allan Quatermain*: 'supposing […] we divide ourselves into twenty parts, nineteen savage and one civilised, we must look to the nineteen savage portions of our nature, if we would really understand ourselves'.[21] Keating comments that 'it can be argued that great writers of the past had long understood the essential message of Freudianism without the benefit of Freudian terminology'.[22] Etherington concurs, recording that

> the idea of an unconscious mind was casually expounded in the last two decades of the nineteenth century; the shock of Freud lay in the content rather than the concept of the unconscious.[23]

The significance of Haggard's proposal, in his early romances, of another layer of the self, lies not in any derivativeness but in its connection to his underlying proposal, both in his novels and in his romances, of the ubiquity and the compelling nature of the sexual imperative.

There was nothing remarkable about this latter proposal. Dever has observed that 'eroticism saturates the world of Victorian fiction. Yet it does so in terms that remain strangely invisible.'[24] Keating has discussed a number of the difficulties facing literary representations of sexuality. He observes that the Obscene Publications Act of 1857 was open-ended. The definition of obscenity, in a legal judgement of 1868, revolves around the question of 'whether the tendency of the matter charged as obscenity is to deprave and corrupt those whose minds are open to such immoral influences', and late Victorian novelists were 'vulnerable to a strict interpretation of the law'. The morally conservative circulating libraries too 'could exert pressure on publishers and authors by refusing to stock particular books'.[25] George Gissing remarks that 'English novelists fear to do their best lest they should damage their popularity and consequently their income'.[26]

Keating has observed that the situation eased somewhat in the early twentieth century through the advent of 'private presses' and 'the spread of public libraries'.[27] But in fiction of the late nineteenth century, as Dever has commented, 'direct expressions of sexuality [...] are the exception to the rule [...] sexuality [...] emerges primarily in disfigured and coded terms and by means of displacement rather than express representation'.[28] It was against this background of a moral ambiguity regarding sensuality and of the prevailing need for authorial prudence in the fictional representation of sexuality that Haggard commenced his own literary consideration of the sexual imperative. And while his consideration of how to cope with the destructive capabilities of the sexual imperative develops throughout the course of his fiction, his moral platform on the tension between the sanctity of marriage and personal emotional fulfilment remains notably consistent, and it is only in his final novel, *Mary of Marion Isle* (1929), a product of a much later period, that he permits himself to propose a happy and permanent union outside the legal confines of wedlock. But even this proposal is an uneasy and caveated one.

What is remarkable, then, is not that Haggard considered these issues concerning relations between the sexes, since they were familiar literary currency at the time, nor that he treated them with a ground-breaking, or even notable, degree of explicitness or moral tolerance, for he did not, but that they dominated his novels and permeated his romances to a degree that can only be explained by their having a deeply personal resonance for him. It was not unusual for writers around the fin-de-siecle to elide autobiography and fiction. Max Saunders points out that from the late nineteenth century to the early twentieth 'autobiography, biography, fiction and criticism began to interact, combining and disrupting each other in new ways'.[29] But the strikingly insistent and transparent way in which Haggard deploys fictionalized autobiography is suggestive of a psychological imperative. Haggard himself suggests a link between his fiction and a personal and unshakeable sense of, what appears to be sexual, sin. In 'A Note on Religion', which appears at the end of the second and final volume of his autobiography, he writes that the consequences of sin are inescapable: 'our virtues [...] are dwarfed and lost in the dark shadows thrown up by our towering crime' and nothing except divine forgiveness can free humans from 'that black mount of evil which our stained hands piled, and the icy gloom it throws'.[30] Haggard was essentially a religious man, and this surely represents a deeply personal sentiment. It develops in significance when considered in the light of a passage in his article 'About Fiction' where, writing of the artist's subject matter, he states, with what appears to be an equally personal conviction, that 'sexual passion is the most powerful lever with which to stir the mind of man for it lies at the root of all things human'.[31]

It is Haggard's novels, with their broadly realistic plots, that show most clearly his ubiquitous pursuit of the overarching theme of the sexual imperative and resonate most obviously with his personal emotional experiences. Viewing his romances through the same lens reveals less immediately apparent, but nevertheless identical, bedrock, and proposes a substantially greater similarity between novels and romances than has been observed.

In subsequent chapters I shall examine how Haggard sets up his novels as he continues sporadically to write them throughout a forty-year career of fictional writing, and how this reveals his engagement with several contemporary genres: Sensation fiction, New Woman writing and Modernism. I shall also consider the relationship between his novels and his romances. And I shall argue that the sum total of these explorations is that Haggard made real, if modest, contributions to the fiction of his time and offers the surprising conclusion that he can be partially acquitted of the familiar charge that, after his spectacular if brief early successes, he cynically capitalized for commercial reasons on a repetitive and empty literary formula. In reality the vast majority of his fiction represents a morally valid, if self-indulgent, attempt to explore and document what he regarded as the prime human driver.

Chapter Two

THE ORIGINS OF HAGGARD'S FICTIONAL WRITING

Haggard continued writing novels throughout his literary career despite the fact that it was his romances, particularly his early ones that established his reputation, bringing him fame and fortune. Although his novels were less commercially successful, Haggard had a personal regard for them. He states of several that he wrote them to please himself, and of others that he considered them to be amongst his better work, and he implies that he would have preferred writing novels rather than romances were it not for the need to earn a comfortable living. His valuation of them seems to reside in his belief that in them he was able to consider subjects he regarded as important. Although, by his own frank admission, Haggard was not a truly 'literary' writer he had a personal sense of the worth of some of his fiction and an apparently sincere concern that at least some of it would continue to be read. Although he does not specify which of his books he had in mind, it seems reasonable to assume from his comments about their worth that they included some of his novels and, since the theme of the sexual imperative features consistently and prominently in them, that this was a theme he regarded as significant. It is a theme that reverberates through his closest personal experiences as an exploration of his relationship with the five key women in his life reveals.

Romance and Realism

Haggard wrote 58 works of fiction and 10 works of non-fiction, published variously by Trubner; Hurst and Blackett; Cassell; Longmans, Green; Smith, Elder; J. W. Arrowsmith; Kegan Paul, Trench, Trubner; Ward Lock; Hutchinson; Hodder & Stoughton; Eveleigh Nash; John Murray; and Stanley Paul. But it was not until 1904, with the publication by Cassell of *The Brethren*, that his publishers took to dividing his fictional works, in the frontispiece of his books, into novels and romances – of which, when his last book had been published, 11 were classified as novels and 47, including 3 collections of short stories, as romances. There is no extant evidence to record why Haggard, his publishers or his literary agent decided to advertise the obvious differences between the two categories into which his fiction falls. The novels, generally dealing as they do with relations between middle-class English men and women and set, for the most part, within English society, differ immediately and strikingly – if on closer analysis only superficially – from the romances, which for the most part depict English men on voyages of exploration encountering exotic foreign societies, locales and individuals, notably women. Although it was not common practice, other contemporary writers also categorized their works, partly in order to bring them into sharper focus for the reading public. Thomas Hardy, for example, divided his novels into three categories, Novels of Character and Environment, Romances and Fantasies, and Novels of Ingenuity, in his General Preface to the Wessex edition of 1912:

> I have found an opportunity of classifying the novels under three heads that show the author's aim, if not his achievement, in each book of the series at the date of its composition.[1]

Simon Gatrell observes that this 'has ensured until recently an authorized two-tier class-system for his fiction: the upper crust of novels of character and environment, as he called them, and the rest as second-rank'.[2] The division of Haggard's fiction was, of course, much more general, but it, too, effectively served to differentiate for the reader the popular romances from the less popular novels, as well as advertising a certain range in his writing.

This division also reflected the revival of the romance in the late nineteenth century and the debate upon the respective merits and definitions of the literary modes of Realism and Romance. Kenneth Graham opines that 'in many ways 1887 is the year of recognition for the new romance', and goes on to point out that in that year George Saintsbury, associate editor of the *Saturday Review*, Andrew Lang, man of letters, author and frequent contributor to literary journals, and Haggard himself, 'all issue manifestos on its behalf'.[3] Peter Keating records that

> all of these writers saw romance as serving to deflect attention away from the dangerous unpleasantness of realism, a classification that in this context allowed for no distinction between Zolaesque documentation and Jamesian psychological analysis: both types of realism were seen as equally guilty of fostering introspection, unmanliness and morbidity, and of favouring a literary method that was mechanical and monotonous.[4]

As Graham observes, the distinction between the romance and the novel is 'as old as the beginnings of prose fiction', and to substantiate this assertion he quotes from Clara Reeve's essay *The Progress of Romance* (1785):

> The Romance is an heroic fable, which treats of fabulous persons and things – The Novel is a picture of real life and manners, and of the times in which it was written.[5]

The romance writers of the late nineteenth century were to collapse this distinction in that they depicted ordinary contemporary men encountering the fabulous. In his romances Haggard depicted these ordinary men as experiencing in that context the same emotional and sexual tensions that they might have done in an English domestic setting.

Nineteenth-century proponents of the romance felt the need to assert a literary case for its superiority. R. L. Stevenson was one of the first to give voice to a concern about the condition of the novel in his 1882 article in *Longman's Magazine*:

> English people of the present day are apt, I know not why, to look somewhat down on incident, and reserve their admiration for the clink of tea-spoons and the accent of the curate. It is thought clever to write a novel with no story at all, or at least with a very dull one.[6]

He proposed that it was the task of literature to take readers outside the confines of their own experience and to satisfy their unarticulated, almost unconscious, fantasies:

> The great creative writer shows us the realisation and apotheosis of the daydreams of common man. His stories may be nourished with the realities of life, but their true mark is to satisfy the nameless longings of the reader and to obey the ideal laws of the daydream.[7]

Haggard reiterated the same proposal in 'About Fiction', published in *The Contemporary Review* in 1887, in language similar enough to Stevenson's to suggest conscious imitation:

> More and more […] do men and women crave to be taken out of themselves […] to be brought face to face with Beauty and stretch out their arms towards that vision of the Perfect, which we only see in books and dreams.[8]

Wendy Katz connects this sentiment of Haggard's with his frequent use of imperial settings, observing that his writing satisfies

> the need for a fuller emotional existence in an increasingly oppressive and matter-of-fact industrial society. For those like Haggard, who faced the passing of a rural existence, the imperial landscape became more and more appealing.[9]

Elaine Showalter sees the proliferation of romance during this period as 'a man's literary revolution',[10] an overwhelmingly male response to the domination of the market by women writers. Refining this proposal, Stephen Arata connects the romance and its frequently imperial setting with an emphatic masculinity and with an expression of loss both at the national decline and at the collapse of the tradition of English letters, observing that 'while the empire in works of male romancers provides a stage on which fantasies of a revitalized masculinity are played out' and although 'it has often been read […] as unambiguously celebratory of late-Victorian masculinist ideals, the male romance is in fact deeply imbued with a sense of loss'.[11] Haggard develops Stevenson's proposal that 'the realities of life' can inform romance. Claiming that 'the ordinary popular English novel represents life as it is considered desirable that schoolgirls should suppose it to be', he asks 'Why do *men* hardly ever read a novel? Because in ninety nine cases out of a hundred, it is utterly false as a picture of life.'[12] Authors, Haggard argues, 'ought, subject to proper reservations and restraints, to be allowed to picture life as life is, and men and women as they are'.[13] He seems to be arguing not for a Zolaesque Naturalism, but against the mannered self-censorship of the authors whom Stevenson had characterized as representing in their novels 'the clink of tea-spoons', and to be proposing that romance is capable of presenting an expanded form of truth about life. Robert Fraser observes:

> For the advocates of romance, the esoteric and outlandish were newly worthy of attention, not simply because they permitted an escape from the commonplace tedium, but because they opened onto the wider excesses of fact.

He adds: 'Though it resembled an act of escape, quest romance was in effect a search for the truth' about 'the nature of man himself'.[14]

Haggard's comments must be interpreted in the context of the question about the relationship between fiction and life, which had been one of the principal subjects of a debate about fiction, conducted by way of journal articles in 1884 and fuelled mainly by Walter Besant, Henry James and Stevenson. In a lecture delivered at the Royal Institution on 25 April 1884 Besant proposes that 'The very first rule in Fiction is that the human interest must absolutely absorb everything else.'[15] James, broadly in agreement, claims 'The only reason for the existence of the novel is that it *does* compete with life.'[16] Stevenson takes the contrary and more interesting view in an assertion that harks back to his comments about 'the daydream of the common man' in 'A Gossip on Romance': 'The novel [...] exists, not by its resemblances to life [...] but by its immeasurable difference from life'.[17] Both James and Stevenson seem here to use the term 'novel' to denote fictional writing in general rather than to differentiate between the novel and the romance. Haggard's observations should not be interpreted as evidence that he aligned himself entirely with James rather than with Stevenson on the question of the novel's relationship to life. He makes it very plain that he has no time for the then current school of American novelists whose 'laboured nothingness' he compares unfavourably with 'the swiftness, and strength, and directness of the great English writers of the past', nor for the naturalistic French school, of whose female protagonists he writes: 'Lewd and bold and bare [...] the heroines of realism dance, with Bacchanalian revellings across the astonished stage of literature'. And he concludes: 'it is things heroic and their kin and not petty things that best lend themselves to the purposes of the novelist, for by their aid he produces his strongest effects.'[18] Haggard does, however, reveal a concern with the realistic depiction of men and women, a concern Stevenson does not appear to share.

As Graham has pointed out, Haggard's article was succeeded in the same year by articles by Saintsbury and Lang, but a plea for a greater degree of colour and imagination in literature appeared as early as 1882 in an article in the *Saturday Review* that applauds Stevenson's 'A Gossip on Romance' (published some ten days earlier), criticizes both the American school and the French naturalists, and regrets that 'incident, romantic event and complication, the grand situation [...] require imagination and our age [...] is not pre-eminent in imagination'.[19] Saintsbury's 1887 article in the *Fortnightly Review* reiterates these observations and welcomes 'the return to [...] the pure romance of adventure' and the abandonment of 'minute manners-painting and refined character-analysis' exemplified in Stevenson's *Treasure Island* (1883) and Haggard's *King Solomon's Mines* (1885).[20] Two months later Lang's article 'Realism and Romance', while criticizing 'modern' English and American novels for their 'unrelenting minute portraiture of modern life and analysis of modern character' and their 'unrelenting exclusion of exciting events and engaging narrative', acknowledges that 'there will always be room for all kinds of fiction, *so long as they are good*'. But, at the same time, he makes it plain, in a typically stylish and amusing conclusion, where his personal preference lies:

> The dubitations of a Boston spinster may be as interesting, by one genius, as a fight between a crocodile and a catawampus by another genius [...]. But if there is to be no *modus vivendi*, if

the battle between the crocodile of Realism and the Catawampus of Romance is to be fought out to the bitter end – why, in that Ragnorak, – I am on the side of the Catawampus.[21]

So too, at this point in his literary career, with the very recent great successes of *King Solomon's Mines* and *She* (1887), was Haggard. But the distinctions that form the basis of Stevenson's propositions, the association of incident with romance and character analysis with the novel, do not substantially differentiate Haggard's romances from his novels. Incident prevails in both, while psychological analysis does not feature. Incident, however, is not employed in the romances purely as a route into fantasy, but also to illustrate what Haggard regards as the crucially important universal human susceptibility to the sexual imperative. And his romances and novels reach the same destination, albeit by different routes.

The Attractions for Haggard of Romance Writing

At least in his public utterances, Haggard could hardly afford, at this stage, to distance himself from romance. His first two works of fiction, both novels that had initial print runs of only 500 copies, earned him a mere £50.[22] They were published in the three-decker format that was associated with the domestic, female-gendered fiction from which the writers of romance fiction broke away. It appears that it was probably chance or commercial opportunism, rather than literary conviction, that caused him to write his first romance. Haggard's daughter Lilias records that its origin was a bet with his brother Andrew that Haggard could not write a book as good as *Treasure Island*.[23] In his autobiography Haggard offers the more flattering version that his reading of a review of Stevenson's recent great success prompted him 'to try to write a book for boys'.[24] The association between romance and the juvenile market had already been established in the mid-nineteenth century by authors like G. A. Henty, R. M. Ballantyne and Frederick Marryat – before the appearance of *Treasure Island*. After the publication in 1885 of his first romance, *King Solomon's Mines*, which had an initial print run of 2,000 copies and was published, not as a three-decker, but in a one-volume edition, and which Haggard specifically dedicated to both the juvenile and adult markets ('big boys and little boys'), the first editions of Haggard's immediately subsequent romances, *She*, *Allan Quatermain* (1887) and *Maiwa's Revenge* (1888) had respective print runs of 10,000, 20,000 and 30,000[25] and consolidated his reputation. Haggard supported a comfortable lifestyle and a substantial family entirely from the proceeds of his writing, a point he makes in his autobiography, reflecting that he would prefer in his writing to focus on agricultural and social matters were it not for the fact that he had 'many dependent' upon him 'directly or indirectly'.[26] There was also pressure from at least one of his principal publishers to concentrate on mainstream romance. Charles Longman, writing to Haggard in January 1907 advised him:

> Hunting, adventure, some of the peculiar vein of humour of those early years, Romance – all these I can do with but no mysticism if you please […] there are a lot of other thick heads who want just the same.[27]

Romance appeared to be what most of the British reading public demanded. Katz notes that

> romance by virtue of its immunity to the ties of actuality, is a literary form characterized by freedom and expansiveness. These two attributes [...] suggest a natural kinship not only between romance and the geographical immensity of the imperial world, but also between romance and the mood of imperial Britain.[28]

Haggard's Perseverance with His Novels

However, despite the facts that his romances generated the vast majority of the income upon which he lived, and that his two initial novels had been financial, as well as largely critical, failures, Haggard continued throughout his career to write novels of contemporary life, although with diminishing frequency, which suggests that he felt the need to maximize his income as he grew older and realized that his productive life was drawing to a close. It was hardly because he had an inclination to experiment in the style of realism. His novels are of a completely different order and touch variously upon melodrama, fantasy and occasionally the exotic. He does not make any definitive statement explaining his persistence with them, although he records of the writing of *Jess* (1887): 'I determined to try my hand at another novel,' despite the tepid reception of his two earliest attempts in the genre and the overwhelming success of his first romance, *King Solomon's Mines*, 'being somewhat piqued by the frequent descriptions of myself as "a mere writer of romances and boy's books"'.[29] This is an interesting, and somewhat confusing, statement about Haggard's intentions and motivations in 1886 when considered in the light of his recorded resolution the previous year to write 'a book for boys', particularly since both claims appear in his autobiography, which he began in 1911. It seems likely that the claim about the earlier resolution may be taken at face value, and that the claim that he wished to dissociate himself from the popular conception that he was merely an author of children's books amounts to a retrospective attempt to embellish his reputation.

To confuse matters further, he also claims: 'I have never really cared for *novel*-writing: *romance* has always made a greater appeal to me.'[30] While such an apparently unequivocal pronouncement cannot simply be set aside, it is unclear precisely what Haggard understands 'novel-writing' to mean in this context, and how he believed it differed from the writing of romance. He may be making reference to novels concerned with 'the clink of tea-spoons'. It is clear, however, that his statement is some distance from the cumulative balance of available evidence, and appearing as it does at the beginning of the first autobiographical volume, which Morton Cohen points out Haggard 'began to write [...] when he was in low spirits',[31] it may well be that it reflects his *ennui* at the time. Cohen later quotes from an unreferenced letter from Haggard to an anonymous reviewer in 1915 that suggests he set store by his novels:

> My name, as you remark, is connected in the public idea with a certain stamp of African story [...]. Therefore Editors and Publishers clamour for that kind of story [...]. If I write other things I am told that they are 'not so good' although I well know them to be much better.[32]

Moreover, in the second volume of his autobiography, Haggard writes: 'even now, if circumstances allowed of it, I do not think I should write much more fiction, at any rate of the kind that people would buy.'[33] It is clear that Haggard is referring here to his profitable romances, and his final phrase suggests that he is alluding to the creation of non-romance fiction that would need only to conform to his own authorial inclinations rather than to the tastes of the book-buying public. This hypothesis is reinforced by the fact that, in an author's note to two of his later novels, Haggard specifically apologizes to his readers for failing to provide them with that which was generally expected of him. In producing *Stella Fregelius* (1904), he says, its author neglected to offer them a 'romance' but 'wrote it purely to please himself.'[34] In *The Way of the Spirit* (1906) he acknowledges his 'deviation from the familiar, trodden pathway of adventure', recording that he wrote the book because it 'interested me'.[35] And when he came to write his penultimate novel *Love Eternal* (1918),[36] which focusses upon spiritual love, he dedicated it to the Vicar of St Thomas, Regent Street (which Haggard 'attended for many years when in London'), the Reverend Philip Bainbrigge, whom he describes as 'My dear friend from whom I have received more spiritual help and comfort than from anyone else in my life-time.'[37] The fact of its dedication to a man whom Haggard apparently regarded as such a central influence in his spiritual life strongly suggests the seriousness of the book in its author's estimation. He was to say as much with respect to another two of his novels. He rates *Beatrice* (1890) as 'one of the best bits of work I ever did'.[38] And writing about *Stella Fregelius* to his literary agent, A. P. Watt, he refers to the book as a work 'by which I set some store'.[39] This strong sense of ownership is enhanced by a further letter from Haggard to Watt that exhibits a protective tone: 'Please do not hawk it around. Than that I would rather it were held over for a while.'[40] The evidence available suggests Haggard may have written his novels because he felt able to consider and express in them, more directly and more intensely than in his romances, issues in which he had a personal investment, and because he felt he did not need to fulfil a literary formula.

Doctor Therne

While 10 of Haggard's 11 novels focus centrally on the question of the sexual imperative, it is important to consider the exception, *Doctor Therne* (1898), since it offers an instructive measure both of what Haggard is capable of achieving in the novel form and of the serious purpose that informed his use of it. The plot turns upon James Therne, a young doctor who encounters a smallpox outbreak while travelling in Mexico but, fearing to catch the disease himself, flees rather than offering help. He returns to England and sets up in practice only to fall foul of a pompous and duplicitous rival, Dr Bell, who shifts onto Therne the blame for the death of an influential patient. Therne is sent for trial but is supported morally and financially by a rich tradesman, Stephen Strong, who is both a Radical and a virulent campaigner against compulsory vaccination against smallpox. Therne thereafter becomes associated with the anti-vaccinationists, accepts money from them and is eventually elected to Parliament as a Radical. He privately believes in vaccination but declines to say so publicly, fearing to lose his livelihood, and he refuses to have his daughter Jane vaccinated. Smallpox strikes the town where they live, and Jane catches the disease. Therne is later discovered by Jane in the act of vaccinating himself. She dies, and he is ultimately exposed as a hypocrite by Jane's fiancé, Dr Merchison.

Haggard explains in an author's note that the subject of the book is 'the Government [...] surrender to the [...] anti-vaccinationists' and the 'importance of the issue to those helpless children from whom the state has thus withdrawn its shield'.[41] Haggard is referring to the 1898 Vaccination Act that allowed parents who did not believe vaccination was efficacious or safe to obtain a certificate of exemption for their children. The act was passed as a result of pressure by the Liberals and Radicals on the Conservative government of Lord Salisbury. *Doctor Therne* therefore has a political dimension. But although the book effectively makes its assault on the anti-vaccination lobby through its uncompromising accounts of the effects of smallpox, it also offers a compelling consideration of the drivers behind the deterioration of the character of Therne, and of the consequences of his decisions.

It is interesting to note the points of similarity between *Doctor Therne* and Anthony Trollope's *Doctor Thorne* (1858). Both Thorne and Therne are doctors of medicine. The setting of Trollope's book is Barchester, Haggard's Dunchester. Both books deploy the theme of feuding between rival doctors. Both feature a rich, self-made, but heavy-drinking, Radical whose money, inherited respectively by Thorne's niece and by Therne, is a crucial element in the plot. It is hard to believe that these similarities are coincidental. While Haggard makes no attribution to the influence of Trollope's book and there is no documentary evidence to explain why he chose to structure his own work on a novel published forty years earlier, it seems likely that he was consciously drawing on the resonances of *Doctor Thorne*.[42] It is also of interest that a presumably unauthorized sequel to *Doctor Therne* was published in 1901 under the title *Lord Dunchester or The End of Dr Therne: An Autobiography*. It was written by Lieutenant-General Arthur Phelps who in 1897 had been elected president of the National Anti-Vaccination League. The book depicts Therne losing his mind and being incarcerated in an asylum as a result of vaccinating himself with contaminated calf lymphs. It was obviously intended as a riposte to Haggard's book.

Doctor Therne is told in the first person, giving it something of the immediacy of the confessional. The crux of the book is introduced at the outset as Therne imagines himself being addressed by those for whose deaths he has been responsible: 'for your own ends you taught us that which you knew *not* to be the truth' (3). Of the death of his daughter, 'the only being whom I ever truly loved', he says:

> No future mental hell that the imagination can invent would have power to make me suffer more because of her than I have always suffered since the grave closed over her – the virgin martyr sacrificed on the altar of a false prophet and a coward. (4–5)

But Therne's tone is part self- accusatory, part self-exculpatory. He writes: 'ground down [...] by poverty from babyhood [...] I desired money above everything on earth' (7). He frankly records his cowardice in abandoning the smallpox victims in Mexico but submits in his own defence: 'For this I am not to blame. The fear is a part of my nature' (33).

Several pages later he states: 'I have not scrupled to show I have constitutional weaknesses [...] I am a sinner', but then goes on to claim:

> Yet I am not altogether responsible for these sins, which in truth in the first place were forced upon me by shame and want and afterwards by the necessities of my ambition. (43)

And he tries to shift the blame for his sins, arguing that the root perpetrator was the duplicitous Dr Bell: 'Surely on his head and not on mine should rest the burden of my deeds' (44). Therne is finally driven to contemplate suicide rather than living on as 'an object of pity and contempt among the members of my profession' (106), and his anticipation of the process of death and its aftermath is powerfully rendered: 'it would creep forward, now pausing, now advancing, until at length it wrapped me round and stifled out my breath like a death mask of cold clay.' Thereafter there would be 'silence while the stars grew old and crumbled, silence while they took form again far in the void' (111). Haggard achieves an effective sense of the insignificance of the individual in the cosmic scale, of his inability to help himself when caught in the grip of powerful emotions like ambition, of the social pressures surrounding him and of the insidious advance and the morally decaying capacity of evil. Therne's account becomes more urgent, self-lacerating and painful as events unfold swiftly and inevitably. Haggard's portrayal of a weak, ambitious, but disturbingly human, man caught up in a situation out of which he has not got the resolution to escape is exceptionally well drawn. There is something of Dr Jekyll in R. L. Stevenson's *Strange Case of Doctor Jekyll and Mr Hyde* (1886) and of Henchard in Thomas Hardy's *The Mayor of Casterbridge* (1886) about Therne, one of Haggard's most interesting creations, as he mechanically and helplessly persists down the path of self-destruction. There are also discernible autobiographical resonances. It seems likely that in depicting Therne's abandonment of the villagers afflicted with smallpox Haggard is contemplating his own abandonment in South Africa of his mistress and their child. Therne's continuing moral weakness resulting in the death of his daughter references the same episode. Haggard believed that his conduct had been sinful and that it resulted in the death of the infant daughter who was born to his mistress. And, in Therne's proposal that Bell is the root cause of his sins, Haggard appears to be referencing his own father. In the book's consideration of the extent of Therne's culpability it is possible to read an element of the same attempted self-exculpation by Haggard that appears in some of his other fiction. *Doctor Therne* speaks in ways similar to the consideration in Haggard's other novels of the potentially destructive nature of the sexual imperative, of a man's inability to control the urges of his ambition and of the consequent moral and practical destructiveness it produces. Its intensity and effectiveness demonstrate what Haggard is capable of achieving and imply a personal involvement with the overarching theme of humans entrapped by urges they cannot control.

Haggard's Attitude towards Writing

Haggard's initial literary ventures were in non-fiction. He began to write when he was a young man in South Africa, and his first published article 'A Zulu War Dance' appeared in *Gentleman's Magazine* in July 1877, when he was 21. That September this was followed in the same publication by 'A Visit to the Chief Secocoeni'. His first substantive work, *Cetewayo and His White Neighbours* (1882), which discussed the question of the reinstatement, in the wake of the Zulu War of 1879, of the Zulu chief Cetewayo, was published in book form by Trubner, Haggard being required to pay an advance of £50 towards costs. He records that when he came to write his first work of fiction, *Dawn*, he was motivated primarily by money for 'any reward in the way of literary reputation seemed to be beyond my reach'.[43] And of course *King Solomon's Mines*, the book that assured his financial future, was written in a conscious attempt to imitate *Treasure Island* and to replicate its commercial success. According to his own account, Haggard was not a man steeped in the works of other writers. Shortly after the publication of *She*, he states in a journal article: 'I have never been a very great reader [...] I have always preferred to try to study human character from the life rather than in the pages of books'.[44] He goes on to cite *Robinson Crusoe* (1719), *The Arabian Nights* (1706) and *The Three Musketeers* (1844) as books that influenced him when young, and *A Tale of Two Cities* (1859) and Bulwer-Lytton's *The Coming Race* (1871) as his favourite novels. The list is hardly suggestive of wide or imaginative reading, although, with the exception of *A Tale of Two Cities*, it does show a taste for romance.

Haggard's first and last substantial venture into the territory of literary theory was his article 'About Fiction', published in February 1887, very shortly after the publication of *She*. He adopts in it an unfortunately pompous tone and is both immodest about his own work and critical about the work of his fellow writers. Having just written, in *She*, an immensely popular romance, it is difficult to credit his insensitivity and lack of judgement in observing:

> With the exception of perfect sculpture, really good romance writing is perhaps the most difficult art practised by the sons of men. It might even be maintained that none but a great man or woman can produce a *really* great work of fiction.[45]

And he goes on to assert: 'If [...] a person is intellectually a head and shoulders above his or her fellows that person is *prima facie* fit and able to write a good work'.[46] Adjacent to these naively immodest observations is a dismissal of the majority of contemporary fiction:

> A writer in the *Saturday Review* computed not long ago that the yearly output of novels in this country is about eight hundred [...] most of this crude mass of fiction is worthless.[47]

In his autobiography Haggard expresses regret for these remarks, confessing that to write them 'was little short of madness'. He claims that he was 'worried into writing [the] article' and advises young authors of the future 'never to preach about your trade' and 'never criticise other practitioners'.[48]

It is almost certain that long before commencing his autobiography in 1911 Haggard regretted the article, for it attracted adverse attention from the reviewers. Cohen records the aftermath: 'in the months to follow critics pounced concertedly upon him', and:

> Denunciations of his work and charges of plagiarism appeared on both sides of the Atlantic [...] and the *Literary World*, the *Spectator*, the *Whitehall Review* and the *New York Post* in turn accused Haggard of plagiarism in *King Solomon's Mines*, *She* and *Jess*.[49]

And the attacks continued into 1888. In January an article entitled 'The Culture of the Horrible' appeared in the *Church Quarterly Review* which, although not necessarily representative of literary opinion, was certainly an arbiter of moral standards. It associates Haggard with

> writers whose books are disfigured by extravagance of assertion, unrestrained indulgence in semi-sensual and repulsive detail, and a pernicious familiarity with topics which good taste and Christian feeling prompt us to handle reverently.

It goes on to state that when such works are praised by the 'acknowledged guides of English literary taste [...] they become so serious a nuisance as to call for loud and immediate protest'.[50] While it acknowledges Haggard's 'very remarkable imaginative power',[51] it is substantially critical of *King Solomon's Mines*, *She* and *Allan Quatermain*. From the perspective of a specifically literary point of view, William Watson's article 'The Fall of Fiction' appeared in the *Fortnightly Review* in September of the same year. It levels further criticism at Haggard's 'gloating delight in details of carnage and horror', characterizes him as 'a writer from whom the qualities of noble style, delicate humour, and subtle pathos are [...] conspicuously absent' and, in an ironic barb clearly deriving from Haggard's pretensions in 'About Fiction', describes him as 'a clever man, well able to take the measure of his own charlatanry – very likely the last person in the world to mistake his own charlatanry for genius'.[52] These attacks damaged Haggard and his reputation. Cohen points out that they made him 'the fashionable target of parody, farce and rebuke', although 'anyone examining the charges of plagiarism can recognize their absurdity at a glance'.[53] They affected Haggard deeply. His daughter Lilias writes that they 'embittered his whole existence at this period'.[54] And they tainted his view of writing articles; possibly of writing fiction.

When he came to write a chapter on romance writing in his autobiography he prefaced his comments by the claim:

> With the exception of certain stories that I should like to tell for their own sake, and not to earn money by them, I should occupy my time with writings of a different sort, connected, probably, for the most part with the land, agriculture and social matters.[55]

Such subjects, he records in the introduction 'are quite unremunerative'.[56] What he has subsequently to say about the writing of romance is economical, careful, demystificatory and almost self-deprecating in tone. It is also transparently self-serving, justifying his own hurried and unrevised writing by enshrining this as a technique, a kind of literary principle. Romance writing should, Haggard states, 'be swift, clear and direct' and 'should be written rapidly and, if possible, not rewritten, since wine of this character loses its bouquet when it is poured from glass to glass'. In contrast to 'About Fiction' he is quite unpretentious: 'Tricks of style and dark allusions may please the superior critic; they do not please the average reader and [...] a book is written that it may be read'.[57] Given Haggard's statements about the need to generate income from his writing it seems likely that in Haggard's mind 'read' is here synonymous with 'sold'. In any interpretation of his apparently dismissive attitude towards fiction, it must be borne in mind that in making these remarks in his autobiography, one of his objectives was to create the reputation he wished to leave. Cohen points out that *The Days of My Life* (1926) 'is in the traditional sense an *apologia*' and that Haggard is seeking 'to leave to posterity the picture of himself he wants the world to have'.[58] And the book is characterized by an unconvincing modesty. In fact, there is an underlying immodesty in Haggard's effective claim that he was able to succeed in producing profitable fiction without engaging with it at anything but a superficial level. But it is also clear that he did care about his literary legacy, for in the introduction to his autobiography he writes: 'I can only hope that my belief in the vitality of at any rate some of my books may be justified.'[59]

However, not even Haggard's closest literary friends and associates regarded him as a truly literary writer. Lang comments in his article 'Realism and Romance' that it is futile to attempt to compare his skills to Stevenson's and that

> he only resembles Mr Stevenson in natural daring and inventiveness and in having written admirable tales of adventure. He is as far as possible from being a born student, or a born master of style. He does not see the world through books and he writes like a sportsman of genius.[60]

Rudyard Kipling, one of Haggard's closest friends, especially in his later years, shared this opinion. Haggard records in his diary for 15 November 1918 that they had had a long talk: 'one of the greatest pleasures I have left in life', and that Kipling had told him that he had 'no acquaintance with literary people', adding 'I don't think I am really "literary", nor are you either'.[61] Both Lang and Kipling became Haggard's intimate friends and at the same time he derived significant professional advantage from his relationship with them. The friendship with Lang dated back to the publication of *King Solomon's Mines*, and Haggard subsequently dedicated both *She* and its sequel *Ayesha* (1905) to him. Cohen has recorded that 'Lang admired Haggard's [...] imagination, and Haggard respected Lang's learning and judgement',[62] and so close were they and so complementary did they regard their separate skills that they were eventually to co-author a book, *The World's Desire* (1890). Cohen goes on to point out that 'Lang added considerable prestige to Haggard's reputation',[63] although there was the potential danger of being pigeon-holed by reviewers in any close association with Lang, notorious for his log-rolling influence in literary culture. Similarly, Haggard and Kipling became close friends and collaborators after their meeting in 1899. They had much in common; a colonial background, a love of the countryside and a deep interest in spiritual matters. Cohen notes:

> Kipling suggested the idea for at least one of Haggard's tales (*When the World Shook*), he took a considerable hand in plotting five others (*The Ghost Kings, Red Eve, Allan and the Ice-Gods, The Mahatma and the Hare* and *The Way of the Spirit*), and read (or was read) at least six stories in manuscript (*Child of Storm, The Wanderer's Necklace, When the World Shook, Wisdom's Daughter, The Way of the Spirit* and *Moon of Israel*).[64]

Haggard acknowledges that they shared reservations about the worth of literary creation in his dedication to Kipling of *The Way of the Spirit*, writing: 'Both of us believe that there are higher aims in life than the weaving of stories well or ill.'

One such aim of Haggard's was to make a contribution to the improvement of the state of society and specifically of agriculture. Of his ten works of non-fiction, five concerned agricultural or social matters. *The Farmer's Year* (1899), Haggard writes, had the

> twofold purpose of setting down the struggle of those who were engaged in agriculture during that trying time, and of preserving [...] for future generations [...] a record of the circumstances of their lives and of the condition of their industry in the year 1898.

However, he continues: 'it brought me in but a small amount of money [...] He who treats of such subjects must do so at his own cost and be content to take his pay in honour and glory.'[65] *Rural England* (1902), which Haggard refers to as 'the heaviest labour of all my laborious life',[66] was the result of his resolve to 'emulate Arthur Young, who more than a century before had travelled through and written of the state of agriculture in the majority of the English counties'.[67] This was a major undertaking for Haggard, who devoted a substantial part of 1901 and 1902 to travelling the country to gather material and writing it up. Once again he earned little from the book, commenting that 'what can be earned from the sale of such volumes will not suffice to pay their expenses.'[68] *A Gardener's Year* (1905) and *Rural Denmark* (1911), the record of a visit Haggard paid to that country in order to attempt to derive from its agricultural system lessons applicable to agricultural practice in the British Isles, were equally unremunerative and time consuming. *Regeneration* (1910) resulted from a request from General William Booth, head of the Salvation Army in Britain, to undertake an account of its social work. Haggard refused to accept a fee for writing the book,[69] although the project took him about three months.[70] It seems clear from the effort Haggard put into these books and the insignificant remuneration he received from writing them that his concern with the issues they addressed was genuine.

It is also plain that Haggard wished to establish his frustration at his need to concentrate on his fictional writing at the expense of subjects he would have preferred to pursue. In the same vein he writes to his brother Andrew in 1903 that

> up to the present [I] can earn a decent living out of writing – But the worst of it is that my real tastes are for my work of the *Rural England* type and that don't [sic] bring in anything except honour and glory. I am one of those persons who are fated to earn their livings by means of a bye-product of their intellects – in my case a certain capacity for writing stories. But that ain't my real capacity which I so seldom get a chance of using.[71]

He is even more unequivocal in the introduction to his autobiography, in which he records that it has been his 'lot to cater' for 'persons wishing to be amused' and

> as there is other work which I should have much preferred to do, I will not pretend that I have found the occupation altogether congenial, perhaps because at the bottom of my heart I share some of the British contempt for the craft of story-writing.[72]

It is unclear in what precisely Haggard believes this 'contempt' consists, but he may be referring to suspicion of the sedentary in an age that respected vigour, enterprise and exploration. He himself reflects this spirit of the age when he writes, 'Active rather than imaginative life has appealed to me more.'[73] While there seems little doubt that Haggard found satisfaction in compiling his works of non-fiction and considered them worthwhile, it is also evident that he was badly bruised by the hostile critical reception of some of his fiction, and especially of his venture into literary theory, and that this reception had shaken his confidence in his literary abilities. It seems therefore persuasive that Haggard, a sensitive personality who was concerned about his literary legacy, adopts in his autobiography a dismissive attitude towards fictional writing in general and towards his own fictional writing in particular in order to inoculate himself against any possible future judgement of history that it was insignificant.

The fact that – despite his often-transparent protestations – Haggard plainly was concerned about the worth of his fiction, proposes an informative interpretation of his repeated consideration of the sexual imperative in his novels especially since, although they were less commercially successful than his romances, he continued to write them throughout his career, primarily because, as he records, their themes interested him. It suggests a connection between his fictional representation of the sexual imperative, the origins of the theme in his personal experiences and his estimation of its fundamental human significance. It proposes that he believed it enhanced the worth of his novels. And, accordingly, it makes a similar proposition in respect of a significant number of his romances. It may also offer the explanation that the apparent imitativeness of setting, character and plot discernible in his novels but most apparent in his 44 full-length romances – while it may partly lie in Haggard's essential literary uninquisitiveness – is primarily attributable to a belief that subjects and settings that had a personal resonance gave his work conviction and strength. But in any consideration of Haggard's persistent fictional representations of personal issues and experiences it is of course important to document his background, early influences, character and emotional pathology and, crucially, his relationships with five key women in his life.

Haggard's Early Life

Haggard was born into a long line of country gentry. His father, William Haggard, was a qualified barrister who did not practice but derived his income from the rentals of farms and land. His mother, Ella Haggard née Doveton, was the daughter of a prominent member of the Bombay Civil Service, and was born and spent part of her youth in India. Haggard was the eighth of ten children, seven boys and three girls. As a boy, his daughter Lilias records, he was regarded as 'without any particular ability',[74] an assertion Haggard himself verifies in his autobiography, where he writes: 'I was stupid [...] I remember when I was about seven my dear mother declaring that I was as heavy as lead in body and mind'. But he also claims: 'I was very imaginative, although I kept my thoughts to myself which I dare say had a good deal to do with my reputation for stupidity.' He recalls that at the age of about nine, alone in a gloomy bedroom, he realized dramatically and for the first time the inevitability of death: 'it was an awful hour.' Five of his brothers were sent to public school, and two went on to Oxbridge, but Haggard attended Ipswich Grammar School. He writes, slightly sadly: 'As I was supposed to be not very bright, I dare say it was thought that to send me to a public school would be a waste of money.'[75] While Haggard's childhood was a comparatively privileged and generally happy one, it is clear from his references to it that the stigma of apparent academic mediocrity was uncomfortable for him to bear and caused him to take refuge in an imaginative life, which he felt constrained from expressing.

Haggard's Relationship with His Father

It seems that at least part of the reason for Haggard's childhood problems lay in his relationship with his father. Haggard writes circumspectly about this in his autobiography:

> Nobody could be more absolutely delightful than my father when he chose and [...] I am bound to add that nobody could be more disagreeable. His rows with his children were many and often on his part unjust.[76]

Lilias Haggard, no doubt drawing upon what she had been told by her father and other members of the family, characterizes William Haggard as 'a man of violent temper, impatient and autocratic to a degree' although she also observes that her father had 'a certain super-sensitiveness to harsh criticism.'[77] It seems that for Haggard the most wounding episode occurred in March 1877,[78] when he intended to return from South Africa in order to formalize his engagement to his first love Lilly Jackson, of which he asserts 'there was no doubt I could have done [so] at that time', but he was forbidden to make the journey by his father who wrote to him in unequivocal terms. Haggard records that he never forgot the harsh tone of his father's words: 'the sting of them after so long an absence I remember well enough, though some four-and-thirty years have passed since they were written, a generation ago.' And he considered his father's intervention to have changed 'the course of two lives'.[79] It appears that Haggard never fully forgave his father. Certainly, his fictional representation of fathers is almost universally negative. They are portrayed as overbearing and insensitive, predominantly as interfering with the protagonist's emotional relationships, in eight of Haggard's novels. In *Dawn*, *The Witch's Head* (1884), *Colonel Quaritch V. C.* (1888), *Beatrice*, *Stella Fregelius* and *Love Eternal* (1918) fathers, for selfish financial reasons, urge their daughters, using various degrees of coercion, to desert their lovers and marry men they detest. In *Joan Haste* (1895) the heroine is consigned to a life of shame and unhappiness in love by a father who, for his own selfish reasons, declines to acknowledge her legitimacy. In *Jess* the heroine and her sister are neglected by a drunken father. In *The Way of the Spirit* and *Mary of Marion Isle* overbearing uncles and male cousins are surrogate father figures, more or less directly pressing the hero into marriage with an unsuitable woman. This overwhelming pattern in Haggard's novels finds a significant echo in his romances, in 16 of which fathers are similarly portrayed.[80]

Haggard's Relationship with His Mother

It may well be that his difficult relationship with his father deepened Haggard's relationship with his mother. Victoria Manthorpe has observed that Ella Haggard was 'a highly intelligent young woman with a flair for literary analysis'.[81] Her early diaries confirm Manthorpe's assertion. She was also well travelled. In addition to her familiarity with India, where her father was posted, Ella made an extensive European tour in 1841.[82] It would appear that her interest in reading was fired by her paternal aunt Ella with whom she stayed when her parents sent her to England to attend Gough House School in Chelsea, and to whom she dedicated her first published work, a poem entitled 'Myra or The Rose of the East', published in 1857, styling her dedication: 'To Her Who First Fostered in My Young Heart The Love of Poesy.'[83] Ella Haggard's journals for 1837 to 1839, written when she was in her late teens after her return to India, bear striking testimony to her intellectual maturity and perceptiveness, and to her literary inclinations.[84] They also suggest a melancholy, a mysticism, a spirituality and a moral scrupulousness that resemble those of Haggard himself. On 9 December 1837 Ella records that 'there is a charm in recalling to our minds our hours of melancholy and grief', which recollection of pleasures cannot rival. And she goes on to note that

> about the time of my birth [...] there was a tremendous earthquake [...] I consider this circumstance to have been as ominous of my future fate as 'the front of Heaven being filled with fiery shapes' was of Owen Glendower's.

On 2 July 1838 she records a conversation with an unidentified Mr Eastwick about 'our immortality', in which she argued that as mind and spirit are separate from each other as well as from matter, the decay and death of the one does not necessarily imply that of the other. She goes on to note: 'I lent him the "Economy of Human Life" to teach him Philosophy' (presumably this is Robert Dodsley's *The Economy of Human Life*, 1750). It is clear that there was a romantic dimension to her relationship with Mr Eastwick, for on 10 July she writes: 'if he really likes me, I must be careful not to coquet with him', since she is conscious of the 'pain which I might be the means of inflicting on him'. And on 14 August of the same year she records that the need had arisen to disabuse the expectations of an admirer, perhaps Eastwick: 'Poor man! How painful a task it is to crush the hopes of those who have flattered us by their preference.' And she concludes: 'Ten thousand times rather, had I live and die *alone*, than become wife of a husband I could not love.' It is possibly significant, and at the least interesting, that the issues of the immortality of the soul, the relationship between the body and the spirit, the inequitable nature of the marriage contract, and the impact upon a man of rejection by the woman he loves are all central to Haggard's fiction, especially to his novels.

Ella was also interested in the feminist movement, although it is clear that she was sceptical about aspects of what it advocated. On 29 June 1838 she writes of a work published the previous year:

> Read part of third volume of Miss Martineau's *Society in America* [...] I approve highly of her sentiments regarding our moral and intellectual degradation [...] I do not however hold that we should sustain a prominent part in public life, at least at present.

She adds that this must be achieved 'by the steady progress of civilisation, and the consequent enlargement of the ideas of men'. But she still lamented her situation, writing on 23 June 1838:

> Unfortunately with me, the mere love of acquiring knowledge is not sufficient inducement for me to apply. I want some definite object in attaining information [...] I cannot, as a woman, look to any particular inducement to learn – unless indeed I determined upon turning authoress (for which my abilities are far too slender).

She is too self-deprecating, for she was to become a published author, albeit in a modest way. In addition to 'Myra or The Rose of the East', Haggard arranged to have published in 1890, shortly after Ella's death, a further poem 'Life and Its Author'.[85] This is a plea in a post-Darwinian era for men not to abandon God, and it argues that scientific advances confirm his existence, a view shared by Haggard as his novel *Stella Fregelius* makes clear. While 'Life and Its Author' is less than compelling, it is competently written and expresses ideas that are not unsophisticated. Ella was also an extensive and discerning reader. Her journal for 1838 records that between June and September of that year she read *The Pickwick Papers* (1837); Paley's *View of the Evidences of Christianity* (1794); some of the work of Jean-Francois Champollion – the French classical scholar, philologist, orientalist and decipherer of Egyptian hieroglyphs – presumably in the original French; *The Heart of Midlothian* (1818), about which she commented that Scott's 'style of writing is not sufficiently *imaginative* to please me'; works by Wilberforce; Edward Young's *Night Thoughts* (1742); Disraeli's *Venetia* (1837); Scott's letters; and Cottle's *Recollections of Coleridge* (1837). She also read Mrs S. C. Hall's *Uncle Horace* (1837), about which she makes the interesting comment that

> l'art consiste a cacher l'art – and the consequence is, that her work, from her not having employed sufficient artifice, appears burdened with too much [...] The characters which she evidently intended to be most striking imitations of Nature, are all overdrawn.

Her favourite author was Bulwer Lytton, and she refers to having read *Alice* (1838) and *Leila: or The Siege of Grenada* (1838), of which she comments: 'the whole secret of Authorship lies in the power of awakening *sympathy* by investing *familiar* things with new beauty or novelty.' It is perhaps more than coincidental that Haggard refers to Lytton's later novel *The Coming Race* as one of his own favourites.

Ella Haggard, then, was well travelled and well read, and it seems her literary preoccupations were similar to Haggard's. He dedicated his romance *Cleopatra* (1889) to her, trusting she would appreciate the portrayal 'of the old and mysterious Egypt in whose lost glories you are so deeply interested'.[86] He records in his autobiography that he chose the book 'because I thought it the best book I had written', although he adds that 'since then I have modified that opinion in favour of one or two that came after it'.[87] His mother responded in an affectionate letter that appears to make reference to an earlier letter of Haggard's:

> I cannot object to your appreciatory dedication if you really think you inherit your literary tastes from me. Perhaps you do, *from me and mine*, for there was much intellectual power on

my side of the family, but your inventive imagination has brought our obscure and unknown attempts to the surface. Circumstances in my case, have always been steadfastly against me.[88]

Haggard highly regarded her intellectual qualities, writing: 'Of all women I have known she was certainly the most charming, as taken altogether she was the most brilliant.'[89] He was deeply attached to Ella, as a further passage from his autobiography makes clear:

> Twenty-two years have passed since she left us, but I can say honestly that every one of those years has brought to me a deeper appreciation of her beautiful character. Indeed she seems to be much nearer to me now that she is dead than she was while she lived. It is as though our intimacy [...] has grown in a way as real as it is mysterious.[90]

It is clear that Haggard felt they shared an intensely spiritual bond. Lilias Haggard provides collateral evidence of the strength of her father's feelings for his mother when she writes of accompanying him on his last visit to the family home before it was sold and of Haggard's attempt to tell her 'a little of what his mother had meant to him' but, overcome with emotion: 'He who spoke so seldom of the things which lay nearest his heart [...] could not go on'.[91]

It is instructive to consider briefly Haggard's close relationship with his eldest sister Ella who was 11 years older than he was. Manthorpe makes reference to 'the Haggard children's affection for Ella as almost a second mother'.[92] She was, according to Manthorpe, 'literary in her tastes',[93] and it was she who taught Haggard to read, as he acknowledges in his dedication to her of his romance *The Brethren* in which he writes:

> Let us for a little while think as we thought when we were young [...] when you opened [...] to my childish eyes that gate of ivory and pearl that leads to the blessed kingdom of Romance.[94]

Ella was also a confidante, notably in the context of Haggard's first love, Lilly Jackson, and he writes expressing his appreciation for her support: 'I am very glad that you saw Miss J in London and that you admired her.'[95] He records Ella's death in his diary entry for 29 March 1921, writing that of all his siblings:

> She was [...] perhaps the best beloved. I remember with gratitude that to the best of my recollection we never had a cross word or even a difference of opinion; indeed we loved each other very dearly.[96]

Haggard is notably sparing in his fictional portrayals of mothers of grown men (as opposed to unmaternal wives). They scarcely feature in his novels, appearing only in *Joan Haste* and *The Way of the Spirit*. In his romances – while conventional mothers are almost equally rare – strong, often destructive, matriarchal figures like Ayesha are depicted, although these women have more about them of the femme fatale than of the maternal. This lacuna may indicate that Haggard felt able to write openly about his mother in a way that he could not about the other women who were influential in his life, or it may be that he hesitated in attempting fictional representations of someone to whom he was so close. In any event it seems highly probable that he derived his interest in writing from his mother and, perhaps to a lesser extent, from his sister. And he also appears to have derived from his relationship with them, as he did obliquely from his difficult relationship with his father, a belief in and an admiration for women that verged upon the excessive.

Lilly Jackson

The completeness of this belief was destroyed for Haggard, with apparent lifelong emotional consequences, by his experience with Mary Elizabeth Jackson, known as Lilly. Born in October 1854, and therefore two years older than Haggard, Lilly was the daughter of John Jackson, an expert in blood-stock who amassed a considerable fortune as a bookmaker and who died in 1869, leaving his 'vast wealth' in trust for his family.[97] Haggard, who does not identify Lilly, writes in his autobiography that, at the time that he was studying at a crammer in London (which was in 1874), he attended a private ball and that 'I fell truly and earnestly in love' with 'a beautiful young lady a few years older than myself to whom I was instantly and overwhelmingly attracted'.[98] It seems that Haggard confided his love for Lilly to his mother and to his sisters Ella and Mary,[99] and in June 1875 he wrote to Ella recording that he had sent 'Miss J' a letter 'which I may perhaps characterise as impetuous [...] I was dreadfully afraid of being snubbed, however I was not but got a very kind and clever answer'. He tells Ella that Lilly replied 'that it would decidedly not be right or for my own good that she should give me the word of encouragement I asked for' but that 'she trusted this answer would cause no estrangement between us' and 'it pained her beyond measure to write anything adverse to my wishes' but 'she could not answer as *she* would wish'. He concludes from her letter 'that she must either care for me or be a disgraceful flirt'.[100]

It seems from Haggard's rendition of her letter that Lilly was indeed an intelligent and sensitive young woman, and that she had a genuine affection for him. He appears to have been in no doubt about how he felt towards her. At any event they were separated a month later when Haggard went out to South Africa to join the staff of Sir Henry Bulwer, the newly appointed lieutenant-governor of Natal. D. S. Higgins believes Haggard's father saw an opportunity 'to find work for his apparently feckless son and end his inappropriate desire to marry' and prevailed upon Bulwer, a friend and neighbour, to take Haggard onto his staff.[101] Higgins provides no evidence for this assertion, but given Haggard *père*'s subsequent behaviour towards his son's wish to conclude a formal engagement, it may indeed have been the case.

Lilias Haggard claims:

> It is quite obvious from those various fragments that lovers leave behind them [...] that when Rider left England he had little hopes that this unusually passionate attachment would come to anything.[102]

It appears Lilias is basing her assertion on unacknowledged documentary evidence. Certainly, Haggard's own account corroborates his daughter's version, and he records that in the first half of 1878 (he is unspecific regarding precise dates) 'The love affair [...] unexpectedly developed, not at my instance, with the result that for some little space of time I imagined myself to be engaged and was proportionately happy'. Some months later, however, he received a letter from Lilly announcing that she was to marry someone else, and he writes that: 'It was a crushing blow [...] I should not have been sorry if I could have departed from the world [...] it left me utterly reckless and unsettled'. He concludes that 'even now I feel it painful to write' of the subject.[103] It is unclear why, when Haggard was apparently confident that in March 1877 he could easily have concluded a formal engagement with Lilly,[104] that he characterizes the development in early 1878 as unexpected. It may be significant that both assertions serve to shift the moral responsibility for the emotional impact on Haggard of, as he saw it, Lilly's betrayal, onto other people; his father, who prevented the almost certain engagement in 1877, and Lilly who, after encouraging him, jilted him shortly afterwards – and thus to confirm his consequent status as victim. In this context it is instructive to consider the attitude Lilias adopts towards Lilly in her biography of her father. Although she does not identify her, she refers to Lilly by the sobriquet Lilith, who is variously defined as, in Rabbinical terms, the first wife of Adam who was supplanted by Eve, and as an Assyrian demon, and whose name, in late nineteenth-century lexicography, was shorthand for a femme fatale. It is clear that Lilias has not chosen this name at random. She also characterizes Lilly as 'gentle and rather stupid' and 'weak'.[105] Lilias is thus, either deliberately or unconsciously, reinforcing her father's self-interested version of events. While it is not possible to be certain which is the case, the balance of probability, given the generally protective tone of Lilias's biography, seems to lie in the former alternative. Certainly, the evidence of Lilly's letter to Haggard suggests that she was far from stupid. What is not in dispute is that the results of this experience, as Haggard interpreted it at the time or subsequently, remained with him all his life.

On 4 June 1878 Lilly married Francis Bradley Archer, banker and stockbroker, and sole trustee of the Jackson fortune.[106] There is evidence that during the succeeding years Haggard maintained contact with the Jackson family. His younger brother Arthur had been at school and at Cambridge with Frederick Jackson, Lilly's half-brother, and Haggard and Frederick had become friends. Higgins records that it is certain he met the other Jackson sisters both in Norfolk and in London.[107] But there is no documentation to suggest that he had further significant, if indeed any, contact with Lilly, although she sent a gift to his sister Mary on the occasion of her marriage in November 1886,[108] so she certainly had some contact with the Haggard family. In December 1895 a warrant was issued for the arrest of Francis Archer on charges of embezzlement. It seems he had been systemically embezzling the funds of both the Jackson trust and business clients. He fled to Africa and was declared bankrupt. Lilly and her family were left virtually destitute, and Haggard found them a home.[109] Lilias records that 'after a year or two' Archer wrote to Lilly asking her to join him in Africa and that 'against the judgement of others she consented to go'.[110] In 1904 Haggard learned that Archer was dying in Africa of tertiary syphilis and that Lilly, also suffering from the disease, intended, on his death, to return home with her youngest son to join her two other boys for whose education Haggard had assumed responsibility.[111] Lilias writes that when she eventually did so in 1907 Haggard established Lilly and her unmarried sister in a house in Aldeburgh, and he and his wife visited her regularly until her death in 1909: 'the ravaged shadow of the woman Rider

[…] still loved, with an affection which transcends all earthly passion and stretches out hands beyond the grave'.[112] Lilias's language is unfortunately contrived, but her contention that Haggard regarded his love for Lilly as eternal finds echo in his novels and in his autobiography where, after recording his first meeting with Lilly in 1874, he writes:

> Some thirty-five years later I was present at her death-bed – for happily I was able to be of service to her in later life – and subsequently, with my wife, who had become her friend many years before, was one of the few mourners at her funeral.

As he followed Lilly's coffin from the church, they passed under an arch, 'exactly like that other arch through which I had followed her to her carriage on the night when we first met'.[113] In this image of the dual bridal arches Haggard is not only inferring a spiritual marriage between himself and Lilly, but he is also making reference to the immutability of human love. Lilias writes that his experience with Lilly 'increased the mysticism of Rider's nature, convincing him that in this world the perfection of human love and companionship cannot, for more than a very brief period, reach its fruition'.[114] Haggard's relationship with Lilly manifests itself variously in all of his ten novels which consider the sexual imperative, and in a significant number of his romances, in terms of the themes of sexual betrayal and of a lost first love, recuperable for eternity in an afterlife. But although these were the longer-term effects on Haggard, the immediate result of his jilting was, as he himself says, to leave him unsettled and reckless.[115]

Johanna Ford

The recklessness to which Haggard refers took the form of an affair in Pretoria with a married woman whom Manthorpe has identified as Mrs Ford.[116] Stephen Coan has further identified her as Johanna Catherine Ford née Lehmkuhl, the daughter of German immigrants and wife of Peter Lewis Ford, the acting attorney general. Ford was born in England and moved to South Africa with his parents in 1851. He seems to have been unfortunate or careless in marriage. His first wife deserted him in Kimberley and, after Johanna's death, he married twice more, fathering a total of 19 children. In Pretoria Ford became friendly with Haggard and Arthur Cochrane, with whom Haggard shared a house, and who had a relationship with Johanna's unmarried sister Josephine. Presumably the friendship with Ford was a close one because Haggard and Cochrane were godparents to Ford's son Rollo.[117]

In early 1879 Johanna became pregnant with Haggard's child,[118] although it is unclear how it was established that he was the father. At any event Haggard decided that the time had come for him to leave Pretoria, and he resigned from government service and made preparations to set up an ostrich farm with Cochrane at Newcastle in Natal, some two hundred miles away. Lilias writes that 'feminine complications' made it 'obvious that they would both be better out of Pretoria'.[119] Haggard records: 'On my part it was a mad thing to do, seeing that I had a high office and was well thought of,'[120] but he sheds no light on the reason for his decision. While Cochrane organized the purchase of the livestock, Haggard left for England, not to return to South Africa for some 18 months, when he did so with his wife. Manthorpe quotes from several letters from Cochrane to Haggard during the latter's time in England which record, in Cochrane's often flippant style, both amusingly and poignantly, the unfolding of events. The earliest announces the arrival of Mrs Ford's baby who was, perhaps unwisely, christened Ethel Rider: 'We are to be Godfathers – at least I am – Mr Ford said he felt highly honoured at the compliment we paid him and his family – what a rum world this is.' Ford appears, at least at this point, to have been ignorant of the child's paternity. In October 1879 Cochrane, who seems to have been backing out of his relationship with Johanna's sister, strikes a more anxious tone:

> It would be utterly impossible for either of us to think of going back to live in Pretoria [...] you [...] may think yourself devilish lucky if you get out of the whole business all clear.

On 8 November he wrote to Haggard again, informing him

> of the sudden death of my young God child and of your –? [...] perhaps it is a good thing for all concerned [...] I hope to goodness there will be no ravings etc, or any unhappy sentences which may be spoken while under the influence of the great grief.

And two weeks later he writes:

> Mrs F seemed awfully cut up at the loss of the baby [...] Phinny [Josephine] seems to have had a great affection for it and mentions casually that it was not like any of *Mr Ford's* children.[121]

Haggard's letters to Cochrane have not survived, but it is reasonable to assume he was in a fragile state of mind during this period. Meanwhile, very possibly as a means of flight from the situation in which he found himself, he wasted little time in settling down. He was engaged to Louisa Margitson by 21 December 1879[122] and married on 11 August 1880. Cochrane writes to Haggard, apparently shortly before the marriage, telling him that Johanna was becoming agitated about the forthcoming wedding:

> I suppose it will be a case of 'prussic' when the morning arrives for the celebrations of your nuptials but joking apart, she seems really to be entirely crushed and she is very anxious to know the day of your marriage.[123]

The whole event seems to have left Haggard with a profound sense of sorrow and of guilt. Manthorpe quotes from his 'Commonplace Book' of 1882, from which Haggard's nephew Godfrey had copied the following passage:

> When I die, I shall find my little child waiting for me, and we two shall together wait for one who is our soul, for you know that in heaven each shall be with the one most beloved and desired.[124]

It is unclear whether this is a rhetorical entry or whether it represents a draft of a real or imaginary letter from, or perhaps to, Johanna. What is indisputable, however, assuming that Godfrey has transcribed the correct date, is that at 1882 Ethel Rider was the only child Haggard had lost. His sense of guilt was greatly intensified after the death in England in 1891 of his only son, Jock, while Haggard and Louisa were in Mexico, where he was researching background for his romance *Montezuma's Daughter* (1893). Lilias Haggard writes:

> The bitterness of his loss grew almost unbearable. Added to this there was undoubtedly the psychological obsession that his child's life had paid the price of the father's sin; that it was required in expiation of transgression, and being so required increased his guilt. That belief (to judge from chance remarks and pencilled passages in his well-worn Bible) he carried with him, an unhealed wound, until the day of his death.[125]

Haggard writes little in his autobiography about Jock's death but acknowledges the lifelong impact the event had upon him: 'The wound has been seared by time [...] but it will never heal.' Indeed, so greatly was he bruised that would not speak of Jock: 'I who never speak of this matter, who never let that dear name pass my lips.'[126] But he does speak at some length about the consequences of youthful, and by implication fleshly, sin in 'A Note On Religion', which forms an addendum to the second volume of his autobiography, referring to the time 'When we rode the wild horses of our youthful sins, the red blood coursing through our veins like wine.' He is even more explicit in a passage in which he depicts the unequal struggle between Nature, or innate human sexual urges, and Law, or the dictates of religious and social morality:

> Nature says to Everyman who is a man: 'See where She stands with longing arms and lips that murmur love. Hark to what She says who would be the mother of your child [...] Seek for Heaven hid in those dark eyes of mine and find all Earth's desire.' [...] cold, stern Law [answers] 'Pass on, she is not thine'. [But] often enough it is Nature that prevails and, having eaten of the apple that She, our Mother gives us, we desire no other fruit. But always the end is the same; its sweetness turns to gravel in our mouth. Shame comes, sorrow comes; comes death and separations. And greater than all of these, remorse rises in the after years and stands over us at night.[127]

It is not difficult to trace here resonances of Haggard's affair with Johanna. And he is unequivocal about the permanently disabling results of sexual incontinence.

Coan notes Haggard's diary entry for 30 March 1914 when, in the context of a trip to South Africa, he visited Pretoria cemetery, and records that 'I saw Oom Paul's [Kruger's] tomb [...] and others of those whom I had known, some of them already neglected and in decay like those who lie beneath'.[128] And a parallel entry on the same date in Haggard's Rough Diary, which was not intended for publication, reads: 'Went graveyard. W patience found graves surrounded by stone wall. Monument to A of weeping woman. Gate rotten. Some of bulbs she planted still growing.' In a separate note at the back of this diary Haggard has written, 'Ethel Rider b. Sept 79 d. Nov 79. Johanna Catherine Ford d Aug 30 1885. Aged 31.'[129] It is not clear who Haggard intends to represent by 'A'. Perhaps it is a shortening of Johanna. But there is little doubt that it is she to whom he is referring since his description resembles a photograph of Johanna's grave in Coan's book.[130] Like his jilting by Lilly Jackson, the emotional aftermath of his affair with Johanna, for whom, to judge from these references in his diaries, he appears to have had a genuine affection, compounded as it was by the death of their child and by the subsequent death of his son Jock, seems to have remained with Haggard throughout his life. Ten of his novels and the majority of his romances speak of male susceptibility to the sexual imperative, and three novels – *Colonel Quaritch*, *Beatrice* and *The Way of the Spirit* – specifically consider sexual and quasi-sexual relations outside a marriage, the sense of guilt involved and the destructive outcomes. Four of his novels and thirteen of his romances include the death of an infant, and *Montezuma's Daughter* and *The Heart of the World*, written shortly after the death of Jock, directly consider a connection between the death of a child and the moral dubiety of its father's sexually driven behaviour. And three of his earlier romances, *Cleopatra*, *The World's Desire* and *Eric Brighteyes* (1891), speak of a man's sexual capitulation to a seductive woman as a betrayal of his oath of loyalty to a first and true love.

Haggard's Wife, Louisa Margitson

His affair with Johanna certainly seems to have influenced the timing of Haggard's engagement, his choice of wife and his consequent marital relationship. In early August 1879 he arrived back in England[131] and moved into his parents' home at Bradenham. Lilias records:

> A school friend of his sister Mary's came to stay for a week […] in the autumn and at the end of the week she and Rider were engaged. Even for the impulsive Haggard temperament this was quick work.[132]

The young lady concerned was Louisa Margitson, an orphan, and heiress to what Higgins describes as a "modest but worthwhile estate".[133] In getting engaged to Louisa, Cohen asserts, 'Rider's […] "good sense" […] brought his father over to his side immediately'.[134] Cohen's implication that this paternal approval was based substantially on Louisa's financial attributes is strengthened by an apparent defensiveness on this point on the part of both Haggard and Lilias. Haggard addresses the subject directly in his autobiography, in which he takes pains to dismantle the assertion, 'I see recorded in works of reference that I married an "heiress"', by claiming of Louisa's estate that 'we do not get much out of it'.[135] Lilias, once more appearing to defend her father's reputation, writes that her mother came into 'a small property'.[136] Cohen however quotes from a letter of 20 March 1880 written by Haggard's father to Frederick J. Blake, a solicitor, in which Louisa is referred to as 'a lady of some considerable landed property'.[137] It seems likely that Louisa's independent financial position was not a negligible part of her appeal to Haggard, who was at the point of his marriage far from well off, with no definable qualifications or prospects. He writes to his brother William of his engagement: 'I think we have as good a prospect of happiness as most people.'[138] Haggard's tone can hardly be construed as other than tepid and world-weary, and it exudes little passion for his future wife. He seems to be adopting, for the first time, a real as opposed to an ideal view of love.

And it is clear that at the time of his engagement he was very conscious of the potentially serious complications that might arise from his recent past. Manthorpe quotes an unreferenced letter from Haggard to Louisa, written shortly after their engagement, in which he makes clear reference to his experiences with both Lilly and Johanna:

> My past life has been so lonesome and unhappy, that the prospect [...] of your true love seems almost too good to be true. It is like coming out of the darkness with light [...] my past may have been reckless enough, but my future shall atone for it.[139]

It is not documented whether Haggard confided in Louisa about these episodes, although his letter suggests that at some point he did. But it does seem that in rapidly becoming engaged to a woman who was conveniently well-off, sensible and dependable, he may have been taking refuge from a threatening past.

Sensible as she was, Louisa was perhaps not the ideal wife for the emotionally fragile Haggard. Lilias writes of her mother:

> In later years the faults which sprang from her virtues sometimes troubled the relationship of their married life [...] her common sense temperament lacked, almost entirely imagination [...] she was in no sense a maternal woman [...] the deeper sympathies and ties of motherhood passed her by.[140]

Manthorpe quotes an unreferenced letter from Haggard's sister-in-law Alice to her son in which she writes that Louisa 'is not a person who shows her feelings at all'.[141] And Haggard's nephew Godfrey writes in his foreword to Lilias's biography of her father that Haggard's 'marriage went with him as far as it needed and for the rest of the time he was with his own thoughts'.[142] There appears to have been a family consensus that Haggard and his wife were temperamentally ill-matched.

This emotional disparity came to a head with the death of their son Jock. Whereas Haggard's response was emphatic and prolonged, Louisa's was infinitely more private and practical and, according to Lilias, 'there is no doubt she suffered much from Rider's violent grief'. In 'after years Louisa never spoke of' the weeks immediately succeeding Jock's death:

> Nor at the time did she give any indication of what she must have suffered [...] she had an iron self-control [...] so rigid that all her life those who were nearest to her seldom knew what her thoughts or feelings were.[143]

According to Higgins, this apparent lack of communication between them provoked Haggard and Louisa to blame each other for having both left Jock to make the trip to Mexico. The upshot of their bereavement was, again according to Higgins, that having 'after the birth of Dorothy in 1884 [...] ceased sexual relations', the Haggards resumed these with a view to producing another son.[144] Lilias may have generated this assertion, which she certainly tends to corroborate, in observing that when Louisa found herself pregnant in the spring of 1892 she 'resented it greatly [...] Never a maternal woman, she had long considered her family complete'.[145] The result of the pregnancy, the birth of a daughter, was a further disappointment to Haggard, and he writes, 'the event has come off – resulting in a girl – as a boy happened to be wanted', although he concedes 'I would much rather have a girl than nothing at all.'[146] This gender misfire, so frankly acknowledged by Haggard, can hardly have improved his marital relationship.

But Louisa's emotional placidity also proved a positive factor in the course of their marriage. When Lilly's husband fled to Africa in 1895 in the wake of the embezzlement charges against him, leaving her virtually destitute, Haggard installed her and her sons in a small house and offered them whatever assistance he could. This re-engagement with Lilly on Haggard's part was of course potentially delicate, and Lilias records that 'it was only owing to Louie's good faith and good sense that it worked as well as it did. She undertook all the arrangements.' When Lilly returned from Africa in 1907, suffering from tertiary syphilis, Louisa behaved towards her in an identically kind manner, despite being well aware that Lilly remained the woman Haggard loved.[147] Lilias was three when Archer absconded and seventeen when Lilly died, so these assertions about her mother's generous behaviour to a woman towards whom she had every reason to feel resentment are probably not drawn exclusively from her own direct experience. It seems likely that Lilias, whose biography reflects a closeness to her father and an admiration for him, is drawing her record from Haggard's own account and, if this is indeed the case, that at this point in his life Haggard felt a keen appreciation of Louisa's loyalty and understanding. In a letter to his wife on 13 August 1905, two days after their silver wedding anniversary, he writes with an obvious affection: 'Thank you dearest, for all your love and help [...] I hope that we may be spared to spend a good many years together'.[148] Higgins comments that 'despite his somewhat strange relationship with his wife, it was she who provided the continuity and stability.'[149] It seems that, at least later in his life, Haggard realized this, and in 1911 he writes that in becoming engaged to Louisa, 'I did the wisest and best deed of my life.'[150] Depictions of protagonists pressed, often by their own family, to make expedient, unloving marital unions generally for financial reasons – of lost first, and lifelong, loves; and of wives who, although they may sometimes be loyal and affectionate, cannot inspire real passion – appear in ten of Haggard's novels and in a number of the romances. But his later fiction, reflecting his autobiographical comments, begins to contemplate the virtues of stable and dependable wives.

Agnes Barber

Louisa was not, however, the only school friend Mary Haggard invited to stay. Agnes Barber came from a family, Manthorpe records, that was 'well educated' and 'devoted to antiquarian pursuits'.[151] Her sister Marjorie, under the pseudonym Michael Fairless, wrote the best-selling *The Roadmender* (1902). But, for all its gentility, the family was relatively impoverished.[152] Haggard was clearly drawn to Agnes and wrote in a character sketch dated 16 September 1879 (the month in which Ethel Rider was born) and entitled 'Character of Agnes Marion Barber as told under the influence of paint and worry' that she was 'one of the most peculiar individuals that I ever came across [...] All her passions are strong especially her love and hate'. He observes that she thinks herself very plain [but] she has unconsciously a little coquettish way with her [...] She has plenty of energy and a good deal of perseverance and is of a sensible turn of mind [...] but with a vein of romance running through her nature [...] She will never marry till she finds her master and then will make a devoted but no [*sic*] jealous wife.[153]

Haggard seems to have met Agnes and to have written this, fairly intimate, character study, which he gave to her some short time before he met Louisa. Given that he admired Agnes's qualities sufficiently to write about them, that he considered himself familiar enough with her to show her the results of his work and bearing in mind that he was fairly plainly considering marriage at the time and that he became engaged to Louisa within a week of meeting her, it appears likely that the prime reason that deterred him from translating his admiration of Agnes into active pursuit was the fact that she had no significant money of her own.

After Haggard and Louisa were married, Agnes came to stay with them for three separate and protracted periods between 1882 and 1886 in order to help Louisa with her young children. Haggard, who in the former year published his first book, *Cetewayo and His White Neighbours*, frequently discussed his writing with Agnes and sought her advice. In September 1882 he wrote to thank her for her comments on *Cetewayo*, claiming of her critical assessment: 'I am a little dazed by its scathing and brilliant flashes.' He goes on to say

I also agree with your remarks about Louisa's pencilled criticisms. She is perfectly crushed with your just indignation – I wonder however that you could allow [such] remarks [...] to move you to any indignation. That was a mistake, it might, had I not hastened to remove the impression, have made her think that there was something in them after all.[154]

It is eloquent of the trusting and confiding nature of Haggard's relationship with Agnes that he permits himself to express to a close friend of hers such apparent contempt for Louisa's intellectual qualities. And just over a year later he is still more open with Agnes about his view of his union with Louisa: 'Marriage is generally speaking very good fun for about three months mais après.'[155] Even making allowance for Haggard's wish to be amusing, his comments can only be read as signalling a dissatisfaction with his marriage. Higgins notes that Haggard and Agnes 'spent many hours talking about books and the art of writing' and points out that Agnes 'had many attributes that Louie lacked. She was sensitive, creative, intellectual and had become a sympathetic conversationalist.'[156] She became Haggard's secretary, and he discussed with her the manuscripts of all of his early fiction – that is *Dawn*, *The Witch's Head*, *King Solomon's Mines* and *She* – and after she left to marry his brother Jack in January 1886 he continued to send her copies of his books, seeking her opinion of them and dedicating to her, in her authorial pseudonym John Berwick, his novel *Stella Fregelius*. She seems in fact to have been a kind of muse for him. Her departure and marriage disturbed Haggard's equilibrium. 'During the three years he had been writing fiction she had almost permanently been his charming, stimulating companion' and when she departed 'Haggard was all too aware that the situation in which he was left was unsatisfactory and unsatisfying.'[157] Although Haggard says surprisingly, but perhaps significantly, little about Agnes in his autobiography, and his daughter Lilias follows suit in her biography as she very often does, the eponymous heroine of his novel *Jess*, which he was writing at the time of her departure, bears a significant resemblance to Agnes, and the theme of the book, that of a man regretting his choice of wife, seems to have personal resonances for him.

Certainly, financial considerations apart, it appears that Agnes might have been a more appropriate wife for Haggard than Louisa. In addition to offering useful criticism of his drafts, she was a published author in her own right, although only modestly successful, writing two novels under the pseudonym John Berwick: *The Secret of Saint Florel* (1897) and *A Philosopher's Romance* (1898), both serialized in *Macmillan's Magazine*, and translating from the original French, *Uncle* by Jean de la Brete (1892) republished under the title *The Cure of Buisson* (1895), in addition to various poems. She was also a robust and incisive personality, quickly seeing off Haggard family objections to her proposed marriage to Jack (probably on the grounds that she brought little money to the union) as a trenchant letter she wrote to Haggard's sister Ella testifies:

> I am very pleased to find that you do not object to *me* personally, as though of course it could have made no difference to my marrying Jack, still one prefers to be, to a certain extent welcome to the relatives of one's future husband.[158]

In any event Haggard maintained his friendship with Agnes until the end of his life. When in 1908 Jack died while serving with the Consular Service in Spain, Agnes and her family moved back to England, and Haggard extended practical and financial assistance.

Conclusion

The key to the nature of Haggard's relationships with women seems to have been his relationship with his mother to whom he was especially close, partly because of their similar temperament, partly as a refuge from his father's emotional brutality. His idealization of her appears to have extended, at least in his early years, to an idealization of women in general. This took a traumatic reverse in his jilting by Lilly Jackson (with whom he apparently fell thoroughly in love), for the apparent reason that she perceived, or was persuaded that, a marriage with an older, more mature and financially established man was a better bet than a liaison with a penniless youth whose prospects seemed to be modest. Haggard's grief, anger and bitterness at what he saw as Lilly's betrayal resulted in a poorly calculated and impulsive act of sexual assertiveness in his affair with a married woman. The outcome, her pregnancy, his abandonment of his respectable and promising position and flight from South Africa, the birth and death of their daughter, and Johanna's grief at these events left Haggard with a deep and abiding sense of personal guilt and the emotionally devastating conviction that the price for his dual sins of sexual incontinence and the betrayal of his love for Lilly was exacted in the deaths both of his daughter and, a few years later, his young son.

It seems clear that the impact of these emotional storms caused Haggard to seek to settle down as soon as possible into a socially respectable and advantageous marriage, ironically prompted by much the same reasoning as Lilly. In the course of this action he eliminated from his consideration of suitable brides a woman who, it appears, would have suited him temperamentally and intellectually and to whom he was genuinely attracted but who possessed no financial ballast. His marriage seems to have been characterized by a degree of affection and respect but no genuine passion and a constant subtext was his continuing love for Lilly, which translated into supporting and caring for her in her sad final years. Haggard's entire fictional oeuvre is studded with reflections of the lacerations of these experiences and represents a continuous imperative to attempt to work through, contextualize and comprehend the emotional geography of his life.

Chapter Three

THE EARLY NOVELS (1884–95): YOUTHFUL ANGER

Dawn, The Witch's Head, Colonel Quaritch V. C. and *Joan Haste* are the most transparently angry of Haggard's early novels. They also abound in transparent biographical resonances. The anger is levelled at the emotional disruption that women, virtuous and benign as well as malign and seductive, can cause to a young man, and at the outcomes of the sexual imperative expressed in terms of sexual jealousy, moral disintegration and violence. This anger is intensified by the proposal that marriage has few positives to offer, and it is scarcely modulated by suggestions of the merits of spiritual love or by the prospect of the continuation and culmination of passionate love in an afterlife. It is a demonstrably, and notably, personal statement by Haggard. In exploring this theme in these four early novels, which focus intensely upon the sexual imperative, he draws freely upon the tropes associated with the sensation novel. Defining perhaps the best-known of these, Lyn Pykett makes reference to 'the popular sensation novel of the 1860s, with its bigamous or adulterous heroines and complicated plots of crime and intrigue'.[1] The violence associated with the genre gives an appropriate frame to Haggard's visceral anger. Inter alia, this chapter notes the sensation echoes in the four novels in question but concludes that Haggard's end result was significantly different to that of the sensation novels of the 1860s. The anger and intensity of Haggard's early novels also informs his contemporary romances. But sexually inspired male anger is not left entirely unchallenged as their sum total. There is also a sense, which Haggard develops and amplifies in his later works, that the sexual imperative and the emotional turbulence it is capable of causing are inevitable parts of the human predicament.

Haggard's Contemporary Biographical Experiences

Haggard completed *Dawn*, his first work of fiction, in 1883. The preceding five years had been a time of concentrated emotional turmoil for him. He had been jilted by his first love. He had subsequently involved himself in an affair with a married woman who became pregnant with his child, who subsequently died. He had hastily married a woman he respected but probably never truly loved. It was against the background of these sexual and emotional experiences, the resulting wounds of which were still raw, that Haggard commenced his literary career, and it is evident that he sought an outworking of these personal experiences in his fictional writing.

Dawn and Its Biographical Resonances

Morton Cohen refers to *Dawn* as 'a shapeless anthology of two-dimensional actors, vague symbolism, stringy plots and blood-curdling stories'.² It is difficult to contradict this judgement. Haggard himself confesses of his writing of *Dawn* (1884): 'How to compose a novel I knew not, so I wrote on, trusting to the light of nature to guide me.'³ He references the sensation tropes of intrigue, crime, marriage and domestic relations, but none of these are pursued in any depth, nor are they particularly effective in enhancing the book. There is a plot, conceived by an unscrupulous woman of mystical tendencies and involving the forgery of letters, not unlike that in Rhoda Broughton's *Cometh Up As A Flower* (1867), to force a young woman into a loveless marriage with a roué twice her age, which nearly succeeds but ends with the roué being torn apart by a bulldog. There are sexually liberated and dangerously seductive women. There is an unloving, materialistic parent. But when Cohen goes on to allege that 'the tale's greatest difficulty is that its author seems to know nothing about character motivation',⁴ he appears to miss the entire point of the book – for virtually all the characters in *Dawn* act as they do out of sexual passion, and the book, in all its aspects, speaks in unequivocal terms of the inevitable consequences of both unlicensed sexual passion and sexual betrayal. These are depicted as warping moral judgement, decaying character, ruining lives, provoking violence and incurring awful punishment. *Dawn* also considers an alternative in terms of a love that has a pronounced spiritual, as well as a sexual, element. Three distinct foci correspond with the book's three overlapping plots: a consideration of the inescapability of the human instinct for purely sexual passion and of the consequences it can involve, as played out in Philip's relationships with Maria and Hilda and in Mildred's desire for Arthur; an angry depiction of unrestrained sexual lust in George's attempts to possess Angela; and a consideration of the virtues of a spiritual ingredient to passion, which is represented in Angela's relationship with Arthur.

Haggard's brother Andrew observed in a letter to him that 'there is a little too much of your personal experiences in the book', and Haggard's daughter Lilias agrees that it contained 'a great deal of Rider's own experiences'.⁵ These can readily be identified. Devil Caresfoot shares some characteristics with Haggard's own father. The description of Maria as 'not very pretty [...] but [...] a perfect specimen of a young English country girl, fresh as a rose, sound as a bell'⁶ bears a marked similarity to Haggard's description of his wife Louisa in his letter of 21 December 1879 to his brother William in which he records that he is to marry 'a brick of a girl [...] she is good and sensible and true-hearted'.⁷ Philip's abandonment of Maria for the beautiful Hilda who, like Johanna, is German; Arthur's flight to the sexually available Mildred when he believes himself betrayed by Angela; and Mildred's grief at his eventual return to Angela, almost certainly find their origin in Haggard's affair with Johanna. And it seems likely that Hilda and Philip's daughter Angela, who becomes the heroine of the book, has resonances of Ethel, Johanna's daughter by Haggard, especially since Angela's name is suggestive of a woman translated to an afterlife.

But it is in the narrator's interjections on the subject of love betrayed that it seems we may most distinctly hear Haggard's voice. He describes the impact upon a young man of first and genuine love:

> In youth [...] we love [...] with an ardour and an entire devotion that we give to nothing in after-life. It is then that the heart puts forth its most tender and yet its most lusty shoots, and if they are crushed the whole plant suffers, and sometimes bleeds to death. (311)

He speaks too of the perversity and enormity of sexual betrayal by a woman who, 'truly loving one man whom she can marry if she wishes it, deliberately gives herself to another. It is not only a folly, it is a crime' (311). It is difficult not to associate the raw quality of this voice with Haggard's own personal devastation at the loss of his first love. But he also apparently perceives or wishes to salve his conscience in connection with his own guilt over his subsequent affair with the reflection that the human condition places inescapable limitations on love: 'even among the purest of us, there are none who can altogether rid the whiteness of the love they have to offer of its earthly stain' (139). Expressed in Christian imagery, this proposition that human love derives from divine love but is incapable entirely of replicating it because of the inescapable spiritual limitations of human beings is to find echo and amplification in Haggard's subsequent fiction. It is also discernible in 'A Note on Religion', the final chapter of his autobiography, in which he states that 'all Love is immortal. It is God's light permeating the universe' but also recognizes that 'the laws of Nature differ from the laws of God'.[8]

It is instructive to note that Haggard's original draft for the book, which he called *There Remaineth a Rest*,[9] has a plot that focusses on Arthur and Angela, and after their enforced separation and Angela's marriage to another man, has Arthur in South Africa learning that Angela's husband has died and that Muriel (called Mildred in *Dawn*) is expecting his baby. Intending to return to England to marry Angela, he is killed by natives and, broken hearted, Angela falls dead into an open grave.[10] Not only was it Haggard's original intention to make the book darker but, in the inclusion of Muriel's baby, even closer to his own experience. The themes of lost first love, the emotionally and practically devastating consequences of sexual betrayal and the involuntary human imperatives reverberate through all of Haggard's fiction, although as time progressed Haggard's focus altered. *Dawn* illustrates his earliest, and rawest, perceptions.

The Witch's Head and Its Biographical Resonances

As he had in *Dawn*, Haggard introduces a number of sensation tropes into *The Witch's Head* (1884), in this case intrigue, marriage and domestic relations. They sit oddly with the plot. The head from which the book derives its title is discovered in an ancient cemetery and rests in a glass case in the family home; its sole obvious connection with the action of the book is that it bears some resemblance to Florence, Eva's sister and the chief architect of evil. Bearing in mind that Haggard believed Lilly's elder sister played an important role in persuading her to marry Archer,[11] it may be that he intended it to represent the eventual humiliation of a destructive woman, a symbolic forerunner of the physical disintegration of Ayesha in *She*. If so, it is not an artistic *tour de force*. Similarly, the murder of Cardus by Atterleigh – the mad father of his first love who pressed his daughter into an unloving marriage out of financial motives – which he effects with an assegai before embarking on a wild ride on a black stallion, which ends in their immolation in a quicksand – seems entirely gratuitous.

Whereas *Dawn* represents, in several overlapping plots, the often violent and character-decaying consequences of misplaced sexual passion, *The Witch's Head* focusses on the impact on both parties of sexual betrayal as played out in a single unified plot. If *Dawn* is informed by episodes from Haggard's personal experience, *The Witch's Head*, written immediately afterwards, is even more overtly autobiographical. Lilias writes of the book's relation to her father's personal life that 'The English scenes reflected his own unhappy love affair,'[12] and, perhaps significantly, Haggard is uncharacteristically silent about the book in his autobiography. Ernest's history, his trip to France; his jilting by his first love Eva under pressure from her family while he is in South Africa and its effect upon him; his subsequent libidinous behaviour; his return to England and marriage to a sensible woman for whom he feels affection rather than passionate love, all closely replicate Haggard's relationship with Lilly, her marriage to another man and the outcome for Haggard of what he perceived as her betrayal of their love. Eva's immediate emotional impact upon Ernest is similar to Lilly's upon Haggard. Haggard records in his autobiography that he first encountered Lilly at a ball, that he was 'overwhelmingly attracted' to her and that she was 'one of the three really lovely women whom I have seen in my life'.[13] Ernest similarly first meets Eva at a ball and considers her a 'radiant creature', and the narrator asserts: 'something passed [...] into his heart that remained there all his life'.[14]

Haggard takes an ownership of Eva that is not entirely dissimilar to Thomas Hardy's ownership of Tess in *Tess of the D'Urbervilles* (1891). Haggard asserts that Eva was forced into acting as she did by both the genetic, and ineradicable, weakness of her character and by the irresistible evil machinations of Florence, but at the same time he punishes her and, through the voice of the narrator, criticizes her directly. He offers images of her sexual liaison with a man, Plowden, whom she finds physically repugnant. He depicts her passion for Ernest as inextinguishable. And he affirms the prospect of the reuniting of Eva and Ernest in an afterlife and the subsequent eternal celebration of their love. Haggard is creating for himself a fictional version of his own experience and fashioning a view on it. The veering and sometimes contradictory judgements of Eva and the representations of her remorse, together with the detailed depictions of Ernest's feelings, are suggestive both of a personal concern and of an uncertainty on Haggard's part about how to interpret his own experience. The book makes clear that despite Eva's failings, any attempt on Ernest's part to forget her and to draw comfort from marriage to a good woman is merely whistling in the dark. *The Witch's Head* handles the same preoccupations as its predecessor, but it projects a gloomier vision; there is no earthly reconciliation and marriage of the lovers. At an autobiographical level it is a sad, occasionally violent, sometimes spiteful and profoundly self-consolatory attempt by its author to achieve a degree of resolution of a personally wounding episode in his life.

Colonel Quaritch V. C. and Its Biographical Resonances

Haggard uses sensation tropes again in *Colonel Quaritch V. C.* (1888). They may be colourful (and include buried treasure, bigamy, blackmail, prostitution, murder and attempted murder) but, as in *The Witch's Head*, they become sideshows as shaded characterizations, and insistent issues predominantly engage attention. *Colonel Quaritch* is concerned with the same overriding question as *Dawn* and *The Witch's Head*: that of the destructive potential of sexual passion. But while *Dawn* primarily depicts the triumph of first love over these destructive forces, and *The Witch's Head* illustrates the capacity of sexual betrayal to inflict visceral and lifelong wounds, *Colonel Quaritch*, in common with sensation novels like Ellen Wood's *East Lynne* (1861) and Hardy's *Desperate Remedies* (1871), considers the often violent consequences of illicit sexual relationships. The book picks up the theme of marriage from the conclusion of *The Witch's Head* and, like the earlier novel, culminates in a representation of a stable union with a morally admirable, if physically undistinguished, woman. But as in *The Witch's Head*, this is neither the prevailing note of the book, nor the most ultimately convincing. *Colonel Quaritch* depicts a series of sexual liaisons and actual and potential misalliances, driven variously by sexual passion and financial considerations that lead to wrecked lives, and an emotional and physical violence that harks back to *Dawn*. But there is a perceptible advance in the subtlety of the representations since Haggard's first novel, as might indeed be expected given that in the interim, with the publication of his romances *King Solomon's Mines* (1885), *She* (1886) and *Allan Quatermain* (1887), he had become a successful author. The tragic protagonists Quest and Belle emerge as something more than merely two-dimensional villains. And there is an implicit recognition of the inevitability of human emotional entanglements.

Although *Colonel Quaritch* is less directly autobiographical than *The Witch's Head*, the book considers issues and situations that reflect deeply personal episodes in Haggard's earlier life, notably his jilting, his youthful affair with a married woman, and his subsequent marriage to a sensible, loyal and comfortably well-off wife. These are apparent in the representations of sexually led youthful indiscretions and miscalculations, denoted by Haggard as sins and which later prove emotionally disabling, of unloving marriages contracted for material reasons, and in a consideration of the merits and consolatory capacity of a union driven by affection rather than passion. It is interesting to note that Quest, like Johanna's husband, Peter Ford, is a lawyer. And it may well be that in making reference to Quest's past sexual liaisons, which have poisoned his relationship with his wife Belle, Haggard is representing the background to Johanna's apparently poor relationship with her husband, and offering a degree of exoneration for her marital infidelity. There is also present a new element in the questioning of the ideal of first love, and an amplification of the implicit suggestion in *Dawn* and *The Witch's Head* that sexual sin constitutes a betrayal of an ideal of love, that Arthur's return to Mildred and Ernest's indulgence in love affairs in the wake of their betrayal, or assumed betrayal, by Angela and Eva, respectively, are unworthy actions. In autobiographical terms this latter element translates into a sense that Haggard felt, in a contradictory fashion, that in indulging in his affair with Johanna he was transgressing against the love he knew he would always have for Lilly, despite the fact that it was Lilly's betrayal that predisposed him towards the affair in the first instance. This same issue of the betrayal of an oath to the ideal of love features more overtly in the three romances, *Cleopatra* (1889), *The World's Desire* (1890), and *Eric Brighteyes* (1891), which were published immediately after *Colonel Quaritch*.

Despite its happy ending, or perhaps because of the transparently unconvincing nature of that ending, there is no mistaking the prevailing tone of *Colonel Quaritch*. It is a book concerned with the inevitable nature of human misjudgement in the sexual arena and with the emotionally devastating and life-wrecking consequences that flow from such misjudgement. It appears to reflect Haggard's personal history and his continuing psychological preoccupations, and is in part a replaying and in part a development of the themes apparent in his two earliest novels.

Joan Haste and Its Biographical Resonances

Joan Haste (1895), published some seven years after *Colonel Quaritch*, exhibits the sensation tropes of bigamy, adultery, intrigue and interfering and sometimes treacherous relatives. They fit more comfortably into this melodrama. The book considers the situation of a socially disadvantaged and sexually passionate young woman who is disinherited by an overbearing father and who gives birth to an illegitimate child, and there are echoes of Hardy's *Tess of the D'Urbervilles* (1891) and George Moore's *Esther Waters* (1894). The likely reference in the book's title to Joan of Arc, which would probably have been readily decipherable to its contemporary audience as indicating a bold, liberated and admirable woman finally overwhelmed by events, provides a clue to Haggard's intentions. But he does not permit the book to throw an unrelieved and truly exploratory focus on the theme of a courageous and embattled young woman and through the voice of the narrator continually attempts to corral the reader's moral responses, both in respect of Henry's degree of blameworthiness and of the sinfulness of Joan's behaviour. Haggard had been dismayed by the public outcry that followed the publication in 1890 of his novel *Beatrice*, which depicted an affair between a young woman and a married man and, in 1894, he had added an advertisement to *Beatrice* in which he stated that 'the man or woman who falls into undesirable relations with a married member of the other sex is both a sinner and a fool'.[15] In *Joan Haste* Haggard made doubly sure of his moral escape hatches. Neither of the protagonists is married. And their behaviour, particularly that of the woman, is constantly pilloried.

In common with *Dawn*, *The Witch's Head* and *Colonel Quaritch*, *Joan Haste* reflects powerful personal concerns of Haggard's, but here the focus has moved. Not only had Haggard's illegitimate daughter died in infancy, as Joan's daughter does, but in 1891 his only son had died. Lilias asserts that her father was devastated, and that he interpreted Jock's death as a punishment for his own sexual 'sin'.[16] Like the romance *Montezuma's Daughter* (1893), the first book Haggard wrote after his son's death, *Joan Haste* explores the theme of the sins of the father determining the life of the child. It also constitutes an uncomfortable examination of sexual imperatives and moral duties. Haggard pursues the themes of *Dawn*, *The Witch's Head* and *Colonel Quaritch*, but the rendition is sadder, more reflective, chastened and philosophical. The strong autobiographical overtones remain. The possibility that in *Joan Haste* Haggard was offering a conscious, if oblique, fictional representation of some of his own most intimate experiences is not diminished by the fact that Joan is rendered in German as Johanna and that Henry was Haggard's given name. In his exposition of Henry's behaviour, Haggard is almost certainly reflecting upon his own and, in the book's tragic outcome, indulging in further self-excoriation.

The Stereotypical Nature of Haggard's Male and Female Characters

In his four early novels Haggard gives expression to aspects of sexual passion, both through a number of recurring but developing themes and through recurrent images that find striking and repeated echoes in his romances of the same period. The prevailing emphasis is upon the sexuality of women, variously dominating and manipulative or virtuous and redemptive, their sexual responses to men and their capacity to provoke overwhelming, violent, sexually driven responses in men. Pykett has observed that one of the most sensational aspects of the sensation novels, especially those that were female authored, 'was the apparently and variously transgressive nature of their heroines'.[17] While the heroines of Haggard's early novels are redemptive rather than transgressive women, his early romances (for example, *She*, *Allan Quatermain*, *Cleopatra* and *The World's Desire*) depict female protagonists who are equally as transgressive as the sensation heroines Isabel Vane in *East Lynne* (1861) and Lady Audley and Aurora Floyd in, respectively, Mary Braddon's *Lady Audley's Secret* (1862) and *Aurora Floyd* (1863). But both sets of heroines are capable of causing men emotional damage.

Haggard's fictional protagonists in his early and indeed in his later writing, male and female alike, are stereotypes. The male heroes of his novels are English gentlemen; in his romances, while his heroes may not all be English, all behave as gentlemen, and as Simon Dentith has pointed out, Haggard accords his Zulu heroes 'some attribution of heroic qualities'.[18] Odysseus in *The World's Desire*, Eric in *Eric Brighteyes* and Umslopogaas in *Nada the Lily* (1892), are admirable, physically brave men who are unmanned by exploitative women. Their epic status defines them and at the same time calibrates the extent of their moral fall. Haggard's English gentleman protagonists work in an identical way. They are one-dimensional, decent but emotionally limited and unimaginative, and constrained by clichéd ideas about duty, masculinity and Englishness. They, like the epic heroes, are defined by the recognized attributes of their class. By contrast, his male villains are defined by not being gentleman or heroes. Haggard makes a point of applying the template of gentlemanliness to his male English characters. Robin Gilmour has observed that the concept of gentlemanliness with its moral content was 'one of the most important of Victorian notions' and that a public school education was generally accepted as defining a gentleman.[19] Haggard was therefore following convention, but it also seems likely that, sensitive as he must have been that he himself had not received a public school education, he was taking pains to distance himself from any possible charges of familiarity with the lower classes.

Similarly, the female protagonists of Haggard's early novels and romances, and indeed of all of his fiction, are either malign or virtuous. He has little interest in exploring the psyches of his protagonists, male or female. In his early fiction his unrelenting focus is on the power that women have to wound men, to cause them to act outside their recognized codes of behaviour, to take them onto unfamiliar and intimidating terrain, to disrupt their lives. And the woman is conceived and expounded, admired, feared, criticized and punished, uniformly through the voice of a frequently interventional male narrator. Peter Keating has observed that 'The general reaction against Victorianism and the doctrine of realism both pointed to the overthrow of mid-Victorian fictional stereotypes, and those of women were prominent' and has instanced 'the less conventional portraits of women throughout the 1880s and 1890s'.[20] Elaine Showalter, more specifically, identifies three prominent fin de siècle types of literary representations of women. First, she observes that 'The odd women – the women who could not marry – undermined the comfortable binary system of Victorian sexuality and gender roles,' and she notes 'the period's construction of unmarried women as a new political and sexual group'. She adds that 'moving away from a mid-Victorian notion of female "passionlessness"' there developed 'a recognition of female sexual desire'. Second, she documents the fictional representation of the New Woman, 'an anarchic figure who threatened [...] to be on top in a wild carnival of social and sexual misrule'. Third, Showalter makes reference to the fictional femme fatale, 'The [...] woman who is dangerous to look upon', signifying 'the quest for the mystery of origins'.[21] Haggard's female protagonists may resemble the Odd Women in their initial independence, but they are subsequently confined by marriage. Some of them may share certain attributes with the New Woman, but it is their self-sacrifice that is Haggard's focus. Nevertheless, they are all women of pronounced sexuality whose sexual allure is dangerous to men. Haggard is writing for men, warning them about women and at the same time documenting and working through his own, recent, painful experiences. But as his early fiction progresses, his focus changes from a visceral anger at sexually exploitative women to a consideration of the blame attaching to the male in an illicit sexual liaison and to the proposal that the sexual imperative carries the seeds of moral and emotional destruction.

Sexually Potent and Sexually Vulnerable Women, and Their Roots in Haggard's Biography

The most striking and most familiar type of female Haggard represents is the powerful, compelling, cruel, sexually potent and sexually driven, but sexually vulnerable, woman who is depicted frequently in his romances, appears regularly throughout his fiction and finds her fullest and most widely recognized expression in the character of Ayesha in *She*. In fact, such women first feature in his early novels. Lady Bellamy in *Dawn* is Haggard's earliest rendition of the type. She is a sexually powerful and exploitative woman who tyrannizes her husband in a fashion that has a sexual edge and foreshadows Ayesha's cruelty towards her subjects: 'Jealousy [...] is a luxury which *my* husband is not allowed to indulge in' (24). The emphasis is in the original text. She gloats over the fact: 'Can you imagine anyone being afraid of me, except my husband, of course?' (24). But Lady Bellamy is also a sexually vulnerable woman. Her passion for George resulted in her desertion of her first husband and their child and, blackmailed by him, 'her own taskmaster' (115), she plots pitilessly to help him possess the virtuous and virginal Angela. She is a morally powerful, ambitious and unscrupulous woman who is driven by sexual passion to acts of sexual violence and who is herself destroyed by it. Her sexually humiliated husband plots against her and, her wickedness revealed, she attempts to poison herself, but this results only in her becoming 'a hopeless paralytic for life' (328). Her physical disablement is itself a kind of sexually humiliating punishment similar to Ayesha's physical reduction in *She* and to Isabel Vane's disfigurement in *East Lynne*.

Florence, in *The Witch's Head*, is another such woman. In her violent jealousy at rejection by Ernest and his preference for Eva, she dedicates herself to punishing and ruining Eva by manoeuvring her into a loveless marriage with Plowden – sexual retribution for a perceived sexual crime. Haggard is again depicting the potentially destructive and life-changing consequences of sexual passion. He illustrates Florence's violent sexuality in violent metaphor. When she observes that Ernest is attracted by Eva, in her jealousy she bites her lip 'till the blood ran' (46), and she snaps her fan in rage. She makes it plain that she is not to be slighted: 'I mean to have my revenge […] he shall suffer […] but […] not […] so much as she' (49); and she warns Ernest: 'as I can love, so I can hate' (41). Like Ayesha in *She*, Florence is driven by thwarted sexual passion. But there is a subtlety and ambivalence about the portrayals of Florence and Ayesha. In a transparent attempt by Haggard to manipulate the reader's view of her, the narrator comments that 'Florence was a very remarkable woman […] the love that she bore Ernest was the strongest thing in all her strong and vigorous life' (113). And she has only contempt for Eva's behaviour towards Ernest, telling her that 'you have fallen very low indeed' (221). Haggard is not only using Florence to express a point of view about Eva, but he is also signalling that, wicked though her behaviour and misplaced though her revenge, she has at least been prompted by genuine and unshakeable love. She has demonstrated a level of loyalty that Eva does not approach. In her own way, Florence, unlike Eva, has stood by her man. And, in this respect she foreshadows Ayesha, who also remains faithful to the man she loves, in her case down the centuries and in the respective incarnations of Kallikrates and Leo. This insistence on the redemptive quality of loyalty to the man she loves, in an otherwise dangerously destructive woman, almost certainly derives from Haggard's personal reflections on the emotional shortcomings of his first love.

Haggard's depictions in his first two novels of intimidating and sexually driven women find immediate echo in his first two romances, written directly afterwards. Gagool and Foulata in *King Solomon's Mines* represent contrasting facets of the same woman. Foulata is sexually compelling, faithful and redemptive, both morally and physically. She counterbalances the evil Gagool and saves the explorers' lives by sacrificing her own. Gagool is 'the wise and terrible woman who does not die',[22] and just as Ayesha is a serial and eternal seductress, so Gagool is a serial and eternal betrayer. And her betrayal has a sexual edge. Although she is too old and withered to exercise any direct sexual power over men, she derives a displaced sexual satisfaction through the violent application of her supernatural power. She 'smells out' alleged traitors to the king and delivers them over to be bludgeoned to death (167). She attempts to entomb the explorers, having enticed them into the treasure chamber and entrapped them through their sharp, materialistic desire for the treasure – to stifle them, as it were, in the very act of consumption. She is an experienced procuress, remarking, 'I have seen the white man, and know his desires'

(148), and she knows too what will be the outcome of the male quasi-sexual imperative, asking: 'why will ye run to meet the evil that shall befall ye?' (256).

Haggard's portrayal of dominant women finds its fullest and most celebrated expression in Ayesha, who first appears in *She* and who incorporates aspects of both Foulata and Gagool. Like Foulata, she is sexually alluring and faithful to her lover. Like Gagool, she is eternal, in her case an eternal femme fatale who seduces Leo and murders his lover Ustane just as, frustrated in her attempt to seduce him, she killed his ancestor Kallikrates, and in the process separated him from his lover Amenartas, some eighteen centuries before. Her overwhelming sexual potency is continually emphasized. She deliberately uses her sexuality to torment Holly through acts of emotional violence, and gloats over the fact that he cannot resist her as she unveils for him 'slowly, very slowly' in a provocative strip tease. She mocks his involuntary response: 'perchance thou wouldst eat out thy heart in impotent desire.'[23] Showalter has pointed out that 'the most popular veiled woman of the fin-de-siecle is Salome' and has observed that 'veiling was associated with female sexuality and the veil of the hymen'.[24] Haggard draws on these resonances in his presentation of Ayesha. His overtly sexual imagery is reinforced by the fact that Ayesha's flimsy garment is fastened by a golden snake, representing male lust. He uses this image even more explicitly and powerfully in *The World's Desire*, where Meriamun, as a preamble to her seduction of Odysseus, breathes on the stone snake that fastens her dress, and causes it to come alive:

> Greater it grew and greater yet [...] and wound itself round the body of Meriamun, wrapping her in its fiery folds until it reached her middle. Then it reared its head on high, and from its eyes there flowed a light like the light of a flame.[25]

The permissions of the romance mode enable Haggard to express without reservation the ability of women to inflame an inextinguishable lust in men, something that at this period would have been morally unacceptable to express as openly in 'realistic' novels. Ayesha is also capable of physical sexual sadism: beautiful, passionate, but sexually unfulfilled and waiting impatiently over the centuries for the return of her lover Kallikrates, she vents her sexual frustration in acts of violence against her own subjects. But she is more complex than the Salome of popular conception as described in J-K Huysmans observations on Gustave Moreau's eponymous painting of 1876: 'she had become [...] the symbolic incarnation of undying lust [...] indifferent, irresponsible, irresistible, poisoning [...] everything that she touches'.[26] Haggard's depiction has breadth and a measure of sympathy. About to enter the flame, Ayesha's thoughts are for Leo, and she becomes simply, and touchingly, a sincere woman: 'Oh my love, my love [...] wilt thou ever know how I have loved thee' (291). Haggard himself comments in his article 'Who Is She?' that the power of her love becomes 'a saving grace and a gate of redemption'.[27] His dominant woman is not merely a stylized tyrant but primarily a woman with a woman's range of emotions. This sense, which is reflected in his subsequent powerful and destructive women, suggests a personal emotional investment in the representation.

Sorais in *Allan Quatermain*, like Florence in *The Witch's Head*, is consumed by violent jealousy because Curtis, for whom she has conceived a sexual passion, is in love with her sister. This prompts her to wage war against her sister. And in sexual terms that recall Ayesha's treatment of Holly she taunts Good with his inextinguishable desire for her: 'for a reward thou shall eat out thy heart with love of me and not be satisfied [...] I hold *thee* in chains that cannot be broken'.[28] Sexually frustrated, Sorais and Ayesha feel the need to wound men in the same coin. Meriamun, in *The World's Desire*, uses her mystical feminine power to oblige Odysseus, the man she desires, against his rational inclinations, and in a kind of inversion of rape, to have sex with her, at once satisfying her own passions, humiliating her male partner and disrupting his genuine love. The book is unequivocal about the sinfulness of the act, recording that the snake entwined around Meriamun's body awoke and 'twined itself about the body of the Wanderer [Odysseus] and the body of her who wore the shape of Helen [Meriamun], knitting them together in the bond of sin' (216). Conscious of her own guilt, Meriamun is also aware that she is a victim of overwhelming passion, and she tells Odysseus: 'if I have sinned, I have sinned from love of thee' (254). The motif of rape is even more starkly drawn in *Cleopatra* when Cleopatra, in order to generate funds for her lover's campaigns, metaphorically rapes the corpse of Pharaoh, thrusting her hand 'again, again, and yet again'[29] into the body in her fevered search for the jewels hidden within it. Haggard's malign, destructive women are capable of both extraordinary violence and extraordinary love. They are not simply sexually driven tyrants capable of profoundly, and humiliatingly, unmanning men. They are themselves victims of their inherent, exceptional, uncontrollable, passionate sexuality. And despite their obvious moral failings there remains the implication that their unshakeable passion for the men they love is admirable.

In his depiction of women who less consciously, certainly less malignly, provoke men to acts of sexual frenzy, immorality and betrayal through their exceptional sexuality, Haggard reinforces, broadens and darkens the concept of the innate capacity of female sexual magnetism to ignite men's emotional responses and disrupt their lives. Angela, Mildred and Hilda in *Dawn*, Joan in *Joan Haste*, Nada in *Nada the Lily* and Helen in *The World's Desire* are such women. As he does with his morally culpable women, Haggard licenses himself to depict in his early novels these women's greater than average sexual potency by investing them with an otherness. Hilda, who inflames Philip's passions to the point of causing him to jilt Maria and thereby to damage his own prospects, is a foreigner. Angela is the unwanted offspring of an irregular marriage. Joan's sexual passion and her fornication with Henry is interpreted and modified through the voice of the narrator:

> In the ordinary sense of the word it was not love that possessed her [...] but rather [...] some absorbing influence that included both love and passion [...] Fortunately, with English women such infatuations are not common.[30]

The narrator is delivering a social as well as a moral indictment. In the assertion that Joan is somehow un-English in her emotional comportment, Haggard allows himself, as he had done with Hilda, to represent her permissive sexual morality. Hardy does the same thing in *The Return of the Native* (1878) in his portrayal of the emotionally destructive Eustacia Vye, whose 'Pagan eyes' are described as unusual in English women.[31] Female sexuality was a theme considered in Victorian medical and scientific discourse, but its representation in fiction was altogether a more delicate proposition. As Keating has observed, Victorian novelists 'became adept in the use of allusions and symbols which would communicate directly what they hesitated to express openly'.[32] Haggard's exporting abroad of the sexuality of some of his female protagonists was a similarly convenient device.

In *Dawn* Mildred, like Lady Bellamy, is invested with Egyptian attributes that effectively signpost their exotic otherness. Lady Bellamy is described as possessing 'clearly carved Egyptian features' (23) and later as an 'Egyptian sorceress' (112). When her plotting is revealed, she compares herself to Cleopatra and, like Cleopatra, takes poison, proclaiming: 'Come, life unending, I have conquered death!' (309). Philip, in a recognition of her otherness, finds her 'bizarrely beautiful' (24) and is at a loss to know whether she fascinates or repels him, a response similar to Leo's and Holly's when they regard Ayesha in *She*. Mildred, who has sexual relations with Philip while he is on the rebound from Angela, is perfectly aware of her attraction for men and is compared, albeit obliquely, to Cleopatra, a comparison reinforced by her museum of Egyptian artefacts, which seems to consist largely of mummies housed in a building she calls 'The Hall of the Dead' (an early foreshadowing of the tombs of Kor in *She*). The narrator compounds the sense of the moral dubiety of Mildred's behaviour when, in a further affirmation of her exoticism, he compares her to Calypso trying to get Ulysses 'into her toils' (193). Bradley Deane has pointed out that for the late Victorians the contemporary interest in Egypt was popularly presented through sexual and historical themes, and the fascination, for Victorian men, of the veiled Arab woman was linked to 'the majestic queen of antiquity'.[33] For Haggard, the Egyptian references were a convenient and transparent shorthand for a kind of sexual exoticism.

Establishing the otherness of his sexually potent English women enabled Haggard to explore their sexual vulnerability and to document their sexual responses in a way that convention would not permit him to do with quintessential English women. Mildred is unable to resist falling in love with Arthur, although she is fully aware that he 'was not one little bit in love with her' (189). She is a victim of the addictive aspect of love: 'she had tasted of a new wine, and it burnt her, and was bitter sweet, and yet she longed for more' (189). She wants him 'at any price' and listens 'with wrath and bitter jealousy' (192) when he talks about Angela. Belle in *Colonel Quaritch* has a strongly sexual response to her lover, Cossey. When she sees him 'her whole delicate and lovely face [lit] up like a flower in a ray of sunshine, the lips slightly parted' and 'she flushed up to the eyes […] and her breast heaved'.[34] Her response echoes Nyleptha's equally physical reaction to Curtis in *Allan Quatermain*: 'Red grew her fair bosom and shapely arm […] the rounded cheeks blushed red […] and then the crimson flood sank back to whence it came and left her pale and trembling' (140). Belle, like Nyleptha, is a passionate woman who is genuinely in love. The narrator comments of her: 'there are women with whom all things melt in that white heat of anguished jealousy – honour, duty, conscience and the restraint of religion […] Belle was one' (153). Like Florence in *The Witch's Head*, Belle's love is so strong that it cannot withstand rebuff without precipitating a violent response.

Joan too is reckless in her desire for Henry: 'now her whole being was dominated by her passion' (129). She is both sexually alluring and highly sexually charged. She holds

Henry in her arms after his fall, and their eventual rescuer finds: 'beneath the shadow of the spiked tomb, clasping the senseless body of a man in her arms [...] Joan Haste – whose white dress was smirched with blood' (83). Haggard's imagery connects Joan's human warmth and fleshliness with both her sexual desire and her sexual desirability and with the eventual violence that springs from it. He depicts Helen in *The World's Desire* in very similar terms. Her neck and arms are bare, and she is 'clad in clinging white, but in her breast there glowed a blood-red ruby stone [...] and from it fell red drops which stained for one moment the whiteness of her robes'(152). The red on white blood imagery denoting sexual arousal and sexual liaison, appears again in *The World's Desire*, where Meriamun's 'ivory face flushed rosy' (52) at the sight of Odysseus, and in *Cleopatra* where Harmachis records Cleopatra's response to Anthony: 'I saw the red blood run up beneath her skin' (221–22). Haggard is unequivocal that all women, even the home-grown English variety, are as susceptible as men to the physical urgings of sexual desire. If they are sexually dangerous to men, they are also sexually vulnerable.

Feminine Sexual Vulnerability

As part of this feminine vulnerability Haggard depicts the sexual repugnance women can feel for a man with whom they are obliged, by external circumstances, to consort but for whom they can feel no love. In *Dawn*, George, having tricked Angela into marriage in the belief that he is dying and on the understanding that there will be no physical relationship, appears in her bedroom intent on exercising his conjugal rights and finds her undressed, wearing only a nightdress, and combing her hair. She violently rejects his advances and threatens to kill herself rather than give herself to him. 'With her long hair glimmering in the moonlight' and her 'white robes' (287), she resembles an angel. Haggard is clear that George is making a grotesque attempt on virginity. In *Colonel Quaritch*, Quest, having in his youth been seduced and cajoled into marriage by the older and exploitative Edith, finds thereafter that his life is ruined. Belle, whom he genuinely loves, believing that Edith is his lover, imposes upon him terms of 'complete separation in all but outward form, and virtual freedom of action for herself' (64). Joan, in *Joan Haste*, marries Rock, whom she detests, in order to cauterize any possibility of ever marrying, and thus in her estimation ruining, Henry. Haggard underlines the significance of this act by making clear, through physical imagery, Joan's sexual repugnance for Rock. Rock's hands are 'long' and 'white', and there is 'something furtive and unpleasant about them' (9), and he walks 'delicately' in a feminine fashion (128). A woman's distaste for a man with whom she is obliged to consort is also depicted in Haggard's romances. In *The World's Desire*, Meriamun anticipates a politically expedient marriage to Pharaoh: 'mayhap I shall give myself to him – hating him the while' (63). In *Nada the Lily*, Nada would rather die than marry Dingaan. Lysbeth, in Haggard's eponymous historical romance of 1901, is forced by the Spaniard Montalvo to marry him in order to save her lover from the Inquisition. When it is later discovered that the marriage was bigamous, she rejoices that 'never again could she be forced to endure the contamination of his touch'.[35]

The image of a woman yielding sexually, through *force majeur*, to a man she finds physically rebarbative seems to have had a strong personal resonance for Haggard. It is certainly suggestive of the way in which he may have imagined, or wished to imagine, Lilly responding sexually to the man her family persuaded her to marry. This image is most forcibly and, for Haggard most personally, expressed in Eva's physical distaste for Plowden in *The Witch's Head*. Haggard emphasizes her status as a victim. Plowden, whose name suggests both emotional bovinity and sexual rapacity, is no dashing suitor. He confesses that he does not even love Eva and in an autobiographically telling simile, pursues his courtship with 'as much consideration for the lady as the elephant has for the lily it tramples underfoot' (144). In another apparently significant aside, the narrator intervenes to veil the 'hateful story' of Plowden's insensitive pursuit and says that if readers are curious about the details 'let them go and study them from the life' (146). Plowden cleverly accedes to Eva's wishes and 'the usual amenities of courtship were […] dispensed with':

> But in his heart he thought that a time would come when she would have to yield to him, and his cold eye gleamed. Eva saw the gleam and shuddered prophetically. (205, 206)

The passage, the scenario, and the image of female vulnerability and male sexual cupidity are reminiscent of Manston's pursuit of Cytherea in *Desperate Remedies*: 'Manston's eye sparkled, he saw […] that perseverance […] was irresistible by womankind'.[36]

After Eva has finally been coerced into acquiescence Florence sees her, 'very pale […] shrinking with scared eyes and trembling limbs'. Plowden, 'looking big and vulgar, was standing over her' (146). In what can only be interpreted as a further deeply autobiographical reference in which Plowden is nuanced as Lilly's husband, the narrator comments, 'the lily was broken at last' (211). These unpleasant, physical images representing sexual repugnance, sexual violence and sexual conquest underline the emotional and physical price Eva is to pay for her weakness, and at an autobiographical level seem to derive from Haggard's preoccupation with the sexual implications of Lilly's marriage to another man and his wish to believe that these were distasteful to her.

The Punishment of Disruptive Women

Both in his early novels and early romances Haggard portrays women who, as well as being to a greater or lesser degree sexually exploitative and sexually dangerous to men, are also victims of the sexual imperative, and he postulates that, despite their obvious moral shortcomings, these women act as they do as a result of their inextinguishable passion for the men they love, and that this fidelity is, in itself, morally admirable. It seems that, as a man who had personal experience of a disloyal woman, Haggard prized such fidelity highly. But although he has sympathy for these women, the humiliating and physical punishments he metes out to them indicate that he is allocating to them the blame for the disruption they cause to men's lives. The beautiful and manipulative Lady Bellamy is left paralyzed for life. The vulgar seductress Edith, who ruined Quest's life in *Colonel Quaritch*, is drowned. Sorais, whose unrequited sexual passion for Curtis precipitates a civil war, suffers a resounding defeat and commits suicide. Gagool, who seeks to exploit the explorers' quasi-sexual desire for the hidden treasure by permanently entombing them underground, and who murders the virtuous and sexually desirable Foulata, is savagely crushed to death by the same rocks she had intended should bury the explorers alive. Ayesha, a cruel sexual sadist, is punished, as it were, in the very sexual act itself. At the moment of stepping into the Flame of Life, as an encouragement to Leo to follow her, she is consumed by it, shorn of her beauty, reduced to a withered simian form and dies. In January 1887, Haggard recorded that she is punished for 'the insolence of her strength and loveliness'.[37] The humiliator of men is herself humiliated. Haggard's comment on Ayesha, taken together with the overwhelming focus of his early novels, seems to confirm that she derives primarily from his experience of Lilly. Shannon Young has suggested that the depiction springs from Haggard's 'oedipal problems',[38] and Norman Etherington has offered the view that 'Ayesha can be interpreted as a mother in disguise.'[39] But this seems to be an over-reading of Ayesha's undoubted matriarchal attributes.

Haggard's preoccupation is with the femme fatale rather than the mother, as his other early romances and of course his early emotional experiences demonstrate. Cleopatra is poisoned by Harmachis, whose life she has ruined, and dies: 'her face sank in with terror, her great eyes […] pale […] passing with that dread company to her appointed place' (323). In *The World's Desire*, Meriamun, who uses magic to seduce Odysseus, is compelled by an irresistible impulse to leap onto his funeral pyre. As she lies on Odysseus's body 'the Snake awoke in the fire […] it grew, it twisted itself about the body of Meriamun and the body of the Wanderer [Odysseus], and lifting its head, it laughed' (316). The same snake that grew and coiled itself about them in their sexual union, now coils about them in death, suggesting the unquenchable nature of the sexual urge and mocking the outcome of their illicit coupling. Haggard's authorial intensity dispenses punishments in excess of those meted out to the destructive Lizzie Eustace, who is publicly disgraced in Anthony Trollope's *The Eustace Diamonds* (1873), and to the exploitative Becky Sharp in William Thackeray's *Vanity Fair* (1847–48), who is reduced to poverty before going on to persevere in her morally dubious behaviour, and more chillingly adjacent to the disfigurement of Isabel in *East Lynne*. In addition to Isabel, several other transgressive sensation novel heroines are also severely punished. Lady Audley in Mary Braddon's *Lady Audley's Secret* (1862) is incarcerated in a Belgian madhouse. Aurora in Braddon's *Aurora Floyd* (1863) is eventually confined by marriage. Miss Aldclyffe in *Desperate Remedies* dies on learning of her son's suicide in prison.

Haggard, in keeping with his comments on Ayesha's punishment in 'Who Is She?', is postulating heavy punishment for those sexually potent, calculating women who themselves betray, or who cause men, despite themselves, to betray the ideal of first and genuine love. It is as though, in his insistent depictions of these uncompromising punishments of temptresses, Haggard is working through a very personal sense of the power over men of unscrupulous but irresistible women, and alleging that they are the real culprits in man's sexual fall from grace and the root cause of his personal self-loathing, both for his own illicit sexual liaison and his involuntary betrayal of the ideal of his first love.

While Haggard offers violent, retributive, physical punishments for his truly evil seductresses and manipulators, his weak-charactered women – those who have been emotionally disadvantaged by circumstances, and those who are themselves overcome by their own innate sexuality – suffer remorse and lifelong regret. The latter are presented as victims rather than perpetrators, and they are women for whom Haggard has a significant measure of sympathy. Mildred, abandoned by Arthur, to whom she offered an emotional haven after he believed himself betrayed by Angela, remains, a victim of her own passion, lying in front of the statue of Osiris in her museum 'like some hopeless sinner before an inexorable justice' (367), sobbing 'till the darkness of the night covered her, and her heart broke in the silence of the night' (371). Belle, in *Colonel Quaritch*, forced into marriage by an overbearing parent, enters a nunnery to reflect upon the consequences of her illicit passion for Cossey. Even the virtuous Nada, whose beauty prompts men to acts of violence, dies, albeit accidentally, of starvation in a sealed cave.

It is instructive, and revealing of his state of mind at that time, to consider a letter Haggard wrote to his secretary Agnes Barber on 5 August 1883, when he was working on drafts of *Dawn*. In the letter he suggests to her the subject for a long poem to be called 'Farewell'. He begins with reflections that merit quoting at some length:

> Farewell is a big subject. The whole world is one long farewell, it may therefore be said to include all human interest in its eight letters. It is a sad word too whether it deals with the parting of friend from friend, of the individual from his surroundings, of a heart from anything it has cherished, of soul from body or of a fine strong mind from its illusions.

Haggard's proposal is that the poem should be about a young man who is betrayed by his lover, who allows herself to be forced to marry someone else:

> Make the woman weak and let her in spite of the written remonstrance of her absent lover let herself be forced or frightened, with her eyes open into marriage with some other man, but do not make her an injured angel as it is the fashion to do when a woman plays false with herself and her lover. Let the blow fall upon him as heavily as you will but [...] let him also marry.

The lovers meet a little later in life and, in her passion for the man, 'the woman reveals her naked heart to her lover's gaze, when she has forgotten husband, children, honour, friends, everything except that he is there and she loves him.' But he deserts her 'as she in cold blood deserted him' and tells her to return to duty and spouse as he will do. They bid each other farewell.[40] The letter illustrates that at the time Haggard was writing *Dawn* his mind was turning on a fictional representation of a particularly painful episode in his own life and responding to it retrospectively in a sad, angry and occasionally vengeful voice. This theme was to find its fullest expression in his treatment of Eva's punishment for her betrayal in *The Witch's Head*.

If we assume, as the striking similarities with Haggard's personal history suggest we may, that Eva is, at least in substantial part, a portrayal of Lilly, then we may also interpret the attitude the book takes to her, and the punishment it inflicts upon her, as reflecting both Haggard's feelings towards Lilly and the feelings he would have wished to attribute to her. In fictionally depicting her emotions about jilting him for the man she married, Haggard was almost certainly drawing upon his imagination rather than on his clear knowledge, since there is no documentary or anecdotal evidence that Haggard had significant contact with Lilly between 1878, when she married Archer, and 1884, when he completed *The Witch's Head*. The sense of personal ownership by Haggard of Eva is most apparent in the uncertain and veering judgement of her. It seems probable that, in his depiction of Eva, Haggard is exploring both his own attitude to Lilly's behaviour and his current feelings for her and seeking to solace himself by working through this painful episode in his life. Max Saunders draws attention to Stephen Reynolds's essay 'Autobiografiction', published in *Speaker* in 1906, observing that Reynolds argues 'that the chief significance of autobiografiction lies in the psychological consolation it offers'.[41] This certainly seems to be the case with Haggard. *The Witch's Head* oscillates between a partial exoneration of Eva and an insidious but repeated criticism of her behaviour, together with an apparent satisfaction in documenting her subsequent emotional suffering. There is a mismatch between the dramatic action that represents her as a more or less helpless victim of her irresistibly evil sister Florence and what the narrator's voice has to say. And while this voice is evidently Haggard's, his undermining of its generally censorious tone is an indication of the difficulty he found in dealing with the subject.

The earlier parts of *The Witch's Head* identify excuses for Eva's behaviour. 'A weak minded beauty is the most unfortunate of her sex' (31), says her aunt, and the narrator urges: 'Poor Eva […] give her all your pity, but […] purge it of your contempt' (148). From the point of Eva's marriage, however, the perspective begins to change, and the book demonstrates a growing ambivalence towards her. It is as if the physical realities of her union with Plowden have taken over Haggard's interest. He brings two voices to bear on Eva, in both of which it is difficult not to perceive his own. The narrator comments on her behaviour, and Ernest and other characters speak to her directly. Book 2, Chapter 14, which painfully documents her failure to grasp her final but real opportunity to reject Plowden and go to join Ernest, is a good example of the book's veering judgement on Eva. Its title, 'The Virgin Martyr', is subverted by the substance of its critical tone. Cardus offers Eva a home and protection just as Haggard's father had done in respect of Lilly.[42] Like Lilly, Eva declines. Despite having pledged 'eternal fidelity' (87) to Ernest, she marries Plowden, and the narrator comments: 'By her own act, of her own folly and weakness, she was undone' (219–20). And, in a vengeful act of supreme cruelty, Florence reveals her plotting to Eva and vilifies her for disloyalty to Ernest: 'You have deserted him when he was absent and in trouble, and you have outraged his love and your own' (220–21). Eva is no martyr but, rather, weak-willed and unfaithful. The criticism of her is unequivocal and cutting.

In parallel with this increasingly audible critical voice, the book, in this respect unique amongst Haggard's treatment of his heroines, begins to examine and analyze Eva's emotions. But this simply signposts the reader to the conclusion that she is inadequately sensitive. In Book 3, Chapter 3, entitled 'Introspective', which apparently has as much relevance to the author as it does to his character, the narrator reflects on Eva's lack of sensibility: 'Such a fate as Eva's would have killed Dorothy, and would have driven Florence […] to suicide or madness. But […] Eva […] was not sufficiently finely strung to suffer thus' (292). He compares her state of mind about their permanent separation with Ernest's: 'To Eva it had been and was a sorrow, sometimes a very real one; to Ernest, the destruction of all that made life worth living' (292). Having established

Ernest's sensitivity as admirable and Eva's emotional deficiency both as contemptible and a means of interpreting her betrayal, the book veers again to a powerful, if dramatically contradictory, representation of her remorse and her punishment for having betrayed Ernest. It is as if, in personal terms, Haggard is making an attempt to convince himself that Lilly bitterly regretted that she had jilted him, that she suffered for it and that she still continued to love him. At the same time, he appears to be exacting a revenge which, historically, was denied him. This he does through telling narratorial comment and through direct address by Ernest.

When, years after her marriage, Eva sees Ernest again,

> all her smouldering passion broke into flame, and she felt that she still loved him with all her strength, such as it was [...] she realised how great, how bitter, how complete was the mistake she had made, and what a beautiful thing life might have been for her if things had gone differently. (293)

And, after their meeting, the narrator comments: 'For her and those like her are vain regrets and an empty love and longing and the wreath of thorns that crowns the brow when sorrow is enthroned' (302–3). The biblical reference to Christ's crown of thorns[43] is presumably intended to depict Eva as both victim and sinner. Her behaviour is finally captioned as moral criminality in the book's final image of her covertly watching Ernest's marriage to Dorothy in the very church in which she herself had married Plowden and, creeping away, like Christian in John Bunyan's *The Pilgrim's Progress* (1678), 'bearing away with her the haunting burden of her sin' (320). This unequivocal identification of Eva's sexual betrayal as sin and, as such, on a moral par with the extramarital sexual relations of Mildred and of Joan, illustrates Haggard's deeply personal, even obsessive, interest in the matter, and strongly suggests that he regarded Lilly's marital sexual relations with Archer as morally illicit. In Ernest's direct address to Eva there is a real sense of personal catharsis. Through Ernest, Haggard seems to be vocalizing what he would have liked to say to Lilly about her betrayal. The accusation is unvarnished: 'You have wrecked my life [...] you gave me proofs which I could not doubt that I had won your love [...] you deserted and morally destroyed me' (298–99). Writing about the humiliation of Ayesha in *She* in a letter to the *Spectator* reprinted in the *Pall Mall Gazette* in 1887 Haggard says that 'in her lover's presence she is made to learn the thing she really is, and what is the end of earthly wisdom and of the loveliness she prized so highly'.[44] It is clear that these observations apply equally to his treatment of Eva.

The Destructive Impact upon Men of Desirable but Benign Women

In addition to his depiction in them of malevolent, dangerously sexually exploitative and morally flawed women, Haggard's early novels and romances also portray gentle and morally admirable women who are nevertheless sexually potent, having the ability, despite their benign natures, to inflame male passion and, potentially, to disrupt male lives. Into this category fall, with the exception of Eva, the heroines of his early novels – Angela, Ida and Joan – and, amongst his contemporary romances, Foulata in *King*

Solomon's Mines, Ustane in *She*, Nyleptha in *Allan Quatermain*, Helen in *The World's Desire* and Nada in *Nada the Lily*. Etherington points out that 'Haggard distinguishes between the uses to which good and bad women apply their physical charms.'[45] This is certainly true, but what is rather more interesting is Haggard's conclusion that the impact on men is often the same. Angela's long-suffering fidelity is combined with a fleshly beauty that drives George to a frantic lust at the sight of her bathing naked. Unlike Ayesha in *She*, Helen in *The World's Desire* can enter the flames of passion without being consumed. But exactly like Ayesha, she provokes uncontrollable desire in men. Nada is a virtuous woman, but her disturbing beauty moves men to lust and violence. Precisely because of her supposed sexual sin, Joan is probably Haggard's most striking portrayal of a woman who is both virtuous and overwhelmingly attractive to men. She is at the same time beautiful enough to tempt Henry into an illicit sexual relationship and passionate enough to enter it herself. But her love for him, sexual rather than spiritual though it may primarily be, prompts her to acts of extraordinary selflessness. She voluntarily goes away to a sordid and lonely existence in London, declining his offer of marriage on the grounds that it would ruin him. She marries Rock, who is loathsome to her, in order to eradicate any chance of marriage with Henry. Finally, she dies in order to save Henry's life. Joan is a desirable and responsive woman with an immense capacity for love and moral goodness. But her overwhelming attractiveness ruins men's lives. Haggard may not mete out retributive punishments on these morally admirable but still dangerously seductive women, but his conclusion is bleak: Angela and Ayesha may be moral poles apart, but they are equally destructive.

Haggard proposes that all women, even benign ones, are primarily to blame for men's sexual infidelities. Hilda in *Dawn* makes Philip's blood 'run warm and quick' (21), and the narrator says that 'his passion for her burnt him like a fire, utterly searing away the traces of his former affection for Maria' (22). He is so overcome by Hilda's beauty that he 'covered his face with his hand, as though this woman's loveliness was more than he could bear to look upon' (30), and he subsequently jilts the heiress Maria in a way that is both profoundly unkind and profoundly damaging to his prospects. In a similar image depicting the self-mutilating aspect of man's passion for woman, Ernest in *The Witch's Head* is blinded by lightning. In Nyleptha's observation to Allan in *Allan Quatermain*, Haggard makes the point more directly: 'Passion is like the lightning, it is beautiful, and it links the earth to heaven, but alas it blinds' (164). In *She* the Flame of Life is both elemental and destructive. Joseph Kestner asserts that in adventure fiction of the late nineteenth and early twentieth centuries 'Blindness is associated with castration, loss of power, denial of the male controlling gaze and fear of the empowered female.'[46] Rudyard Kipling, for example, uses it to indicate frustrated passion in *The Light That Failed* (1891). Haggard is arguing that, blinded by the heat and luminosity of sexual passion, men can no longer see clearly. Braddon foreshadowed this concept in her depiction of the impact upon Bulstrode of Aurora Floyd: 'A divinity! Imperiously beautiful […] painfully dazzling to look upon, intoxicatingly brilliant to behold'.[47] In *Dawn* Arthur is similarly overwhelmed by Angela's beauty. He falls in love with her at first sight and 'never before had he known any such sensation as that which now overpowered him' (107). He is reduced by it. The corollary of Arthur's passion for Angela is that when he believes she has betrayed him by marrying George, his jealous and wounded response is equally passionate. The narrator reflects, in terms that surely have a personal resonance for Haggard:

> Arthur, to an extent quite unrealized by himself until he lost her, had centred all his life in this woman, and it was no exaggeration to say [...] that she had murdered his heart, and withered up all that was best in it. (311)

Arthur flounces off without a moment's hesitation, to have sexual relations with Mildred via several days of debauchery in London. And while Mildred is punished, as Eva was to be in *The Witch's Head*, Arthur returns to the arms of a forgiving Angela. Haggard exonerates him on the grounds that he could not help himself.

This investment in the woman of sexual powers that have the capacity to overwhelm men, her virtual deification, expressed in biblically derived cadence and imagery, together with her capacity for destruction, foreshadows the unmanning, irresistible beauty of Ayesha in *She* and of Helen in *The World's Desire*. Ayesha sums up the situation: 'if the temptation be but strong enough, then will the man yield' (201). Helen arouses such a frenzy of sexual passion in men that they abandon wives and lovers and flock to see her: 'they could no more withstand their longing' (149). They besiege her temple, seeking to reach her inner sanctuary, 'gnawing at the bars with their teeth, crying to be let in' (151), but are killed by the invisible swords that protect her, while, in just one of the fire metaphors that pervade the book, their wives and lovers burn down the temple in a futile attempt to destroy Helen. The romance mode enables Haggard to render this remarkably raw and striking depiction of the helpless imperative of male passion, humiliating both in itself and in its ultimate unfulfilling outcome. Read in the light of his novels, which project the same proposal in necessarily less direct terms, it takes on a consistent and deeply personal aspect.

It is autobiographically significant, in the light of his first and lifelong love and his subsequent affair, that Haggard depicts woman's betrayal of a man's love, and man's sexually driven response to this betrayal, in the cadre of a first love. The narrator in *Dawn* observes of the significance for a man of a genuine first love: 'Henceforth that love [...] will become the guiding spirit of his inner life [...] He may sin against it but he can never forget it' (108). The personal resonance is unmistakeable. *The Witch's Head* constitutes Haggard's most concentrated treatment of the twin themes, and it is clear from the book's insistence on the subject that he has a vested psychological interest in putting the majority of the blame on the woman. Ernest's first sight of Eva makes a profound physical and spiritual impact upon him:

> The dress was cut low, and her splendid neck and arms were entirely without ornament. In the masses of dark hair, which coiled like a coronet round her head, there glistened a diamond star [...] from those dark eyes there shone a light that few men could look on and forget [...] it was like the light of a star. (45)

Once again Haggard depicts, in the impact upon a man of a beautiful woman, a luminous, incandescent quality, but here it is soft and pure rather than blinding, and it is expressed with a freshness suggesting personal conviction, perhaps even personal reminiscence. This same personal quality recurs in Haggard's equally intense autobiographical romance *Montezuma's Daughter* in which Thomas reflects, in old age, upon his first kiss with his lover Lily: 'the memory of that kiss has gone with me through my long life, and is with me yet, when, old and withered, I stand upon the borders of the grave' (23). In *The Witch's Head* this image of love at first sight intensifies the impact of Eva's betrayal. Like Arthur's reaction at Angela's behaviour, which is to hurry off to the sexually available Mildred, Ernest's grief at Eva's betrayal also expresses itself in sexual wildness. The overwhelming force of a first, genuine passion is transformed by the perceived betrayal of that passion into an equally overwhelming, angry and destructive lust. When, many years later, Ernest again encounters Eva he tells her: 'you have taken that from me which I can never have to give again […] you have […] driven me to sins of which I should not otherwise have dreamed' (298). Ernest has been robbed by Eva of both his first, and genuine, love and of his judgement. Like Arthur he has been driven by sexual betrayal, or perceived sexual betrayal, by the woman he truly loves, to acts of uncharacteristic and humiliating sexual libidinousness. But their illicit sexual liaisons are essentially justified as a man's involuntary and inevitable response to a woman's moral crime. It seems that Haggard is in this respect rewriting autobiography in an act of self-exculpation. In *She* he extends the concept of man's helplessness in the face of sexual temptation. Ustane has been unswervingly faithful to Leo, but nevertheless he is obliged by the sheer force of Ayesha's sexual magnetism, and against all his inclinations, to allow himself to be seduced by her in the presence of the body of Ustane, whom Ayesha has just killed. Leo has been compelled to break his oath of fidelity to his first love, but like Arthur and Ernest, he is exonerated. It is Ayesha who is punished.

Men's Share of the Blame for Their Sexual Excesses

Convenient and comforting though the conclusion that women are to blame for men's sexual peccadilloes may initially have been for Haggard at a personal level, it seems from his immediately subsequent fiction that he was uneasy with it, and that he could not shake off a profound conviction that in his affair with Johanna he was personally culpable for having betrayed his pure first love for Lilly. He expresses this conviction primarily in the three romances published between 1889 and 1891. Harmachis, Odysseus and Eric, in *Cleopatra*, *The World's Desire* and *Eric Brighteyes*, respectively, break an oath to a first and genuine love through being beguiled into an illicit sexual liaison by an exploitative and sexually irresistible woman. All of these men are determined, emphatically masculine, heroic, but unimaginative, figures, unmanned and, in two cases, forced to have sexual relations against their will by a woman's intense sexuality. But even though they are unable to help themselves they are heavily punished for having broken their oaths of fidelity to their first loves, in part by being deprived of these loves, with only a limited hope of reconciliation in an afterlife, and in part because the sexual fulfilment of their lusts is not accompanied by any corresponding emotional fulfilment; the experience is tarnished by remorse and by continuous desire.

Harmachis, buried alive by his fellow priests as a punishment for breaking his oath to an ideal of true love, remains unable to forget Cleopatra and, as Richard Pearson points out, is 'entombed in a frenzy of inescapable desire'.[48] In the same way that Lady Bellamy tells her husband openly that she does not reciprocate his love, that Belle refuses her husband sexual relations, that Holly is taunted by Ayesha for his inextinguishable but unfulfillable sexual passion for her, and that Good in *Allan Quatermain* is similarly mocked by Sorais, so Cleopatra, at the very moment of her death, poisoned by Harmachis, triumphs over him, exposing her breasts to him and mocking his ineradicable desire for her: 'Now put away their memory if thou canst [...] no torture [...] can [...] draw nigh to the rage of that deep soul of thine, rent with longings never, never to be reached' (321–22). Similarly, in *The World's Desire* Meriamun's dungeons contain a chamber, the gate to which is in the shape of a woman, in which imprisoned men are chained and burned alive: 'the last torment by fire' (250). In these early romances, as Pearson comments: 'the narrative climax links the male protagonist not with a satisfying, procreative sex, but with a perverse destructive sex, which arrives as the inevitable fulfilment of his inner drives.'[49] Higgins suggests that in Ayesha's sudden transformation into a wrinkled simian figure after entering the Flame of Life, Haggard is describing 'the nightmare of satiated lust instantly giving way to guilt and disgust.'[50] Higgins's imaginative suggestion is superficially appealing, if only partly convincing, but in these romances Haggard is certainly proposing that part of man's punishment for breaking his oath in his helpless, involuntary lust is the ultimate lack of fulfilment of that lust. Its eternal, gnawing, imperative is an inevitable part of the sexual act.

Haggard's personal obsession with this theme of the sexual betrayal, by a man, of his first love is further underlined by his treatment of it in *Montezuma's Daughter* and *The People of the Mist* (1894), written shortly after the death of his son in 1891. Haggard was devastated by his loss and interpreted it as a punishment for his own sexual incontinence. He found himself unable to work for some months and, when he did, it seems clear that once again self-consolation was a psychological imperative. In *Montezuma's Daughter* and *The People of the Mist* the male protagonists, respectively Thomas and Leonard, having sworn eternal fidelity to their first loves, go abroad to a far-flung land where they fall in love with, and marry, exotic native women. Eventually they return to England: Thomas because his native wife has conveniently died; Leonard, bringing his wife Juanna, to discover that his first love has also, equally conveniently, died. Thomas's first love, Lily, who has remained faithful to him, forgives him for breaking their oath, and they marry. Leonard's first love had married someone else but never forgot her love for him, leaving him considerable property upon which he lives happily with Juanna. In both books first love triumphs and the man is exonerated for his sexual infidelity, very determinedly so in *Montezuma's Daughter*. Thomas appeals directly to the reader for comprehension:

> I was young, and the English Lily, my own love, was far away and lost to me for ever. Was it then wonderful that I should find this Indian poppy fair? (120)

The autobiographical resonances are plain. It seems that Haggard's less excoriating and more comfortable vision of male responsibility in these two books was prompted by the personal tragedy he had recently suffered. It is as if he desperately needed to offer himself some residual reassurance.

But by the time he came to write *Joan Haste* Haggard's pessimistic vision had reasserted itself. His earlier attempts to absolve the man from blame for an illicit sexual entanglement have foundered as the distance between *Dawn* and *Joan Haste* illustrates. Both Arthur and Henry are unfaithful to their first loves, Arthur in his affair with Mildred, Henry in conveniently abandoning Joan for the socially advantageous Emma. Arthur is exonerated from blame, but Haggard is unable to do the same with Henry. He is not a man who conceptualizes his predicament as the excruciating choice between the fulfilment of an overwhelming love and his duty to his family, but rather as the reconciliation of that duty with his perceived obligations as a gentleman towards a woman of modest social standing whose reputation he has ruined in a moment of male sexual weakness. He is unimaginative, controlled, morally blinkered and emotionally tepid. Although he has never before seen a woman to equal Joan, he fails to recognize the true nature of his feelings for her, writing them off conveniently, but erroneously, as infatuation. But the narrator makes a repeated attempt to absolve Henry from blame, arguing that it was Joan who took the first step in precipitating their sexual liaison: 'Her purpose [...] was to make Henry love her, and to the consummation of this end she brought to bear all her beauty and every power of her mind' (131). He proposes that Henry's capitulation is about Joan's power prevailing over his better judgement. Her love for him 'gradually conquered his mind and body and broke down the barrier of his self-control' (132). Joan, looking in the mirror, realizes her own beauty and 'a sense of her own power entered into her' (143); and the narrator comments, 'she was lovely [...] as we may imagine the ancient Helen to have been' (142). This reference to Helen calls to mind *The World's Desire*, which depicts Helen as, almost unwittingly, bringing men to destruction through her irresistible power to inflame their sexual passions. In short, Joan is a reprise of Helen and of Ayesha, Cleopatra and Nada. It is in this context that Haggard invites the reader to assess Henry's susceptibility to her. The narrator spells it out prosaically:

> He was weak and he was worried [...] Under such conditions it was not perhaps unnatural that he should shrink back from the strict path of interest and follow that of a spontaneous affection. (132)

And, anyway, Joan is sexually irresistible. Not only is Henry, like Arthur, Ernest and Leo, substantially exonerated from blame for illicit sexual relations, as, effectively, the helpless victim of an exploitative and sexually irresistible woman, but his feelings for Joan are transparently and leadingly categorized as a mere 'spontaneous affection' rather than love. There are once again echoes of Haggard's own affair with Johanna when, almost certainly aware of her pregnancy, he left South Africa for England where he swiftly married the sexually uninspiring but socially acceptable Louisa, who, like Emma, was an heiress. After sowing his wild oats, Haggard, like Henry, swiftly contracted a socially advantageous union and was able to pass it off as duty. The lofty dismissal, through the mouth of the complicit narrator, of Henry's responsibility is highly suggestive of an attempt at self-exculpation.

But the voice of the moral arbiter exonerating Henry does not constitute the prevailing tone of the book. After their sexual liaison, it is his sense of duty towards Joan rather than his love for her that prevails. After he has had an unpleasant confrontation with Rock he soliloquizes unflatteringly about her:

> Fond as I am of you, had I known half the trouble and insult that I must suffer on your account, I would have chosen to go blind before ever I set eyes upon your face. (232–33)

When he learns of her marriage to Rock, instead of the wild and violent regrets which Ernest experienced in *The Witch's Head* when he learned of Eva's betrayal, Henry coolly and loftily reflects: 'of her own act she had put an end to an imbroglio that had many painful aspects, and there remained no stain upon his character' (358). It is only when Joan lies dying that he tells her: 'I shall love you now [...] and always' (422). Haggard adumbrates Henry's Laodicean qualities in his portrayal of Samuel Rock. Where Henry is tepid and emotionally inarticulate, Rock is patently overwhelmed by his frustrated sexual passion for Joan. The violence and permanence of Rock's passion is in instructive contrast to Henry's passivity. It seems as though, in what appears to be an autobiographically driven exploration of the moral nature of Henry's behaviour towards Joan, Haggard has been forced to the personally painful conclusion that, like his own towards Johanna, it is contemptible.

Henry's self-induced myopia has caused him, until it is too late, to interpret his feelings for Joan as mere transient, sexual passion. Haggard is plain that sexual liaisons conceived out of lust, as opposed to a genuine and pure love, whether or not they are provoked by a woman's betrayal, are, in effect, sins against the ideal of true love, and he represents the consequences in the relationships between Quest, Edith, Belle and Cossey in *Colonel Quaritch*. Both Quest and Cossey, like Haggard himself, are guilty of a youthful affair with an older woman, and like the protagonists in *Cleopatra*, *The World's Desire* and *Eric Brighteyes*, both have been the victims of calculating women. Quest was seduced and cajoled into marriage by the older and exploitative Edith. Cossey was encouraged by the married Belle, whom he has never loved but found himself loved by her, and 'after a more or less severe struggle yielded to the temptation' (99). He hates the deception involved, and the relationship 'became more and more irksome to him' (101) as 'her violent and unreasoning passion wearied and alarmed him' (100). Belle confesses: 'I led you on, I know I did' (58) and later acknowledges that 'all the blame will follow me [...] I am older than you [...] and a woman' (59). The details of Haggard's relationship with Johanna are sparsely documented, but it seems likely that there is something of his personal experience in this depiction. Certainly the reference to Cossey's alarm over Belle's 'unreasoning passion' is reminiscent of a letter to Haggard about Johanna's state of mind, in the aftermath of the death of her child by Haggard, written from South Africa by his friend Arthur Cochrane and in which Cochrane expresses the hope that 'there will be no [...] unhappy sentences which may be spoken while under the influence of the great grief'.[51] Certainly it is not difficult to believe that Haggard, having involved himself in an available and flattering relationship with an older woman, soon began to regret aspects of the entanglement. All the available evidence indicates that Johanna's husband remained unaware of the affair but, apparently entertaining what must have been his worst nightmare, Haggard depicts the wronged husband, Quest, confronting Cossey and exacting from him a large sum of money in compensation.

Even though they have not broken any personal oath, Quest and Cossey are punished, like Harmachis, Odysseus and Eric, for their crime against true love. Quest's punishment is that his love for Belle is not reciprocated and that she denies him sexual relations, insisting on 'complete separation in all but outward form' (64). He weeps 'in the anguish of his soul, praying to heaven for deliverance from the burden of his sins' (124–25). This depiction of male remorse finds echo in *Cleopatra*, where Harmachis records: 'I […] wept tears of agony for the lost unchanging past' (257). Because of 'one fatal error of his boyhood' (135) Quest descends into moral turmoil and finally dies violently. Cossey similarly fails to win Ida, his real love. Edith too suffers for what Haggard presents, in an apparently self-servingly fictionalized autobiographical reference, as her sexual criminality in having seduced the youthful Quest. She had 'entered his life, corrupted him and destroyed him' (124). She becomes a showgirl and part-time prostitute, cheated and despised by her customers. Gerald Parsons observes that the contemporary Christian view of young men like Quest was that 'by yielding to the "lower elements of their nature" through sexual indulgence […] they destined themselves for social and spiritual ruin'.[52] The fact that Quest subsequently married Edith constitutes no extenuation of his sinful behaviour. Roy Porter and Leslie Hall note, 'Preachers condemned premarital fornication as just as sinful as promiscuity.'[53] W. Guest, a Congregational minister writing on sexual sin in 1878 in 'A Young Man's Perils' warns that such sin cannot be atoned for: '*Sin is imperishable* […] *it cannot be undone.*'[54] The italics are original. The proposal that sexual licentiousness is not only a sin against Christian moral precepts but is also a profound sin against the ideal of real love clearly concerned Haggard personally and deeply. Not only does this personal conviction seem to derive from his own Christian faith (he records in his autobiography: 'I believe in the simple and unadulterated doctrines of Christianity.'[55]) but it also seems to originate in his guilt at his own sexual incontinence.

The Consequences of the Sexual Imperative: Sexual Jealousy, Moral Disintegration and Violence

Despite the numerous depictions of punishments of both men and women for sexual incontinence, there is a growing sense in Haggard's early fiction that they do not resolve the problem. They lack a finality. Only in *Dawn*, *Colonel Quaritch* and *Montezuma's Daughter* are there truly happy endings to complement the punishment of the malefactors, and in the last two books, the happy endings lack conviction. Ayesha in *She* dies to reappear. She is as indestructible as the sexual urge itself, and no amount of punishment will prevent her from re-offending. There is a growing darkness and hopelessness in Haggard's depictions of sexual entanglements. They cause moral decay and violence and affect unborn lives. And they are unavoidable; they can happen to anyone. Belle in *Colonel Quaritch*, having renounced her life of sin and become a nun, bids farewell to her former lover Cossey saying: 'The sin was mine; that is it would have been mine were we free agents which perhaps we are not' (280). Haggard is beginning to entertain a fatalism he is to reiterate in his later fiction. But it does not obscure the force of his depiction of the destructive consequences of sexual sin.

The proposition that the grip of sexual passion and its consequences can affect the virtuous but unwary as well as the inherently morally flawed is exemplified in *Dawn* in the character of Philip who, initially presented as physically and morally admirable, undergoes a moral, physical and financial decline as a result of his sexual passion for Hilda. He lies, he performs acts of moral cowardice towards both of the women in his life and finally he becomes, in effect, a murderer. His moral collapse is reflected in his physical state. Maria finds him 'scared […] with dishevelled hair [and] white and trembling lips' (63). He has ruined her life, but thereafter he 'never thought of repentance' (69). He withdraws from society. He is bitter towards the product of his passion for Hilda, his daughter Angela. In short, the result of his surrender to sexual passion is that his moral judgement is distorted. He is haunted by spectres, drinks heavily and is hounded by his conscience, 'His features […] resembling those of a dumb thing in torture […] terror staring from his face' (287). In the grip of apparent hopelessness, he sets fire to George's house in an act of pyromania that suggests an attempt to eradicate by fire the destructive sexual fire that has gripped both of them. Philip is an early rendition of Harmachis, Odysseus and Eric, virtuous men who are compelled to act uncharacteristically by a lust they cannot control.

In Philip's cousin George, Haggard takes a step further in his consideration of the corrupting effects of unbridled sexual passion. George's desire for Angela borders on the pornographic. She is young and beautiful. He is the same age as her father, is morally flawed and physically unappealing. Worse, he is a roué with a former (and perhaps current) mistress in close attendance, and this background, together with his poor physical and mental health, suggests that he may be syphilitic, as was Lilly's dissolute husband Archer. George's lust for Angela comes to an insupportable pitch when he glimpses her bathing naked in a pool at night, her arms lifted in the act of knotting her hair. Her body, illuminated by lightning, 'gleamed whiter than ivory' (203). Haggard's vivid, physical imagery implicates the reader in George's emphatically carnal response and propagates a sense of discomfort about his lust. The narrator comments that the effect of the sort of love that the likes of George are capable of is to 'scorch the heart with fearful heats, and then to crush it, and leave its owner's bosom choked with bitter dust' (205). Lady Bellamy prosaically sums up the situation to George when she refers to Angela as 'the splendid creature you would defile' (211). This portrayal of the defilement of purity is reinforced in the description of George in a state of frenzied sexual anticipation on the morning of his wedding to Angela: 'the first ray of the rising sun fell blood-red upon his wasted form, and then, bathing his thin hands in its beams, he sunk down exhausted' (279). This is strong and angry imagery suggesting a rebarbative act of defloration that both prefigures Haggard's apparent obsession with Plowden's sexual relations with Eva and exudes strong autobiographical resonances of what he probably considered as Archer's defilement of Lilly. What is not in doubt is that George's passion for Angela has turned into grotesque and character-warping lust.

Haggard makes a connection between George's moral behaviour and his social status. He is the physically inferior product of a misalliance. In short, he is not a gentleman. The other male villains in the early novels, whose lust for the female protagonist causes disruption, also possess attributes that cast doubt on their gentility. Plowden in *The Witch's Head* comes from a nouveau riche background. Cossey in *Colonel Quaritch* is Spanish-looking. Rock in *Joan Haste* is a Dissenter. When Haggard portrays this corrupting male lust and its punishment in his romances, the man concerned is, in each case, invested with a similar otherness. De Garcia in *Montezuma's Daughter* and Montalvo in *Lysbeth* (1901), whose sexual desire for a virtuous, and Northern European, woman precipitates the book's action, are both Spanish. In the later romances Meyer in *Benita* (1906) is a German Jew. Acour in *Red Eve* (1911) is not only French, but by virtue of his name and his attributes resembles Lilly's husband, Archer; his lust for Eve is depicted in further fire imagery: 'for I am on fire for this maid, and all her scorn and hate do but fan my flame.'[56] All four are punished by violent death. Ishmael in *The Ghost Kings* (1908), whose passion for Rachel causes him to attempt to murder her lover, may be an Englishman by birth but his adopted name indicates his moral decline and his social marginalization. The narrator records that 'his passion increased daily, burning ever more fiercely for its continued repression'. His fierce lust meets equally fierce punishment. The flames that destroy the town 'leapt out upon him like thin, scarlet tongues'.[57] He is consumed by his own passion. Haggard is depicting men whose uncontrolled lust causes them to try to impose themselves sexually upon virtuous women, as beyond the boundaries of civilized behaviour, as both contemptible and alien.

The violent punishments suffered by those who have betrayed genuine love are reinforced by the proposition, reiterated in all of Haggard's early fiction, that thwarted sexual passion breeds violence. Frustrated and humiliated by Angela's lack of response to his overtures, George threatens her: 'I will crush you to powder' (196) and, later, driven to jealous fury after seeing Arthur kissing her, strikes her twice across the face with a heavy whip. He is shortly afterwards mauled to death by Arthur's bulldog in what may be interpreted as an act of displaced revenge on Archer by Haggard. Quest, rejected by Belle because of his youthful liaison with Edith, is killed with Edith when they struggle and fall from a train. Cossey is mutilated by Belle because he has turned his attentions to Ida. Ernest, jilted by Eva, is symbolically blinded by lightning. Rock's awareness that Joan finds him physically loathsome and that she desires Henry drives him to a violence that has a sexual edge. He flogs the horse pulling their cart, urging: 'Come on, Sir Henry [...] you know that a pretty woman likes to go the pace, don't you?' (402). And he later shoots Joan in mistake for Henry.

In similarly provoked jealous acts of moral violence, Florence in *The Witch's Head* and Elizabeth in *Beatrice*, plot to force their sisters into loveless marriages. There is an autobiographical resonance in Haggard's depiction of the violence inflicted by one sister upon another. According to Lilias, Lilly was advised to marry Archer 'by a strong minded older sister.'[58] The same depictions of jealous violence appear in the early romances. Gagool mocks the beautiful Foulata as she is about to be delivered to the sadistic Scragga. The beautiful and passionate but sexually unfulfilled Ayesha, waiting over the centuries for Kallikrates to return, vents her sexual frustration in acts of hideous violence against her subjects. Meriamun in *The World's Desire* attempts to kill Helen by fire, furiously jealous that Odysseus loves her. Sorais in *Allan Quatermain*, jealous that Curtis prefers her sister Nyleptha, plunges the country into civil war. Swanhild in *Eric Brighteyes*, jealous of Eric's love for her sister Gudruda, arranges for Gizur to kill her.

The Sins of the Father

In a further reflection of a personal preoccupation, Haggard posits that punishment for a parent's illicit sexual liaison may be exacted upon the children. Not only did Haggard regard his affair with Johanna as a sin against his eternal love for Lilly, and interpret his son's death as punishment for this sin, but it is plain that he regarded the early death of Johanna's baby in the same light. So too, apparently, did Johanna. Haggard's friend Arthur Cochrane, who was well aware of his affair, and was himself romantically attached to Johanna's sister, wrote to Haggard on 8 November 1879 informing him of the death of the baby and again on 27 November 1879 recording Johanna's distraction at the death which 'she will look upon as a punishment'.[59]

The theme of the sins of the fathers reverberates through Haggard's early novels. Angela's sorrows are caused at root by her father's passion for Hilda. Belle was forced to marry Quest, whom she does not love, through the pressure of a drunken father. But this preoccupation of Haggard's finds its fullest expression in *Joan Haste*, published of course after the deaths of Ethel and Jock, where the life-defining consequences for a child born out of misplaced sexual passion are exemplified in both the illegitimate Joan and her illegitimate infant daughter. The child dies as a result of her mother's stress-induced sickness, which itself springs from the situation her illicit sexual behaviour has imposed upon her. And Haggard makes it clear that Joan's illegitimate status determines her character, her sexual susceptibilities and the outcome of her life. Joan, from the very start of her life, is conscious that 'some vague and half-understood shame [...] clung to her closely' (3). She has a profound sense of her own unworthiness, and it affects her moral responses. She is inherently morally flawed. The narrator comments: 'From childhood she had lived beneath the shadow of a shame that, in some degree, had withered her moral sense' (130). In this respect Joan resembles Lady Audley who, as Pykett points out, has 'the "shame" of an ignoble father and humble and impoverished family circumstances.'[60]

This portrayal of a child, blighted from the outset and pursued throughout life by the apprehension of a residual inferiority attaching to it from a situation that was in no way its fault and the details of which it does not understand, is replicated in *Lysbeth* by Adrian, who is the product of Lysbeth's union with the Spaniard Montalvo, into which she was forced in order to save the life of her lover Dirk, and which turns out to be bigamous, thus rendering Adrian illegitimate. When Lysbeth later marries Dirk, Adrian is held in contempt by the family and is deceived into betraying it, finally dying by the hand of his father Montalvo. The death of a child, a son in both cases, also features in both *Montezuma's Daughter*, the romance Haggard was researching at the time of his son's death and his first book published thereafter, and *Heart of the World* (1896). In both cases the death of a child is presented as the result of the breaking of an oath, in the first case against love, in the latter against religious precepts. That the subject had a deep personal significance for Haggard is clear from Otomie's words to Thomas about their dead children in *Montezuma's Daughter*:

> Your love for the dead children will always remain [...] and the desire of them, that desire for the dead than which there is nothing more terrible, shall follow you to your grave.[61]

These words find a close echo in a passage in *Stella Fregelius* (1904): 'There is no human passion like this passion for the dead; none so awful, none so holy, none so changeless.'[62]

Consolatory and Redemptive Women

Haggard's dark presentation in his early fiction of powerful and exploitative, and of weak or fickle, women disrupting men's lives, and of the inescapable and destructive grip of the sexual imperative, is to some extent shaded by his depiction of consolatory, virtuous and redemptive women, and also by his developing consideration of the merits of spiritual rather than sexual love and of a love that finds its culmination in an afterlife. In their constancy and dependability his consolation women, who offer the protagonists a practical and affectionate alternative to their lost loves, resemble Haggard's own wife Louisa. In personal terms, Haggard seems to be trying to establish whether, in Louisa, he can or should forget Lilly. But such women do not prevail. In *Dawn*, it is Philip's rejection of the sensible Maria who, like Louisa, is an heiress, for the sexually potent Hilda, which precipitates his disintegration. But it is clear that Philip is incapable of passing up the compelling Hilda for the uninspiring Maria. Unlike Philip, the emotionally pedestrian and dutiful Henry in *Joan Haste* chooses to marry the heiress Emma rather than the passionate Joan. But after Joan's death he realizes too late that he really loved her and that he is faced with the prospect of marriage to a woman who is sensible and loving but for whom he cannot feel as he does for Joan. Ernest's marriage to Dorothy in *The Witch's Head* is similarly second-best. Dorothy is in all respects the polar opposite of both Florence and Eva. She has loved Ernest all her life, but her sexual passion is controlled, channelled and restrained by a deep moral sense. She devotedly takes care of him when he returns, blinded, to England, and she enthusiastically agrees to marry him despite being fully aware that he cannot feel for her as he still does for Eva. The book's final chapter, entitled 'Dorothy's Triumph' (342–44), appears on the surface to vindicate and reward Dorothy's selflessness and enshrine her as the victor over both Florence and Eva. Ernest tells her that she has rid him of his passion for Eva:

> You have cured me my dear wife, for you have crept into my life, and taken possession of it, so there is little room for anybody else [...] now [...] I love you with all my heart. (343)

The book's final sentence: 'And so hand-in-hand they went on homeward through the quiet twilight' (344) appears to set the seal on this interpretation. But the proposal fails to persuade. It is plain that it is Eva who is victorious. Ernest can never forget her and, whatever Dorothy may wish to believe, will claim her in an afterlife. It seems that Haggard is exploring through Ernest the nature of his own feelings for his first love and for his wife.

His conclusion is plain. In this most autobiographical of his novels Haggard's inability to make a convincing case for the success of Ernest's marriage is surely informative about his view of his own.

Negative Depictions of Marriage

All of Haggard's early novels depict marriage in a negative light, often as a burdensome duty towards the family. Angela, Eva, Ida and Henry, under pressure from their respective families, either marry or initially agree to marry partners for whom they feel no real love but who are fortunately placed financially. Talia Schaffer refers to this form of exogamous marriage as the 'gift' marriage.[63] It is only in *Dawn* that the protagonists finally marry for genuine and passionate love. Ida bears a close resemblance to Maria and Dorothy, and apparently to Louisa as well. She is not beautiful 'but there was [...] a force and solid nobility stamped upon the features' (4). Ida is a dutiful rather than a passionate woman. She is totally impervious to the charms of the handsome Cossey, who loves her, and when it appears that she must marry him to safeguard the family fortune it is her distaste for him rather than her loss of Quaritch that concerns her. As she reflects sadly on the necessity of marrying Cossey: 'In the west the lurid rays of the sinking sun stained the clouds blood red, and broke in arrows of ominous light upon the driving storm' (178). The imagery foreshadows, in clear sexual overtones, a physically and emotionally violent union. But despite her sexual repugnance, Ida is calmly prepared to go through with the marriage in 'the interest of the family' (237). The reader is left with a sense of her emotional inadequacy and her sexual ordinariness rather than her capacity for self-sacrifice. She and Quaritch can eventually marry only because he discovers a hoard of buried treasure; a fantasy enabling a fantasy. The nature and the culmination of their relationship represent the unconvincing apotheosis of the pedestrian, the restrained, the dutiful. Haggard's conclusion is in this respect identical to that of *The Witch's Head*. And in *Joan Haste*, published some seven years later, Henry and Emma's comfortable and convenient marriage is not the final note of the book, which concludes instead with Henry's manipulative sister Ellen's cruelly unfeeling comments on Joan's death.

Carolyn Dever has commented:

> The marriage plot is the dominant literary fiction in this period, and it is a plot concerned both with the expression of sexual desire and with its limitation within comfortable, familiar social boundaries.[64]

And Nicola Beauman adds that 'The marriage ceremony is the [Victorian] novel's conventional ending.'[65] Haggard both maintains and subverts this convention by drawing each of his early novels near conclusion with marriage, but only one of these is a romantic alliance, and he makes it clear that this is the only truly worthwhile kind.

Haggard's early romances project an equally unenthusiastic view of marriage. In *The World's Desire* Helen's beauty compels men to desert their wives to pursue what Etherington calls 'the phantasmagorical images of their own making'.[66] The marriage ties are helpless in the face of men's innate lust. And some four years later Haggard makes a more directly jaundiced representation in *The People of the Mist* in which the female protagonist, tellingly named Juanna, goes through two forced marriages (a possible piece of autobiographical self-exculpation on Haggard's part), neither of which has any binding significance and, having formally married Leonard, discovers that she cannot entirely shake off the shadow of his former love. Leonard and his first love, Jane, on the other hand, both marry other people despite having sworn an oath of eternal fidelity to each other, but this does not hinder the prospect of the continuation of their love in an afterlife. In his early fiction Haggard dismisses the proposition that true, but predominantly spiritual, affection could ever be considered as a valid alternative to passionate love, however damaging the latter might be, and enters a sceptical view of a marriage that is comfortable and financially well-judged but that lacked passion. It is interesting to note that, although he considered that illicit sexual liaisons transgressed against an ideal of first love, there is no sense that he felt a practical but loveless marriage did likewise. In a personal context his apparently joyless and, if Higgins is to be believed, for long periods sexless,[67] union with Louisa seems hardly to have constituted a betrayal of his eternal love for Lilly.

Spiritual Love and Love in an Afterlife

In his two earliest and most explicitly autobiographical novels, Haggard begins to entertain a proposition that was to resonate throughout his future fiction, finding its fullest expression in the period between the publication of *Stella Fregelius* in 1904 and *The Ghost Kings* in 1908: that of a first and genuine love that has an emphatic spiritual dimension and that persists throughout life and throughout an afterlife, often finding its fullest expression in the latter. Angela in *Dawn* possesses 'a higher and more spiritual beauty' (85). She is also something of a mystic. She tells Arthur: 'the veil between ourselves and the unseen is thinner than we think [...] communication [...] can pass from the other world to ourselves' (130). There is an inevitability, a fatalism, about their love. She tells him: 'You are my fate, my other self; how would it have been possible for me to love any one but you?' (154). There is also a profound sense of their love's eternal nature. The narrator comments that true love cannot find 'full solace' on earth but 'strives to pass hence with that kindred soul to the heaven whence it came' (175–76). Angela believes that, even if she loses Arthur in this world, in an afterlife: 'we shall be together, and never part any more' (342). When, at the conclusion, they are reunited, the narrator's comments throw light on the book's title and constitute Haggard's earliest reference to a theme that was to appear in most of his subsequent fiction; that of reunification of lovers in an afterlife: 'Happy are those who thus find their Angela, whether it be here – or at Dawn, on the furthest shore of yonder solemn sea' (371). Haggard is referencing a first love that carries an innocence, an integrity, a spirituality, an eternal validity and a quasi-religious conviction. There is a transparent sense of self-solace in his depiction that seems to find its fullest and most poignant expression in the narrator's assertion that those who have experienced genuine first love will discover that it transcends both betrayal and death; that 'having once loved truly it is not possible that they should altogether lose' (176), and that there are many who have the memory of a lost Angela hidden away somewhere in the records of their past, and who are fain, in the breathing spaces of their lives, to dream that they will find her wandering in that wide Eternity where 'all human barriers fall, all human relations end, and love ceases to be a crime'. (176)

There is a similar proposal in *The Witch's Head*. The voice of the narrator sums up the spiritual proximity of the lovers and establishes a yardstick by which to measure the extent of their eventual tragedy:

They were sitting side by side in the stern-sheets of the boat, and the sun was just dipping all red-hot into the ocean. Under the lea of the cliff were cool shadows; before them was a path of glory that led to a golden gate. The air was very sweet, and for those two all the world was lovely; there was no sorrow on the earth, there were no storms upon the sea. (77)

Haggard achieves a sense of suspended passion, of a potential future happiness frozen into an arrested moment which, like that depicted in Keats's 'Ode on a Grecian Urn' (1820), is unattainable in its very perfection. This effectively illustrates the vulnerability of first love and foreshadows the book's conclusion that its consummation will not prove attainable in this life. But it also exudes a strong sense of personal nostalgia and underlines Haggard's close involvement with the book. Despite Eva's betrayal, Ernest's love for her is eternal as he tells her when they meet years later:

I love you now, as I have always loved you, as I always shall love you [...] I believe that the love of the flesh will die with the flesh. But my love for you [...] is of the spirit, unending and [...] when this hateful existence is done with I shall in some way reap its fruits with you. (299)

This affirmation of the eternal nature of genuine love and the promise of its full celebration in an afterlife constitutes the concluding tone of *The Witch's Head*. Haggard's emotional proximity to the book seems to have imposed upon him a psychological obligation to construct a reassuring conclusion, as he did, for the same apparent reasons, in *Montezuma's Daughter*. At any rate, when he came to write *Colonel Quaritch* and *Joan Haste*, the absolute conviction of a consolatory afterlife had receded. Ida, believing that she is to marry Cossey, writes tepidly to Quaritch, 'in the grave [...] I trust and believe we shall find each other' (286–87). Joan, dying, tells Henry, in terms Haggard may have imagined Johanna speaking and which recall Haggard's entry in his Commonplace Book for 1882,[68] that she and their dead child 'shall wait for you together in the place – of peace' (422). Henry makes no response.

In the early romances the tone is equally equivocal. For Harmachis in *Cleopatra*, for Eric in *Eric Brighteyes*, and for Umslopogaas in *Nada the Lily*, there is little or no hope of a reunion with their lost loves in an afterlife. Odysseus in *The World's Desire* will have to await a new incarnation until he finds Helen waiting for him. In the deeply personal *Montezuma's Daughter* it appears to have been a psychological imperative for Haggard to represent a reunion of the lovers in this life and in an afterlife. Thomas, having been reunited with Lily, and after a long and happy life with her, comforts himself at her eventual death by reflecting that 'very soon I shall join Lily where she is' (325). And in the immediately subsequent *The People of the Mist*, Leonard has both the love of the living Juanna, whom he marries, and that of his dead first love, Jane, who has never forgotten him. The dying Maya in *Heart of the World* tells Strickland: 'I trust that in the land which you will reach at last, you may find us waiting for you, the child and I.'[69] Strickland's life effectively ends with Maya's death and some five years later he is happy to die and join her. In *Lysbeth* Dirk tells Lysbeth at the point of their parting: 'it will be sweet to meet again and part no more' (286). But perhaps the most poignant rendition, and the most direct, appears in *She* in which Holly, visiting the tombs of Kor, encounters one in which 'clasped heart to heart were a young man and a blooming girl' (185). They have both died of stab wounds and over their tomb is the inscription 'Wedded in Death'. Holly imagines that the girl, 'purer than a lily' (185), was about to be forced against her will to marry an older man, and that her lover, 'a darkhaired youth' (185), appeared at the wedding and was stabbed by the groom's friends and that the girl then stabbed herself. The reference is plain. Although the level of conviction fluctuates, the reunification of lovers in an afterlife is a concept that appears throughout all of Haggard's fiction, and seems to have been driven by a compelling wish to salvage this final hope from what he saw as the wreck of his life's only real love.

Conclusions

It is unclear why Haggard chose to adopt aspects of the sensation novel in the four novels considered in this chapter. The genre was by then dated and, according to Patrick Brantlinger, had 'flourished in the 1860s only to die out a decade later'.[70] It may be because he judged that they suited his predominant, and turbulent, subject matter, because they were familiar to readers, being striking and colourful, and because they were attractive to a young writer unsure of his literary bearings. In any event, Haggard's early novels differ in key respects from the sensation novels of some twenty-five years earlier, being essentially melodramas involving lost loves and thwarted passions and whose *leitmotif* is the impact upon men of the sexuality of the female.

Nevertheless, in these four early novels Haggard uses some acknowledged sensation tropes, most prominently adultery, criminality, violence and intrigue. But the plots these generate lack the complexity, tightness and real interest of sensation novels such as Wilkie Collins's *The Woman in White* (1860), *East Lynne* and *Lady Audley's Secret*. Nor does Haggard fully engage with some of what Pykett identifies as important sensation novel issues: 'women's covert anger at the limitations of their social and domestic circumstances', their 'legal subjugation within marriage' and 'the nature of femininity'.[71] While in each of Haggard's early novels the marriage issue is referenced in terms of the woman as victim and commodity, his depiction of the effects of this situation upon the women involved lacks detail and intensity. In *The Witch's Head*, for example, the issue is trivialized and Eva, pressured into marrying Plowden whom she does not love, is described as 'not sufficiently highly strung' (292) to suffer unbearably. In contrast to the descriptions of the emotional turmoil of sensation novel heroines such as Isabel Vane, Laura Fairlie and Cytherea Gray, Haggard shows little interest in exploring the psyche and emotions of his female heroines. In *East Lynne* the narrator records of Isabel's remorse at her impetuous elopement with Levison that 'she knew that her whole future existence [...] would be one dark course of gnawing, never-ending retribution'.[72] In contrast, the narrator in *Joan Haste* says of Joan's reflections on her affair with Henry that 'Sorrow and repentance were to overtake her when she learned all the trouble and ruin which her conduct had caused' (183). The contrast in intensity levels is self-evident.

Haggard's focus is on the threats to the male posed by trangressive women. As this chapter has illustrated, *Dawn*, *The Witch's Head*, *Colonel Quaritch* and *Joan Haste* teem with depictions of the overwhelming and potentially morally warping nature of sexual passion, of sexual betrayals, of powerful and destructive women, of the emotional wrecking of lives. While *Dawn* and *The Witch's Head*, although angry and violent, offer final consolation in the form, respectively, of the reunion of the lovers and promise of the celebration of their love in an afterlife, *Colonel Quaritch* and *Joan Haste* are more equivocal about such consolation and project a jaundiced sense of the flawed nature of sexual liaisons. The same preoccupations depicted in identical ways are equally evident in Haggard's early romances. *King Solomon's Mines*, *Allan Quatermain* and particularly *She* represent a male anger at sexually exploitative women, and the violent punishments of such women. *Cleopatra*, *The World's Desire* and *Eric Brighteyes* speak of male inability to resist woman's overwhelming sexuality. It seems plain that the intense and unremitting focus, the anger and the sense of guilt implicit in irregular sexual liaisons, derive from Haggard's still-recent personal experiences. In a reference to the inevitable shame and remorse consequent upon sexual sin, he writes in his autobiography, compiled between 1911 and 1912 and published posthumously in 1926: 'remorse rises in the after years and stands over us at night, since, when our eyes are no longer clouded with the mists of passion, we see and bewail our wickedness.'[73] The similarity between this observation and a comment by the narrator on Belle's punishment in *Colonel Quaritch* is striking, and it is plain that in 1887 Haggard was writing about the same thing:

> Few of us need to want for a place of punishment to get the due for our follies and our sins [...] They are with us day and night, about our path and about our bed, scourging us with the whips of memory, mocking us with empty longing and the hopelessness of despair. Who can escape the consequence of sin, or even of the misfortune which led to sin? (283)

There is a perhaps self-serving fatalism here. In the early novels it sits alongside the voice of the narrator constantly prompting the reader's moral responses, particularly in *The Witch's Head* and *Joan Haste*. Haggard's insistence on signalling the sinfulness of sexual activity, which was unlicensed by the contemporary social mores, is both transparent and unsettling. But, as well as ensuring that he kept within contemporary moral parameters and did not endanger his livelihood, it seems also to indicate a personal emotional intensity about the subject. In *Joan Haste* the inescapably powerful nature of the sexual imperative, which acts upon both Henry and Joan, is not left in doubt. Henry reflects:

> It is useless to try to escape from the facts of life, for at last in one shape or another they overtake us, who, strive as we may, can very rarely defy our natures. (74)

The flesh always wins over the spirit. This is an early rendition by Haggard of the proposal that the seeds of moral destruction, and the consequent remorse it involves, are an integral part of the sexual imperative, which itself is an inescapable part of being human. Harmachis, incurably in love with Cleopatra although she has betrayed him, expresses this humiliating helplessness with a concision that seems to vocalize admirably the burden of Haggard's early fiction:

> For though that thing we worship doth bring us ruin [...] yet must we worship on, yet stretch out our arms towards our lost Desire, and pour out our heart's blood upon the shrine of our discrowned God. (324)

Chapter Four

THE NEW WOMAN, FEMALE SELF-SACRIFICE AND SPIRITUALITY (1887–1901)

Interpretations of Haggard as a chronicler of male angst have tended to obscure other, equally complex, aspects of his fictional writing, notably his treatment of the position of women and of the marriage question in his novels of English domestic life. His most sustained consideration of these subjects is to be found in *Jess* (1887) and *Beatrice* (1890), two novels in which Haggard's primary focus is on the strong sexual responses of two independently minded and highly spiritual young women to men who are already committed to other women. While they self-consciously genuflect towards the concept of the New Woman they have a limited amount in common with the contemporaneous and popular New Woman novels. The themes with which they deal, primarily the impact of female sexuality upon men and female self-sacrifice, are essentially a development of the themes of Haggard's earlier novels and continue to reflect significant personal experiences.

Jess and Its Biographical Resonances

Unlike Haggard's other novels, *Jess* is set entirely outside England, in an African context more typical of his romances. The book has a simple, unified plot and turns on the sexual passions of the four principal characters: Jess; Bessie, her sister; Muller, who desires Bessie; and John, whom Jess loves and who falls in love with her while engaged to Bessie. The focus is on the moral quandary of Jess and John, and on the intense spirituality and overwhelming sexual potency of Jess and her remarkable capacity for self-sacrifice in order to protect her sister. Her altruism is adumbrated by the depiction of the brutal Muller. Both Jess and Muller are highly sexually driven, and both are capable of extreme violence, but morally they are polar opposites. Contemporary critics were divided about the success of the character of Jess. The *Pall Mall Gazette* concluded that Haggard was not 'at home' in 'giving a psychological study of female character',[1] while the *Athenaeum* applauded his 'study of a strange and fascinating being'.[2]

Haggard commenced *Jess* in the late autumn of 1885 and completed it at the end of December of the same year.[3] One month later he began work on *She* (1887),[4] published two months before *Jess*. There are clear structural and plot parallels between the two books. Both are set in Africa, both employ violent natural phenomena as metaphors to enhance the impact of the narrative, crucial scenes in both centre in caves. More significantly, there are also persuasive similarities between Jess and Ayesha. Both are strong, mystical, compelling women whose power over men causes them to act beyond their familiar range of responses. But the self-sacrificial Jess is the moral obverse of Ayesha.

Like *Dawn* (1884) and *The Witch's Head* (1884), *Jess* exhibits clear autobiographical influence. Lilias Haggard records that her father, having written the book, could not bear to look at it again: 'it set down in black and white things which had bitten too deep',[5] and Haggard himself suggests as much in his autobiography: 'I have never reread it, and I think that I never mean to do so.'[6] The South African setting and the fluency with which its geographical features are described reinforce the suggestion that Haggard is drawing upon his own experiences. The description of the farmhouse where John first encounters Jess and Bessie bears a strong physical resemblance to the house in which he and his wife Louisa lived. Probably more significantly, the cottage in Pretoria where Jess and John pass an idyllic few months together during the Boer siege is an exact replica, in description and in name, of the cottage Haggard shared with his friend Arthur Cochrane during the period when he was conducting his affair with Johanna. But the most deeply autobiographical element is the characterization of Jess.

D. S. Higgins has contended: 'Only one woman Haggard knew matches the description of Jess's appearance and characteristics. She was Aggie Barber.'[7] It seems likely that Jess was indeed based upon Agnes. Certainly, Haggard's physical description of Jess as 'small and rather thin, with quantities of curling brown hair',[8] corresponds with contemporary photographs of Agnes. And Jess's mental attributes are also close to those Haggard and others perceived in Agnes. John reflects that Jess is 'the strangest woman he had ever met, and in her way one of the most attractive' (31). In 1879 Haggard had written of Agnes that she was 'one of the most peculiar individuals that I ever came across […] All her passions are strong especially her love and hate […] she thinks herself very plain' nevertheless 'she has unconsciously a little coquettish way with her'.[9] And in a similar pen portrait, Agnes's friend Amy Berry wrote of her on 12 March 1881: 'You are exceedingly independent and strong-willed, decidedly argumentative', and: 'You have gained an early knowledge of the world's hollowness and unsatisfyingness.'[10] These attributes closely resemble Jess's own and her world view: 'Who *can* have a happy mind? Nobody who can feel' (47). And she is certainly passionate, independently minded and strong-willed.

The depiction of Jess as an exceptional and admirable person appears to find its origin in Haggard's personal estimation of Agnes, but it seems he did not admire only her character and intellectual capacity. The frankly flirtatious tone of his correspondence with her strongly suggests a degree of emotional intimacy that is unusual between a young married man and his wife's best friend. In 1882 he sends her a letter when she is away for a few days, complaining that the chores his wife finds for him prevent him from writing at greater length, urging her, for her part, to 'write soon' and regretting that 'having basked in the full effulgence of Intellectual Light' he is now 'left in all his pristine darkness'.[11] Later that year he writes to her again, thanking her for her critical assessment of *Cetewayo and His White Neighbours* (1882), and refers to Louisa's remarks on the book as being 'so trivial, so empty headed and so inapposite'.[12] Haggard's disparagement in this correspondence of the intellectual and literary capacity of his wife of two years is clearly suggestive of a dissatisfaction with his marriage. This finds echo in the narrator's, albeit clumsy, observation on the uncomfortably differing outlooks of Bessie who 'was not an intellectual woman' and John who 'was a decidedly intellectual man' (125). John reflects of Bessie and Jess, 'the one is all flower and the other is all root' and 'breathed a secret hope' that Jess 'would continue to live with them after they were married' (158). Agnes of course did exactly this in respect of Haggard and his wife. After falling in love with Jess while engaged to Bessie, John asks himself 'why had he not waited to see which of the two he really took to?' (166). Given that Haggard knew Agnes at the same time as Louisa, and that therefore he could have decided to pursue either of them, it is difficult to resist the assumption that he is expressing regret at having made the wrong choice, at least at the emotional and intellectual level.

It seems plain that in Haggard's portrayal of Jess he is giving voice to his attraction to Agnes. There is no evidence to suggest a physical relationship between them, but there must be a strong implication that in his depiction of John, engaged to Bessie, and having what amounts to an affair with her sister, Haggard is, post facto, giving imaginative rein to that possibility. It must also be significant that while John finally marries Jess's sister, Agnes had become engaged to Haggard's brother before Haggard commenced *Jess*. If Jess is, in some measure, a representation of Agnes her emotionally testing experience of seeing the man she loves and admires become engaged to her own sister seems to replicate Haggard's own vis-à-vis Agnes and Jack. Haggard had commenced writing *Jess* in 1885, the year in which Agnes became engaged to his brother, having lived with the Haggards for the best part of four years, eventually becoming his secretary. Not only was he under the immediate influence of her intellectual and emotional appeal, but he knew she would shortly be moving out. This background can only strengthen the surmise that his depiction of Jess is a celebration of his regard and affection for Agnes. It is superficially tempting to regard Bessie as an approximation of Louisa. But while it seems certain that *Jess* derives in a substantial fashion from Haggard's disillusionment with his marriage, Bessie has few of the characteristics of Louisa. She is beautiful, and her sexual attractiveness drives Muller, handsome and rich and therefore hardly circumscribed in his choice of women, to a frenzy of passion in a way in which it is doubtful Louisa did to men. It seems more likely that Haggard had Lilly rather than Louisa in mind when he drew Bessie and that he was in fact comparing the highly attractive but, in his view, weak and emotionally flawed Lilly with the physically unremarkable but intelligent, spiritual, compelling and deeply loving and constant Agnes. The autobiographical resonances remain apparent in *Jess*, but they are less literal, more sophisticated and flexible than in the earlier novels.

Beatrice and Its Biographical Overtones

Like *Jess*, *Beatrice* depicts the intersecting sexual passions of four closely connected characters – Beatrice, Geoffrey, Elizabeth (although her passion is also material) and Davies – the moral violence such passion breeds and the extraordinary self-sacrifice of the highly spiritual female protagonist, Beatrice, in order to protect her lover, Geoffrey. But the force of the book resides in the fact that Geoffrey is married. In this respect Beatrice's predicament and behaviour are more extraordinary than that of any other female protagonist in Haggard's fiction. Adultery was certainly not an unfamiliar concept in the late nineteenth century. Michael Mason claims that 'in some upper-class circles there was a very lenient code on adultery especially when this involved sustained liaisons that did not violate the appearance of strict marital decorum', and he notes this 'more emancipated elite having a defrosting effect on middle class moralism'.[13] Jane Eldridge Miller corroborates the contemporary need to maintain marital appearances, noting: 'The concept of the indissolubility of marriage was a powerful and deeply rooted one in British society.'[14] Celebrated legal debates in the mid-nineteenth century had focussed on the issues of adultery as well as sexuality. Barbara Leckie records that 'the debates over the Matrimonial Causes Act, recurrent through the 1850s, discussed adultery [...] at length; the Obscene Publications Act debates in 1857 discussed representations of sexuality in print culture'.[15] The public were no strangers to the subject of sexual infidelity. Leckie observes that 'the publication of divorce cases in the daily newspapers served as the dominant discursive framework through which adultery was made visible in the Victorian and transitional modernist periods', but she adds that considering them in fiction was another matter, noting that 'much less intense and exhaustive representations of adultery in the novel and popular genres were strictly regulated'.[16]

Haggard was careful not to establish adultery in *Beatrice* and, at any event Beatrice, being unmarried, was not an adulteress, but his unmistakeable sympathy for her was both personally groundbreaking in the context of his earlier fiction and dangerous for his livelihood, as he was to discover from the critical reception of the book's moral tone. An unidentified reviewer writing in the *Athenaeum* commented that Haggard 'perhaps was never so bold as when he launched *Beatrice*.'[17] And although both Charles Longman and Andrew Lang liked the book and Marie Corelli wrote to Haggard telling him that *Beatrice* 'is *beautiful* – full of poetry and deep thought',[18] the public's response was less positive. Haggard writes in his autobiography:

> Some years after *Beatrice* was published I was horrified to receive two anonymous [...] letters from ladies who alleged that their husbands [...] one of them a middle-aged clergyman – after reading Beatrice had made advances to young ladies of that name [...] Also I heard that a gentleman and a lady had practised the sleep-walking scene, with different results from those recorded in the book.[19]

Haggard was so upset that he wished to suppress the book and was only dissuaded by Longman. However, in 1894, he modified or removed certain passages (it was the only fictional work he substantially revised) and added an advertisement in which he stated that as its author he 'never dreamed that his study of an ill-disciplined but beautiful character could be chosen as a text for wrong' (iii–iv).

The autobiographical elements in *Beatrice* are less obvious than in *Jess* and the earlier novels as the equations between Haggard's personal experiences and his fictional representations become less transparent, but it is difficult not to believe that in his depiction of a beautiful, highly intelligent, unusually spiritual, eternally loving, sexually potent woman who chooses to die rather than ruin the man she loves, Haggard was proposing an ideal he had failed to find in Lilly, or indeed in Louisa, but elements of which he had identified in Agnes Barber. Similarly, his portrayal of a cold, unloving and unmaternal wife, Honoria, seems to derive, at least partly, from Louisa. The parallel seems to reside most forcefully in Honoria's lack of maternal feeling. She does not love her daughter and does not want any more children. Lilias refers to her mother's resentment in 1892 at the knowledge that she was again expecting a child: she 'had no desire to start all over again with a nursery'.[20] Finally, in his depiction of Beatrice's jealous, malevolent and domineering sister Elizabeth, Haggard is recalling both Florence, Eva's equally malevolent sister, in the deeply autobiographical *The Witch's Head*, and at a similarly autobiographical level his personal belief that it was Lilly's sister who put pressure on her to marry Archer. Lilias records that the merit of 'the rich and desirable match was ably and continually expressed by a strong-minded elder sister'.[21]

The New Woman

Angelique Richardson has observed that 'In 1882 [...] belief systems were in crisis, and traditional, social, political and gendered hierarchies were crumbling', and has listed 'the Women question' amongst 'pressing social questions of the day'. She records that in 1883 'the first New Woman novel, Olive Schreiner's *The Story of An African Farm* was published' (under the pseudonym Ralph Iron).[22] Lyn Pykett identifies some of the issues constituting 'the Women question': 'the New Women writers' exploration of marriage and their exposure of the [sexual] double standard [...] brought [a] difference of view to bear on modern marriage and the gender roles it both required and constricted'.[23] Peter Keating concurs, observing that the work of New Women novelists 'dramatized the woman's point of view with a frankness found only very occasionally in earlier British fiction and [...] helped break the convention [...] that fiction was unavoidably marriage-oriented', and that 'The main preoccupation of New Women fiction was "the immorality and indignity of sexual double standards"'.[24] New Women writers were also concerned with female sexuality. Lyn Pykett notes 'their preoccupation with sexuality and sexual frankness',[25] while Elaine Showalter asserts that 'the sexually independent New Woman criticized society's insistence on marriage as woman's only option for a fulfilling life'.[26] Despite these generally observable characteristics of New Women writers and fiction there were naturally differences of emphasis in respect of individual authors. In 1888, as Carolyn Nelson notes, 'Mona Caird published her article entitled "Marriage" in the *Westminster Review*' and 'provoked a great debate over the marriage question that continued in the periodicals and fiction of the 1890s'. Caird asserts that 'the present form of marriage [...] is a vexatious failure' and claims: 'Give freedom in marriage, and each pair will enter upon their union after their own particular fashion, creating a refreshing diversity in modes of life.'[27] On the other hand, Sarah Grand, as Sally Ledger points out, 'championed sexual purity and motherhood in *The Heavenly Twins*'[28] and was a proponent of marriage. Keating has pointed out that 'the New Woman novelists did not constitute a school of writers in any formal sense',[29] and Richardson has drawn attention to 'competing narratives'.[30] But these modalities did not appear to affect the popularity of the genre. Richardson comments that 'in the closing decades of the century the New Woman [...] rapidly came to dominate fiction, both as theme and writer, becoming synonymous with modernity itself'.[31] As such this genre was attractive to writers. Keating asserts that 'the New Woman theme was highly profitable as well as fashionable'.[32] There can be little doubt that Haggard was aware both of its popularity and profitability, and he explored the genre in parts of his fiction, notably in *Jess* and *Beatrice*.

It is immediately striking about both characters, Jess and Beatrice, that they are repeatedly described as being different from other women, not in respect of their physical qualities, but in respect of their intellectual attributes and their opinions. In this they resemble Angela in *Dawn*, whose tutor tells her, 'You have acquired information denied to the majority of your sex.'[33] John's early impression of Jess is that her mind is 'not like most women's' (31). The narrator reinforces his impression, observing that Jess has

> the god-like gift of brains, the gift that had been more of a curse than a blessing to her, lifting her above the level of her sex and shutting her off as by iron doors from the understanding of those around her. (32)

Beatrice too has about her face 'the stamp of intellect and power'[34] and, unlike Jess, who is a colonial girl of limited formal education, she has attended, as she tells Geoffrey, 'a college where you get certificates that you are qualified to be a mistress in a Board School. I wish it had been Girton' (12). Haggard is signalling that Beatrice is a modern, progressive woman of the type that was to appear in later novels, such as Sue Bridehead in Thomas Hardy's *Jude the Obscure* (1895), who also attended such a college, and Herminia Barton in Grant Allen's *The Woman Who Did* (1895) who attended (and dropped out of) Girton. A Girton education was in late nineteenth-century fiction a hallmark of the New Woman, and it is in this context that Haggard is, albeit clumsily, inviting his reader to regard Beatrice. Both she and Jess have a gloomy, disillusioned view of life. Jess remarks to John, 'How is it possible to be happy, when one feels the breath of human misery beating on one's face' (47). Beatrice opines 'death cannot be worse than life is for most of us' (20) and reflects to herself that 'Life is very dreary when one has lost everything, and found nothing, and loves nobody' (2). But the formulistic nature of their protestations is illuminated by a comparison with the world-weary comment of George Egerton's heroine in *A Psychological Moment* in *Discords* (1894):[35] 'What is happiness? The most futile of all our dreams, the pursuit of a shadow.' Both Beatrice and Jess are depicted as having the aspirations of the enlightened modern young woman to make their name in intellectual circles. Female education was a vexed topic. Richardson observes that 'in the second half of the nineteenth century [...] various reforms in education threatened to undermine "separate spheres" for men and women'.[36] When she considers the educational opportunities Geoffrey has had, Beatrice 'knew if she had half his chance, that she would make her name ring from one end of Europe to the other' (48). Jess expresses herself in very similar terms: 'she would go away to Europe and mix in the great stream of life [...] and see if she could win a place for herself among the people of her day' (147).

But the narrator's assertions about Jess and Beatrice sit uncomfortably with the surrounding texts. They are, for the most part, bald and unconvincing appliqués that are largely unsubstantiated by the dramatic action of the plots. Norman Etherington makes the extravagant assertion that Jess is 'a feminist somewhat like Schreiner's Lyndall'.[37] Haggard had met Schreiner. A letter he wrote to his brother Jack suggests that he, apparently somewhat reluctantly, admired Schreiner's intellect and was well aware of her feminist credentials. Haggard writes that, in her presence

> I feel what I have never felt with any other woman that I have met my intellectual superior. Her insight into human nature is keen and clearer than my own, her reasoning power is stronger and the cast of her mind more original.

Of her desirability as a wife he adds:

> I doubt if she would marry you [...] or anyone else. I dare say that if she was fond of you she would have no objection to living with you [...] Very likely she has already lived with somebody.[38]

Haggard's comments seem to reveal a degree of discomfort at what he supposed was Schreiner's view of marriage and suggest a reservation on his part about that aspect at least of the New Woman. In any event, while it is probable that he had *The Story of An African Farm* in mind when he wrote *Jess*, Etherington's suggestion has little grounding in reality. Apart from the labelling, the only characteristic Jess has in common with the emotionally lacerated, socially unconventional and self-destructive Lyndall is that they both inhabit African farms. It is Jess and Beatrice's passion and spirituality rather than their intellectual or political precocity that drive the action. Haggard seems to be suggesting that feminist progressive thinking collapses in the face of female desire and emotional intuition and, most importantly, in the face of love. He appears to reinforce this argument in the effect Beatrice's passion for Geoffrey has upon her religious belief. She claims that she has lost her faith: 'I have nothing to pray to. I am not a Christian' (20). But her love for Geoffrey restores it. Showalter observes that 'the New Woman was also the nervous woman. Doctors linked anorexia, neurasthenia, and hysteria with the changes in women's aspirations.'[39] And Pykett has similarly pointed out that she was 'a symbol of disorder and rebellion' and, in her fictional form was seen as 'erotomaniac, hysteric, mannish and challenging'.[40] Jess and Beatrice are self-evidently not such women.

Gail Cunningham observes that 'the incidence of death or despair among fictional New Women is extraordinarily high'.[41] She instances, inter alia, Edith Beale in Sarah Grand's *The Heavenly Twins* (1893), Lyndall in *The Story of An African Farm* and Herminia in *The Woman Who Did*. Jess and Beatrice also die but not in despair. Theirs is a noble, spiritually driven self-sacrifice. Cleopatra, Meriamun and Ayesha in Haggard's romances do, however, die in despair (although Ayesha is re-created), but they are not subjected to the same degree of scrutiny as Lyndall, Herminia and the female protagonists of *The Heavenly Twins*. It is only in Maya in *Heart of the World* (1896) that Haggard sustains a convincing depiction of a radical woman prepared to translate her convictions into action. In order to possess the man she desires and to demonstrate that her marriage to a foreigner, Strickland, is sanctioned by the god of her people, Maya sacrilegiously collaborates in forging an edict from the god endorsing it. The narrator is unequivocal about her credentials: 'Maya was the child of the New World filled with the spirit of today.'[42] Maya herself asserts: 'my life is my own and not a possession of the gods' (177). Unlike

Angela, Eva and Ida of the early novels, Maya is unconstrained by the concept that her duty to her family is pre-eminent, and she tells her father: 'my duty to myself and to him who loves me, and whom I love, is higher than my duty to you.' (242). As she says, she is prepared, for love of Strickland, to offer

> deadly outrage to the god of [my] people, to the instinct of [my] blood, and the teachings of [my] youth [...] Is not love everything to me, and is it shameful that this should be so? (271)

Jess and Beatrice are, of course, also driven by love (Jess for John and Bessie, Beatrice for Geoffrey) rather than regard for the social and religious mores of their society, but this love prompts them, in consideration of the social reputations of those they love, to acts of self-sacrifice, whereas Maya's sense of her right to personal happiness prevails over any such consideration, and she and Strickland eventually pay a heavy price in the death of their child, Maya's suicide and their painful separation, at least in this world. In her overwhelming conviction that her right as a woman to pursue an ideal and to disregard the social consequences, and in the outcome of that pursuit for both herself and her child, Maya resembles Herminia Barton, Sue Bridehead and Natalia in George Meredith's *One of Our Conquerors* (1891). Her difference from these New Woman heroines is of course that, while they are English women operating within an English domestic context, Maya is an exotic foreigner operating in an exotic, romance locale. It may well be that Haggard felt that investing her with an otherness not dissimilar to that of Joan Haste and certain other of his female protagonists enabled him to be more adventurous in his depiction of her feminine attributes than he felt the demands of his livelihood enabled him to be with his English domestic heroines.

Haggard certainly modulates and softens Jess and Beatrice's credentials as modern women by emphasizing their femininity and in doing so locates them at several removes from the New Woman. Pykett comments: 'most of the feminist writers of the 1880s and 1890s openly rejected the concept of womanliness.'[43] It is plain that Haggard's interest does not lie in this direction. The narrator describes Beatrice's face: 'it was all womanly; here was not the hard sexless stamp of the "cultured" female [...] She could love and she could suffer' (2). For John, Jess may be different from other women, but she has the femininity and the spirituality to provoke his desire: 'her face was touched with a diviner beauty than he had yet seen on the face of woman' (31). But for all Jess and Beatrice's femininity and spirituality they are, in common with some of the heroines of the New Women novels, and of Haggard's early romances, women of a pronounced sexuality.

Jess and Beatrice as Sexually Passionate and Sexually Potent Women

Jess and Beatrice may be extraordinarily, even inconveniently, intellectually gifted, but their sexual responses are those of Lyndall, Natalia, Ayesha, Cleopatra and in the early novels, of Mildred and Belle. They differ from these women only in respect of their refusal to allow their passion to obscure their moral duty. Jess's response to John is intensely physical: 'her youthful blood [...] rose in her veins like the sap in the budding trees, and stirred her virginal serenity', and she 'knew that she loved with heart and soul and body and was a very woman' (51). The resonance of the intensifier 'very', which seems to derive from The Creed that forms an integral part of the service of Holy Communion,[44] reinforced by the narrator's reference to Jess's 'half-divine, soul-searing passion' (98), suggests a quasi-religious, quasi-sexual transformative experience that echoes Angela's half-unconscious sense in *Dawn* of impending love and 'girlhood's twilight ended, and [...] the advent of woman's life and love' (90). When she learns that John has not, as she feared, been killed in battle with the Boers, Jess is overcome by her passion for him: 'There she stood, her breast heaving with emotion as the sea heaves when the fierceness of the storm has passed' (162).

The physical, post-orgasmic, imagery is echoed in *Beatrice* when Beatrice's account of a dream in which she sees her life intertwined with Geoffrey's leaves her profoundly stirred: 'her breast heaving, and her lips apart' (70). Haggard is clear about the depth of the sexual urges of Jess and Beatrice. He had depicted the physical manifestation of female sexual passion in his earlier fiction but preponderantly in respect of women of dubious moral character like Belle and Mildred in his novels and, still more morally dubious, Ayesha and Sorais in his romances. In Jess and Beatrice he is proposing, unequivocally, the same susceptibility in morally admirable, spiritually remarkable women. And he mirrors this intense physicality in his depiction of the sexual responses of the supporting female characters. Bessie, we are told, when John proposed to her, had 'flushed up to the eyes and then the blood had sunk back to her breast, and left her pale as a lily' (107). Even Beatrice's malevolent sister Elizabeth is susceptible to male charms. She remarks piquantly to Davies of Geoffrey, 'He is one of the finest-looking men I ever saw' (36).

As he had in his earlier fiction, Haggard is depicting women, good and admirable, and malevolent and morally dubious alike, as strongly sexual beings and, as such, equally threatening to men. In this respect his argument is fundamentally similar to that of some of his contemporaries. Carolyn Dever points out that 'Victorian novelists had frequent recourse to the strategy [of] polarizing female identity into two neat categories – virgin and whore, angel and demon [... and] associate goodness with asexuality; badness with hypersexuality'. She goes on to add that 'even as Victorian novelists such as Collins and the Brontës put this representational strategy to use, they subvert it in the next breath.'[45] Bram Stoker did the same in his depictions of Mina and Lucy in *Dracula* (1897). Showalter observes that both 'exhibit the characteristics of the New Woman', Lucy in her 'sexual daring' and Mina in her 'intellectual ambitions'.[46] Both pose a threat to the male protagonists. Lucy's male lovers respond to her hypersexuality, her intense femininity, by each of them in turn transfusing her with their blood and finally, in a grotesque depiction of an especially violent rape, by driving a stake through her body. But they also perceive a threat to their masculinity from the considered, intellectual and masculinized Mina; a threat to which they respond by confining her and by limiting her access to knowledge. Haggard's male protagonists, although they are threatened on a sexual rather than an intellectual level, find their lives disrupted by admirable and malevolent women alike.

The Sexually Passionate Women of Haggard's Romances

Haggard is concerned with the outcomes of these strong promptings of physical passion. In his earlier fiction he portrays women like Ayesha, Meriamun in *The World's Desire* (1890) and Swanhild in *Eric Brighteyes* (1891) prepared to go to extreme lengths, even sometimes rape and murder, to possess the men they desire. In his later romances he depicts the same headstrong, destructive women. In *Heart of the World* Maya's passion for Strickland, 'to win a husband whom she desires' (292) causes her to profane the highest religious tenets of her country, which itself leads to her own death and the death of her child. Atene avows her passion for Leo in *Ayesha* (1905), 'my fancy wandered towards this man.'[47] It leads her to attempt to kill Ayesha, to wage war, and finally to kill herself. Asika in *The Yellow God* (1909) conceives an immediate passion for Alan, which prompts her to hasten the death of her husband in order to marry Alan, telling him: '[I] loved you from the moment that my eyes fell upon you.'[48] Even rational, analytical and morally admirable women like Jess and Beatrice, caught in the vortex of their own passion, indulge in lovemaking scenes, which can be read as amounting to sexual relations, with men whom they fully realize are formally committed to other women, although, for them, a greater, spiritual, passion causes them to renounce their earthly rights to these men. Joan Haste behaves in much the same way. The admirable but erring women of the novels, Jess, Beatrice and Joan, share the same ultimate fate as the morally reckless women of the romances. But for them death is an elective self-sacrifice rather than a mandatory punishment.

Jess and Beatrice's Impact upon Their Lovers

Not only are Jess and Beatrice susceptible to overwhelming sexual passion, but they also, in common with the women Haggard drew in his earlier fiction, have the ability to inflame men and to cause them to act outside the boundaries of their own recognized moral codes. Both John and Geoffrey are decent, restrained, sexually experienced and morally aware English gentlemen, and both are spoken for, but neither is able to resist the powerful sexual and spiritual appeal of, respectively, Jess and Beatrice. The narrator comments that John might have known that to cultivate the society of a woman with eyes like Jess 'was to run the risk of catching fire from them himself, to say nothing of setting her alight' (33). The explicit fire imagery, denoting the highly combustible, involuntary, painful, permanently scarring and judgement-warping effects of sexual passion on both men and women, which Haggard uses throughout his fiction, finds its tersest and bleakest expression in *Love Eternal* (1918), with its reference to 'sex the eating fire that is so beautiful but burns'.[49] When Beatrice, sleepwalking, appears in his room, Geoffrey, whose response to her has to this point been controlled and careful, is thoroughly unmanned and finds himself 'trembling at the sight of the conquering glory of the woman whom he worshipped' (216). There is as much of the spiritual here as of the sexual, and Haggard's use of 'worshipped' and of 'conquering glory' enhance the sense that both the sexual and the spiritual impact of Beatrice (and of Jess) have quasi-religious overtones.

John, who like Geoffrey is temperamentally controlled, experiences identical moments of helplessness in respect of both Bessie and Jess. After Jess's departure for Pretoria he allows his judgement to be warped by Bessie's attractiveness and proposes to her. The narrator comments: 'However strong the rope, it has its breaking strain' (99). The language is virtually identical to Ayesha's declaration in *She* that 'every man, like every rope, hath his breaking strain.'[50] John proves similarly susceptible to Jess. Haggard makes it clear that Jess deliberately overpowers John: 'She [...] had always known, that she could master him, and force him to regard her as she regarded him, did she but choose [...] And now she [...] chose' (163). Haggard is once more depicting the powerlessness of men to resist the sexual imperative and, in doing so, seems to be indulging in self-exculpation in respect of his own sexual susceptibility. There are strong echoes here of Ayesha in *She* forcing Leo to love her in the presence of the corpse of Ustane. For John:

> Everything melted away before the almost spiritual intensity of her gaze [...] the smouldering embers broke into flame, and he knew he loved this woman as he had never loved any living creature before. (163)

Leo and John may be English gentlemen in very different settings, but their responses are identical. In this respect the distance between romance and novel is negligible.

Haggard contrasts these epiphanic moments for strong and morally admirable Englishmen with the readier, coarser, violence-provoking sexual passion of Muller in *Jess* and Davies in *Beatrice*, the former a foreigner, the latter not a gentleman. If John's desire for Jess comes to him as a moment of spiritual revelation and clarity, Muller's for Bessie renders him 'inarticulate with passion' (37) and he adores her 'with the deep and savage force of his dark nature' (118). This primal, animalistic, wordless sense of fleshly passion divorced from a spiritual element is mirrored in the 'ox-like' (97) Davies's passion for Beatrice: 'His blood quivered and his mind grew dim' (98). The sensation is purely physical. Both Muller and Davies resort to moral violence, and the former also to threats of physical violence, in order to force the women they desire to marry them. Their unlicensed, unreciprocated, carnal passion is heavily punished. Muller, troubled in mind, meets a violent death. Davies becomes 'half-witted' (302), contracts what it is plain will be an uncomfortable marriage with the cold and exploitative Elizabeth, and dies prematurely. The violent punishment of men who, in their fierce sexual desire for a woman, try to force her, often through threats of violence, to marry them against their will also finds voice in Haggard's later romances. Tikal in *Heart of the World*, who pressurizes Maya in an attempt to persuade her to marry him, is thrown down a well. Montalvo in *Lysbeth* (1901), who succeeds in compelling Lysbeth to marry him by threatening her lover, Dirk, with the Inquisition, is torn apart by an angry mob. Such men are the heirs of George in *Dawn* and Cossey in *Colonel Quaritch V. C.* (1888). At an autobiographical level Haggard continues to express considerable anger against them.

The Moral Dilemmas in *Jess*, *Beatrice* and *Joan Haste*

In *Jess* and *Beatrice* Haggard is once again addressing the principal theme of his early novels, that of the force of sexual passion upon both men and women. But he is also examining a new but equally autobiographically linked theme – that of the moral legitimacy of a genuine, caring love, in essence a first real love, with a pronounced spiritual element, which occurs between a woman and a man who is already committed, in some degree, to another woman. He considers this same theme, although more obliquely, in *Joan Haste* (1895). The degrees of commitment differ. John is engaged to the attractive and virtuous Bessie. Geoffrey is married, albeit to the cold and materialistic Honoria. Henry's duty and the expectations of his family prompt him towards marriage with the loving and virtuous Emma. Henry is undoubtedly the freest agent. This, together with their widely different social backgrounds, and the fact that Joan, like Jess, makes the running in their early relationship but, unlike both Jess and Beatrice, is a woman without significant intellectual credentials or moral orientation, suggests that *Joan Haste* may be a book about the results of a cross-class casual affair and as such of a different order from *Jess* and *Beatrice*. But it has much in common with them. The narrator's intrusive commentary repeatedly emphasizes Joan's 'sin.' He comments: 'Her conscience was guilty, but Joan was not a woman to take warning from a guilty conscience. Indeed, its sting only drove her further along the downward road.'[51] Later he observes that Joan is restrained neither by 'an inherited sense of the proprieties' nor by 'strong religious principles' (130). But these unsympathetic, accusatory and morally pompous comments are not convincing, as Joan's self-sacrifice shows. The moral thrust of the book is plain. Henry belatedly realizes that he loved Joan and confirms the book's judgement that he should have put his love, and his duty to his lover, before his perceived duty to society and to his family.

John, like Henry, lacks self-knowledge. Despite being more than half-aware that he is drawn to Jess he allows himself, in a moment of male weakness, to be carried away by Bessie's 'pretty face' into proposing to her, although 'he was not violently in love with her' (99). Once they are engaged the moral situation is clear. But later his passion for Jess sweeps over him 'utterly drowning and overpowering his affection for Bessie' (165–66), like the impact of Hilda upon Philip in *Dawn*, which causes him to disregard his commitment to Maria. For John the seriousness of this is brought home to him by Jess who, when he tries to kiss her after she has 'put out all her strength' in order to cause him to love her, ironically and rather perversely rejects him, reminding him: 'You forget […] you are going to marry Bessie'. John, 'Overpowered by a deep sense of shame […] turned and limped from the house' (163). There seems to be a suggestion here of the Fall of Man and his consequent expulsion from the Garden of Eden as depicted both in the book of Genesis and Milton's *Paradise Lost* (1667). Certainly, Haggard is plain that John has allowed himself, like Adam, to taste 'the Fruit/Of that Forbidden Tree'.[52] He has no right to allow himself to fall in love with another woman, and certainly not with Bessie's sister.

Haggard emphasizes the delicacy of this situation by depicting Jess's sensitivity at betraying and potentially wounding her sister through her relationship with John when she tells herself, 'Bessie I have sinned against you' (331). He seems to be referencing the contemporary debate over the merits of the Deceased Wife's Sister Marriage Act of 1835, which prohibited a man from marrying his dead wife's sister. Diana Wallace has pointed out that 'According to the table of kindred and affinity in the Book of Common Prayer the wife's sister became by marriage a "sister" to the husband and sexual relations with her therefore became incest.'[53] The debate culminated in the passing of the synonymous Act of 1907, which finally removed the prohibition of such a marriage. The issue was a significant one in Victorian life, where female death in childbirth was not uncommon, and the unmarried sister-in-law was not infrequently called upon to act as surrogate mother, and it was reflected in Victorian literature. Sarah Annes Brown has observed that Charles Dickens was accused of an improper liaison with his sister-in-law Georgina Hogarth after his rupture with her sister Catherine and has also noted that Hardy reflects the issue in *Tess of the D'Urbervilles* (1891),[54] where Tess, at Stonehenge, anticipating her eventual execution, asks Angel to marry her sister Liza-Lu. Angel replies: 'If I lose you I lose all! And she is my sister-in-law.'[55] While it appears that Haggard is exploiting the issue as a plot expedient rather than taking a position on it, it is interesting to note that in his following book *Allan Quatermain* (1887) he depicts the result of two sisters' rivalry over the same man as bloody civil war.

Haggard thus sets the moral scene for his examination of whether an unsatisfactory marriage in any measure legitimizes extramarital, or what amounts to extramarital, sexual relations in the form of a genuine love based upon a passion that is spiritual as well as sexual. Etherington has suggested that, through this examination, Haggard may be contemplating adultery with Lilly, if only theoretically: 'whether this or any other relationship was consummated physically is not terribly important. The subject was constantly on his mind.'[56] It seems more likely that the morally scrupulous Haggard is concerned to establish whether his marital circumstances justify his unwavering emotional attachment to his first love or his apparent desire for Agnes, or indeed whether Johanna's troubled marriage in any way justified their affair. In any event, in his representation of marriage he loads the dice. While in *Jess* John's marriage to Bessie is happy enough but never succeeds in eclipsing his love for Jess, in *Beatrice* Haggard portrays marriage as disillusioning and burdensome. He makes it plain that Honoria is entirely to blame. She is cold, trivial and materialistic. Her moral deficiency is established beyond doubt by the statements that she is unmaternal: 'Lady Honoria did not belong to that class of women who think maternity is a joy' (54). Lilias records that her mother too was 'Never […] maternal.'[57] Although this reference of course postdates *Beatrice*, it strongly suggests that Louisa's view of children was adjacent to Honoria's.

In a gesture of sympathy towards the position of women, which is perhaps also indicative of an attempt by Haggard to understand Louisa, the narrator concedes that Honoria is a product of her upbringing: 'The passions had been bred and educated out of her, for many generations they have been found inconvenient and disquieting attributes in a woman' (64). Jenny Bourne-Taylor and Sally Shuttleworth note that 'The highly-strung hysteric women of the upper classes were […] directed to look at the bouncing health of the lower classes who did not subject themselves to the idle, artificial lives of society women', and point out that 'commentators throughout the period were […] united in their belief that one of the dominant causes was repressed sexual […] energy'.[58] Honoria appears to be such a woman. Haggard is making the clearest of statements about his view of the merits of spiritually modulated passion in a woman. His verdict on Honoria is confirmed by the violent manner of her death. She dies in a fire in the midst of her material pleasures, consumed, like Meriamun in *The World's Desire*, by her own lust. Haggard's unremittingly critical portrayal of Honoria and his dismissive treatment of her death scene seem to indicate an intense anger at her cold, materialistic and unmaternal behaviour and at the fact that such a morally flawed and contemptible character stood between the sexual and spiritual passion of Beatrice and Geoffrey. Haggard is clearly establishing an extenuating background to Geoffrey's love affair with Beatrice. He was similarly to depict an unworthy, and in this case apparently unfaithful, wife in *The Way of the Spirit* (1906), but although the protagonist, Rupert, strikes up an intimate friendship with another woman, Mea, he steadfastly refuses to have sexual relations with her, choosing sexual renunciation as a response to the condition of his marriage. Haggard does not postulate such a course for Geoffrey, who is forced to choose between cohabitation with Beatrice or separation from her.

What Happens Between the Lovers in *Jess* and *Beatrice*; Moral Judgements and the Drift of the Subtext

A judgement about the moral conclusions of *Jess* and *Beatrice* on the behaviour of Jess and John and Beatrice and Geoffrey must first consider what Haggard intended to convey about the nature of that behaviour. There are two points in *Jess* where John and Jess are overwhelmed by their passion: when Jess finds that John is alive after having believed him killed, and when they think themselves about to die in the storm-lashed river. In the first scene Jess provokes John by the intensity of her spiritualized desire: 'her beautiful eyes were alight with a flame that he had never seen in the eyes of a woman before' (162). John then attempts to kiss her. Jess declines the kiss, reminding him that he is engaged to Bessie. Afterwards they agree to forget the incident, but the narrator records:

> It was all a living lie and they knew it. For behind them stood the irrevocable Past, who for good or evil had bound them together in his unchanging bonds and with cords that never can be broken. (172)

While it is clear that there had been no sexual contact, it is equally clear that they have experienced a deeply spiritual defining moment in their relationship, and that the commitment between them has become total and eternal. Jess feels they are 'growing life to life, knit up in a divine identity' (169).

The scene in the river is loaded with both sexual and spiritual resonance. As the storm rages around them, they believe they are about to die, and this serves to strip away their emotional inhibitions: 'To and fro they swung, locked fast in each other's arms' (223). The sexual imagery is clear. They kiss passionately and are happy 'with a wild joy [...] all things were forgotten, for they were alone with Love and Death' (226) and Jess, 'lost in the depths of her own nature, sobbed out her passion-laden heart upon his breast' (227). Although it is plain from the practicalities of the backdrop that intercourse has not taken place, it is absolutely clear that Jess and John have become intimate at a spiritual level and that this involves a sexual bond between them.

There are three such significant scenes in *Beatrice*. The first, similar to the river scene in *Jess*, is where Beatrice and Geoffrey, immediately after meeting, are caught in a storm at sea, together in a small canoe and, like Jess and John, they are in fear for their lives.

The violent natural setting, their close proximity and shared danger heighten their emotions, and Haggard's imagery connects all three:

> The angry disc of the sun was sinking into the foam. A great red ray […] lay upon the awakened waters like a path of fire. The ominous light fell […] full upon Beatrice's lips. (15)

The sexual connotations of the 'great red ray' and 'awakened waters' and the physicality of 'Beatrice's lips' are clear. Geoffrey's battle against the storm also has an intense physicality and more than a suggestion of sexual intercourse: 'the perspiration was streaming from him at every pore […] he was becoming tired […] Soon he would no longer be able to keep the canoe straight' (18). As the waves finally swamp their canoe they grasp hands, and as they sink Beatrice clings to Geoffrey's unconscious body, promising to herself 'I will hold him till I die' (23). Haggard is proposing an immediate, instinctive, intense and life-changing mutual passion between Beatrice and Geoffrey, albeit perhaps only half-perceived by them, and in the prophetic suggestiveness of 'ominous light' falling directly on Beatrice's lips is indicating that such passion must, and should, culminate in what amounts to a sexual consummation. At a later juncture they go walking together on the cliff top while another storm, denoting their mounting passion, is brewing: 'The sea […] moaned like a thing in pain. The storm was gathering fast' (205). The scarcely ambivalent reference to female orgasm is succeeded by a further depiction of Beatrice's passion: 'The last red rays of the sunset […] lay upon her heaving breast' (206–7). Geoffrey is overcome: 'One moment he hesitated […] then Nature prevailed […] for the next she was in his arms', and 'their lips met in a first long kiss' (208). And while they talk as lovers:

> Above them moaned the rising gale […] the long waves boomed upon the beach, while far out to sea the crescent moon, draped in angry light, seemed to ride the waters like a boat. (209)

The intensity and insistency of the sexual imagery is striking. It is hard to conceive that intercourse has occurred, but as with Jess and John in the flooded river, this second mutual epiphany for Beatrice and Geoffrey has set the seal on a spiritual intimacy between them that has the force of a sexual union.

The episode most overtly suggestive of sexual relations is that in which Beatrice, sleepwalking, appears in Geoffrey's bedroom 'her bosom heaving softly beneath her night-dress, her streaming hair unbound, her lips apart' (216). But the book states plainly that sexual intercourse does not occur, and Geoffrey carries the still-sleeping Beatrice back to her own room. Through the sleepwalking device Haggard has enabled himself to illustrate Beatrice's, albeit unconscious, predisposition to sex and her offering of herself to her lover, and at the same time to construct an unassailable dramatic reason why intercourse cannot occur. A passage from Lilias's biography of her father seems to throw some light on Haggard's motives for this unequivocal denial. She records that 'growing to a deeper understanding of her father's nature, of his realization and sympathy with those passionate extremes which beset the human heart' she suggested to him that his protagonists 'might occasionally have been allowed to stray a little further down the Primrose Path', and that Haggard replied: 'nothing is easier […] than to write a book about men and women as they really are [...] but it just can't be done, my dear – it just can't be done'.[59] It seems that Haggard was constrained by the need to preserve his public reputation and safeguard both his readership and his income. At any event it appears that in *Jess* and *Beatrice* it was not part of his concern unequivocally to establish physical intercourse, to navigate minutely between the desire and the act. What he does present, in both couples, is a profound and eternal spiritual intimacy that involves an equally profound, if physically unconsummated, sexual union.

It is notable that, of these five crucial scenes in *Jess* and *Beatrice*, three take place in the context of violent natural phenomena involving water and storms. These are the key scenes. Free of the constrictions of social or domestic settings, Haggard is able to allow his imagery to speak for him. The waters, sea or river, are profoundly elemental; the storms a natural rendition of human passion. Haggard was using one convention to circumvent another as he had already done in *Dawn*, where Arthur and Mildred in effect consummate their relationship as a storm rages outside (320–21).

This sense of the profound nature of what has occurred and its moral implications can also be read in the considered responses of the protagonists to what has transpired between them. There is an insistence in both *Jess* and *Beatrice* that their behaviour amounts to serious moral transgression against the prevailing religious, if not the civil, code, both in terms of the social crime of an emotional association involving a man who is already committed to another woman, and in terms of the more personal betrayal of a loved one. Casting herself in the role of Eve, Jess reflects, 'she had tempted him and he had fallen' (285). She tells John economically and unequivocally, 'we have sinned, we must suffer' (288). But the real focus of her remorse is her betrayal of her sister: 'she had been false to Bessie' (285). Similarly, although Beatrice recognizes the moral criminality of their love, her chief concern is the potential harm it will do to Geoffrey's career, and she tells him, 'It is wrong, and will bring trouble on you' (211).

Both Jess and Beatrice redeem what they perceive as their sin against, respectively, Bessie and Geoffrey by their acts of self-sacrifice, which involve far greater sins. Jess, on the point of dying after having killed Muller in order to protect Bessie, states confidently to herself, 'Bessie, I have sinned against you, but I have washed away my sin' (331). Beatrice, by taking her own life, the only act that will with certainty terminate her relationship with Geoffrey and, she believes, save him from ruin, is equally confident that she will contract a marriage of eternal love with him. The reviewer of the *Pall Mall Gazette* commented 'If a novelist makes his heroine commit [...] a great crime, he can only retain the full sympathies of his readers by the most skilful treatment'.[60] Jess's act of murder and Beatrice's suicide (a morally culpable act in a Christian society) are however not apparently conceived of by Haggard as sin, while their sexual behaviours are clearly labelled as such. Part of the reason seems to lie in Haggard's own background. He was personally very aware of what he regarded as the sexual sin of the episode of his relationship with a married woman, and his guilt and remorse seem to have been with him all his life.[61] But, most significantly, *Jess* and *Beatrice* make clear that, despite the formal moral and dramatic need to label it as 'sin', the sexual behaviour of the heroines is a part of the natural and inevitable outworking of a genuine, deeply spiritual and entirely admirable love, and that in this context the acts of violence they perpetrate in the belief that they are the only solution to the complications caused, are morally justifiable on the grounds that they spring from a profound and spiritual response to that love.

Although Jess and Beatrice's acts of self-sacrifice are redemptive, the narrator's voice responds to them with reservation. He remarks of Jess that 'Self-denial is a stern-faced angel' (144). Jess herself says to John 'There is no true happiness outside of love and self-sacrifice' (48) but it is plain that her misjudged altruism in deciding to go and stay in Pretoria in order to leave the field clear for Bessie is in fact the cause of the tragedy. Had she remained it is evident that John would have quickly realized he loved her and not Bessie, and that Bessie would have soon got over losing John. The same is true of Beatrice's self-sacrifice. Of her altruism the narrator comments that, admirable though it may have been, in absolute terms and at a practical human level it blighted Geoffrey's life:

> She did not remember that when all is lost which can make life beautiful [...] the poor garish light of our little victories can but ill atone for the glories that have been. (278)

While this can be seen as an autobiographical reflection by Haggard on the success of *King Solomon's Mines* (1885) and *She* and his consequent fame and fortune viewed in the light of his loss of Lilly, it is clear that it is also a comment on the impractical, other-worldly, unintentionally wounding and self-wounding aspects of self-sacrifice, and a statement, which is adjacent to Maya's assertions, about the right of human beings to a fulfilling existence. Hardy was to make a similar statement about the damaging aspects of self-denial in *Jude the Obscure*, where the outcome of Sue's perverse and excoriating self-sacrifice is profoundly destructive.

This same sense is reflected in Haggard's own implied moral conclusions on Jess and Beatrice. While in *Jess* the unsatisfactory nature of the outcome is signalled through the narrator's intervention – 'Let those who would blame them pause a while' (226) – and through John's inability to put Jess out of his mind and his tepid enthusiasm for his consolatory marriage to Bessie, in *Beatrice* it is evidenced chiefly by Haggard's revisions to the narrator's comments. These comments take the form in the first edition of 1890 of an ironical criticism of contemporary, self-righteous, illiberal moral standards, an underlying sympathy for Beatrice and Geoffrey, and a sense of the helplessness of human beings caught up in sexual passion. In an observation on Geoffrey's inability to identify the dangers in his relationship with Beatrice, the narrator remarks, 'human nature in strong temptation is very apt to override artificial barriers erected to suit the convenience or promote the prosperity of particular sections of mankind' (First Edition, 189–90). Later, the same voice urges Beatrice to

> take your chance. You may find that you were right and the worldlings wrong, and you may reap a harvest beyond the grasp of their poor imaginations [...] For of this at least you are sure. If there is no future for such earthly love as yours, then indeed there is none for the children of this world and all their troubling. (First Edition, 227)

That Haggard included these telling comments in his first edition and deleted them in the 1894 and subsequent editions in the face of popular moral criticism indicates where his real sympathies lay and how he intended the book to be read.

A concluding, and equally significant, commentary by the narrator survived revision. Its burden is the inescapability of the human condition: 'if there be any pitiful Principle, well might it sigh over the infinite pathos of human helplessness' (311). This constitutes the earliest rendition by Haggard of a conclusion to which he increasingly comes in his later fiction and which culminates in his final novel, *Mary of Marion Isle* (1929): human beings cannot be held responsible for the outcomes of the irresistible sexual imperatives that are an integral part of their being, and that genuine love is the only dependable good. This sense of helplessness is reinforced in both *Beatrice* and *Jess* by a fatalism that echoes that of Haggard's earlier novels and foreshadows that of his later ones. The narrator's concluding comment in *Beatrice* is: 'We are but arrows winged with fears and shot from darkness into darkness' (312). Jess, having gone away to Pretoria in order to avoid what she anticipates will be the emotional complications of her relationship with John, reflects, when he unexpectedly arrives there: 'His sudden appearance was almost uncanny in the sharpness of its illustration of her impotence in the hands of Fate' (148).

The corresponding additions and amendments Haggard made in 1894, formally strengthening the moral tone of *Beatrice*, probably reflect a concern for his own authorial livelihood. While literary representations of the 1880s reflect a preoccupation with the femme fatale, there was in 1894 a reaction to the New Woman. Pykett observes that 'Sarah Grand's *The Heavenly Twins*, for many the prototypical New Woman novel, sold 30,000 copies in its first year (1893)' but that, increasingly 'The New Woman writers [...] were taken to task for their failure, or refusal, to conform to traditional fictional paradigms, and to observe the formal (and other) proprieties'.[62] She instances William Barry's review in 1894 of *The Heavenly Twins*.[63]

But, although they may have been expedient, Haggard's alterations also point to a clear sympathy for his heroine. He concludes his advertisement of 1894 with the unequivocal statement: 'the man or woman who falls into undesirable relations with a married member of the other sex, is both a sinner and a fool' (iv). The formalistic tone and circumlocutory language are suggestive of parody. His amendments to the narrator's comments include those in the observation of Beatrice and Geoffrey that 'They had broken the law and defied the customs of their world, and the law and the world were avenged upon them and their unhallowed passions' (224). These take the form of the addition of the phrases: 'They had broken the law' and 'their unhallowed passions'. The heavy, pompous, accusatory tone and the evocation of 'the law" is suggestive of irony; the pseudo-sanctimonious reference to "unhallowed passions' equally so. Haggard is criticizing the moral attitude of both Church and State. His sympathy for his protagonists seems to be confirmed by an ironical reference he makes in his autobiography to his revision of *Beatrice*: 'I went through the tale carefully, [and] modified or removed certain passages that might be taken to suggest that holy matrimony is not always perfect in its working.'[64]

The same underlying authorial sympathy for his characters is apparent in *Joan Haste*, published some five years after *Beatrice*, in which sexual intercourse outside marriage unquestionably takes place. Intimidated by the hostile moral reaction to *Beatrice*, Haggard's intention seems to have been to ensure that no one could mistake his attitude towards the extramarital sex depicted. Joan's fate, her social descent, her illegitimate child and her violent death are all punishment for her illicit sexual liaison. The narrator passes judgement on Joan's part in her sexual union with Henry and comments on its consequences for her: 'sorrow and repentance were to overtake her when she learnt all the trouble and ruin which her conduct had caused' (183). The seriousness of her crime is underlined by a biblical reference to Adam and Eve's consumption of the forbidden fruit: 'the red bloom she had gathered was to become a bitter fruit [...] a fruit of the tree of sinful knowledge' (268). The narrator's verdict on Joan's actions echoes the criticism of Eva's 'sin' in *The Witch's Head*. But like the veering response to Eva's moral lapse, the evidence of Joan's behaviour subverts the book's formal judgement of her, and she emerges as a redemptive rather than an errant figure.

In *Jess* and *Beatrice*, Haggard is, in effect, justifying what amounts in both cases to extramarital sexual relations, or at the very least affirming his sympathy for the participants. This seems at first sight to be at odds with his attack on the Naturalistic French school in his essay 'About Fiction', but he makes it clear in the same essay that his interpretation of realism is substantially different, arguing that fictional pictures of life ought to be subject to 'proper reservations and restraints'.[65] But the reservations and restraints of Haggard's domestic novels do not obscure his sympathy for the victims of the marriage question.

It is instructive to consider to what extent such sympathy is common amongst those writers of the period who dealt with the same subject. Ledger has observed that 'one of the defining features of the dominant discourse on the New Woman at the fin de siècle was the supposition that the New Woman posed a threat to the institution of marriage.'[66] But closer examination of *One of Our Conquerors*, George Gissing's *The Odd Women* (1893), *The Woman Who Did* and *Jude the Obscure* reveals an apparent ambiguity in the authors' attitudes towards the moral situations they present. Ledger points out that, in *The Woman Who Did*, 'The wholesale defeat of Allen's heroine implies a limited sympathy towards her. Her point of view is ultimately overridden by that of the narrator who endorses [...] dominant Victorian definitions of womanhood'. Unlike Jess and Beatrice, the female protagonists persist in their socially deviant behaviour. Natalia, Herminia and Sue cohabit with men outside wedlock and give birth to their children. Monica leaves her husband and refuses to return to him despite being pregnant with his child and finding herself abandoned by her lover. Only belatedly do they realize the consequences of their actions. Natalia, Herminia and Monica die, essentially of shame. Sue commits a conscious emotional suicide in returning to Phillotson. Jess and Beatrice cannot be said to 'threaten the institution of marriage' in the same way. They are immediately and keenly aware of their 'sin', and eventually take their own lives, not because they are ashamed of what they have done – in fact they regard it as the fleshly expression of the highest form of love they can offer, and they aspire to recreate it, at least in spiritual form, in an afterlife – but in order to protect the reputations, futures and marriages of those they love. While the motivations of Meredith's, Allen's, Gissing's and Hardy's characters remain uncertain (and complex), there is little doubt about those of Haggard's. And while those author's sympathies towards the behaviour of their heroines is sometimes ambivalent there is no doubt about Haggard's.

The Spirituality of Jess and Beatrice

Haggard presents Jess and Beatrice as women who are remarkable and admirable, not simply because of their capacity for self-sacrifice, but because they are unusually spiritually endowed. Their spiritual attributes constitute the difference between them and misguided, if more convincing, female victims of their own urges and convictions, or lack of them, like Herminia, Natalia, Monica, Sue and indeed Joan Haste. Jess and Beatrice have rarefied, other-worldly natures that elevate them beyond the demands of a purely realistic status and differentiate them from the New Women. Their spirituality connects them with both a kind of divinity and with an extraordinary sexuality and creates an association between the two.

Jess's spirituality – and the eternal nature of her love – is first indicated by song, Beatrice's by dream. Jess sings, and of her song the narrator records: 'Passion [...] echoed in its every line, and [...] unending love hovered over the glorious notes' (12). Exactly the same phenomenon first indicates precisely the same qualities in Helen in *The World's Desire* and later in the eponymous heroine of *Stella Fregelius* (1904). Beatrice dreams that her life, and Geoffrey's, are intertwined and, in her dream, hears him address her as the 'woman whom I knew before the Past began, and whom I shall know when the Future is ended' (69). Jess is animated by a 'half-divine, soul-searing [...] passion' (98). But it is still a sexual passion, and John sees on her face 'a spiritualised desire' (175). Beatrice's dream leaves her profoundly sexually aroused, but she later reflects that her love is not 'mere earthly passion' but 'something grander, purer, deeper and quite undying' (141). Both have experienced, through an unconscious and spiritualized medium, an extraordinary sexual passion that has about it aspects of the divine and the eternal. When this sexual passion re-emerges, it has again the same spiritual dimension. When Jess sees John after having believed him killed, 'something seemed to pass before her eyes and blind her, and a spirit took possession of her' (163). Beatrice's love leads her to conclude that she has a soul, 'something that could love with the body [...] and beyond the body' (141). And the ultimate expression of Jess and Beatrice's fierce sexual spirituality is the moral strength it gives them, both to perpetrate profound violence in its cause, and to achieve absolution for this violence.

The intense spirituality of the woman is the driver for the spiritual proximity of the lovers. Jess felt 'as though they two were growing life to life, knit up in a divine identity" and that this "communion could never be dissolved' (169). For Geoffrey 'in the mystery of that dread communion [...] passion [...] took life and form within him' (143). The rapport between the lovers, enabled by extraordinary and redemptive women, is defined in terms of the divine 'mystery' of the most intimate fleshly and spiritual Christian ritual, the sharing of the body of the Redeemer in the service of Holy Communion.[67] The male lovers express this spiritual intimacy similarly. John as an 'utter sympathy' (159), Geoffrey as an 'unearthly sympathy' (215).

Haggard is speaking of a quasi-religious compact, both sexual and spiritual, outside formal marriage and infinitely more binding and enduring beyond death. Of Jess the narrator says that 'her love was indeed a love deeper than the grave [...] ready, when dissolution had lent it wings, to soar to love's own star' (225). Beatrice believes the answer to her life's problems is 'Unity attained in Death' (144), and that 'Death will be the Priest and that oath which I shall take will be to all eternity' (291). This unequivocal confidence in the apotheosis of love in an afterlife is reminiscent of a similar statement by Nell Lestrange on the death of her lover in Rhoda Broughton's *Cometh Up As A Flower* (1867): 'through the grave and gates of death I should pass to my beloved.'[68] It is apparent that Haggard has a strong personal stake in this proposition. Quite apart from the sympathy he extends to Jess and Beatrice, he intervenes with extraordinary emphasis in *Beatrice* in the voice of the narrator to comment on the love of Beatrice and Geoffrey: 'now reason fell and Love usurped his throne, and at that royal coming Heaven threw wide her gates' (209). This ultimate, incontestable religious endorsement of their love is closely succeeded by the statement: 'Only Love is real; Love shall endure till all the suns are dead, and yet be young' (209). The unequivocal nature of Haggard's assertion has the hallmarks of a personal psychological imperative.

Conclusion

Jess and Beatrice undoubtedly share some of the attributes of fictional representations of the New Woman. They are articulate women of pronounced sexuality who are prepared to flout elements of moral and religious principle in pursuit of their love. But they are also deeply self-sacrificial women who decline to be complicit in causing the men they love to compromise their reputations, careers and actual or intended marriages, and who are prepared to take their own lives to prevent this occurring. Haggard registers a transparent authorial sympathy for the predicament of his heroines and endorses the validity of a sexual relationship outside marriage provided that this relationship springs from a deep and genuine love. This is notable in a male author addressing the subject of the New Woman. But he does not explore in any detail the emotional disruption caused to his heroines, nor does he give serious consideration to adjacent issues such as the outworking of female sexuality or the validity of the institution of marriage. His heroines are in a sense confined by their own self-sacrificial spirituality and are instruments in assuring, or attempting to ensure, the futures of their male partners.

It seems, however clear, that in locating the love of Jess and John and, particularly, that of Beatrice and Geoffrey, outside the contract of marriage and intended marriage, in endorsing it at a religious level and investing it with strong sexual and spiritual elements and the ability to transcend death, Haggard is, in an autobiographical context, contemplating and evaluating the nature of his own marriage and the experiences that preceded it. In examining the relationship between spiritual rapport and sexual passion and the capacity of the former to provoke the latter, he appears to be drawing on his relationship with Agnes and reflecting whether he ought to have married her rather than Louisa. He is also positing an eternal validity and reality for his feelings for Lilly, both justifying his continuing physical passion for her and comforting himself with the prospect of a permanent reunion in an afterlife. He is posing uncomfortable questions about the nature, significance and sanctity of marriage and proposing a greater moral absolute in a genuine and eternal love outside its parameters. At the same time, he continues to be preoccupied with the sexually derived power that women have over men. But the raw anger of his earlier fiction at the sexual imperative and its capacity to wound is beginning to give way to a more reflective, sad, resignation, and he is tentatively proposing a way of coping with the exigencies of the emotional labyrinth. He develops the theme of the profound spiritual and eternal dimensions of real love in his immediately succeeding fiction and explores the proposition that the spiritual could be a viable, and preferable, substitute for the sexual.

Chapter Five

SPIRITUAL LOVE AND SEXUAL RENUNCIATION (1899–1908)

In the period that begins with the publication of *Swallow* (1899) and ends with that of *The Ghost Kings* (1908) Haggard gives consideration for the first time in his fiction to a love that is predominantly spiritual rather than sexual and, most strikingly of all, to the delicate subject of sexual renunciation. His most concentrated focus is found in his novels *Stella Fregelius* (1904) and *The Way of the Spirit* (1906). While both of these books closely examine the merits of a spiritual love that is largely divorced from sexual love, they both ultimately recognize, albeit with different degrees of conviction, that the sexual imperative is an integral and inescapable part of the human condition and postulate that while earthly sexual renunciation may sometimes be necessary, it demands a price from those who adopt it and derives any validity it has from the prospect of an eventual reunion in an afterlife that will have a pronounced sexual as well as a spiritual dimension.

Haggard's Contemporary Biography

In the 19 years from 1889 to 1908 Haggard suffered bereavements and emotional trials, involving family and close friends, that affected him deeply. In December 1899 his mother died. Lilias observes of Haggard's feelings for his mother that he 'loved her so greatly, in one sense above all other women'.[1] Haggard himself provides an insight into what her death meant to him and how often, in his later life, he recalled her, in a passage in his autobiography:

> She seems to be much nearer to me now that she is dead […] It is as though our intimacy and mutual understanding has grown in a way as real as it is mysterious. No night goes by that I do not think of her and pray that we may meet again to part no more.[2]

In February 1891, while Haggard and his wife were in Mexico, they received the news that their only son Jock had died in England at the age of ten. Haggard, fond of all of his children, was particularly attached to his son. As his daughter remarks 'this child he worshipped with all the passion of his over-intense nature'.[3] Of the immediate impact, he records in his autobiography: 'I descended into hell.'[4] And of his belief in a reunion with his son in death, he writes some twenty years later, 'Soon, after all these long years of separation, I shall go to him […] then surely my spirit will find his spirit, though it must search from world to world', and he goes on to quote from *Montezuma's Daughter* (1893): 'there is no comfort save in the truth that love which might have withered on the earth grows fastest in the tomb, to flower gloriously in heaven'.[5] It is plain that, in the years succeeding their death, Haggard thought continually of his mother and his son, that he felt that his love for them was growing, and that he strongly wished to believe in a reunion with them in an afterlife. That this preoccupation finds expression in the fiction he wrote during this period is evidenced by a passage in *Stella Fregelius*:

> There is no human passion like this passion for the dead; none so awful, none so holy, none so changeless. For they have become eternal, and our desire for them is sealed with the stamp of their eternity.[6]

In December 1895 Lilly 'came for the second time into Rider's life'.[7] Her stockbroker husband Archer fled to Africa having been charged with embezzlement of client funds, including Lilly's family fortune. She was left almost penniless, and Higgins records that Haggard 'took a small house where he installed her and the boys, and proceeded to do what he could to start them in life'.[8] In 1898 Archer wrote to her asking her to join him, and 'against the advice of her friends, including Haggard, she agreed'.[9] In 1904 Haggard learned that Archer was dying in Africa and, on his death in 1907, Lilly returned to England 'suffering from the tertiary syphilis that had killed her husband'.[10] Haggard found her a house on the Suffolk coast, and he and his wife visited her frequently until her death in 1909. Throughout this period Haggard and Louisa also remained in frequent contact with his sister-in-law Agnes, and Haggard continued to seek her advice on his fiction, including *Stella Fregelius*, as his dedication of the book to her in her pen name of John Berwick makes clear. In 1900 they holidayed with Agnes and her family at their residence in Florence where they were living during Jack Haggard's inhospitable posting in Noumea. In 1908 Jack died suddenly in Malaga, and Haggard extended financial help to Agnes and her family.

It was against this background of the deaths of his mother, for whom his love was 'profound and long-lasting', and his son whose death, according to D. S. Higgins, 'seemed to prove to Haggard the veracity of his belief that those close to him were destined to suffer because of his own sins', that Haggard wrote *Stella Fregelius* and *The Way of the Spirit*.[11] To compound his emotional turmoil he had to deal with the imminent return into his life, in a tragically reduced physical and financial state, of the woman who remained his great love, and the impending need to provide materially both for her and for a woman with whom he remained intellectually intimate, whom he had deeply admired in a spiritual sense and to whom he had almost certainly been physically attracted. Issues surrounding the relationship between the living and the dead, the afterlife, and the connection between, and relative merits of, spiritual and sexual love were clearly in his mind, and it is unsurprising, given the contemporary interest in spiritualism, that Haggard examined in his fiction its capacity to provide satisfactory answers to these concerns, all the more so because he was himself a man of spiritual inclinations.

The Contemporary Interest in Spiritualism

Haggard's scrutiny of spiritual love has to be seen, not only in the context of his own emotional history, but also of the contemporary popular interest in spiritualism and of similar scrutiny in the work of contemporary novelists and spiritualist writers. Arthur Conan Doyle observes of the origins of spiritualism in England that 'spiritualists are in the habit of taking March 31 1848 as the beginning of all psychic things, because their movement dates from that day'.[12] Joseph McCabe concurs, noting that 'spiritualism began in the year 1848' and adding that its essence is 'the claim of communication with deceased human beings'.[13] He asserts that the movement was 'peculiarly opportune about that date' and cites 'the democratic movement [...] the new scientific movement' and the 'visibly failing authority of the Church' as contributing factors.[14] Alex Owen contends that the ubiquity, and often premature nature, of death predisposed the late Victorians to the spiritualist belief 'that it is possible for the living to contact and communicate with the spirits of the dead',[15] asserting:

> Proof of immortality and the joy of renewed contact with lost loved ones were powerful common factors in the acceptance of Spiritualism. At a time when regular family bereavement was a feature of everyday life, the death of somebody close, often a child, was a strong precipitating factor.[16]

Michael Wheeler notes more succinctly 'the Victorians' obsessive interest in post-mortem existence'.[17]

One contributory factor, Frank Podmore points out, was the influence of the eighteenth-century philosopher Emanuel Swedenborg: 'The idea of intercourse with distinctively human spirits, if not actually introduced by Swedenborg, at least established itself first in the popular consciousness through his teaching.'[18] Owen observes that 'many of Swedenborg's notions were popularized and taken up by the Spiritualist movement as a whole', and she notes that 'Swedenborg's works had been translated and published in London in 1845.'[19] Spiritualism seems initially to have flourished in England. McCabe claims that 'By the beginning of 1874 London had a large and enthusiastic body of spiritualists, and there was a proportionate movement in the provinces.'[20] Part of the reason for its popularity may have been that the teachings of Swedenborg were readily reconcilable with Christianity. Podmore writes that 'the spiritual utterances were regarded as supplementing rather than supplanting Christianity, the doctrines of Swedenborg serving to mediate between the old revelation and the new'.[21] But by the 1880s fraudulent practices by *soi-disant* mediums were discrediting the movement. McCabe records that, in 1882, 'In the face of the constant exposures of popular mediums, few men of cultural distinction now cared to be openly associated with Spiritualism.'[22]

Haggard's Experience with Aspects of Spiritualism and His Fascination with the Concept of an Afterlife

Haggard had experienced at first-hand the more outlandish aspects of spiritualism. In 1874, aged 19 and studying in London, he attended a number of séances. Among these was one at a private house in Green Street about which he writes in his autobiography:

> Two young women of great beauty – or perhaps I should say young spirits – [...] appeared in the lighted room. I conversed with and touched them both, and noted that their flesh seemed

to be firm but cold. [...] [One] was draped in a kind of white garment which covered her head and I asked her to allow me to see her hair. She pushed up the white drapery from her forehead, remarking sweetly that if I would look I should see that she had no hair, and in fact she appeared to be quite bald. A minute or two later, however, she had long and beautiful hair which flowed all about her.

Afterwards [...] she [...] remarked that she was tired. Thereon her body seemed to shrink, [and] the neck elongated enormously, after the fashion of Alice in Wonderland. Then she fell backwards and vanished altogether.[23]

Of these experiences, he concludes:

Whatever may be the true explanation, on one point I am quite sure, namely that the whole business is mischievous and to be discouraged. Bearing in mind its effect upon my own nerves, never would I allow any young person over whom I had control to attend a séance.[24]

And, more generally, he writes of attempts to invoke the spirits of the dead:

The risks are many, and the fruits [...] apt to be unsatisfactory, if not deadly [...] Once I tried to point this moral in a tale I wrote which is named 'Stella Fregelius'.[25]

Nevertheless, in spite of this scepticism about séances, Haggard demonstrates throughout much of his fictional writing a persistent interest in the philosophical aspects of spiritualism, crucially the question of the continuation after death of earthly life and the reunification of lovers in an afterlife. It has regularly been observed that Haggard's fiction, especially his early and best-selling romances, incorporates spiritualist ideas about reincarnation and the immortality of the soul. Wendy Katz, for example, observes that 'in book after book Haggard affirms the inviolability and supremacy of the spirit'.[26] However, his sustained and concentrated focus in his fiction of the turn of the century on some of the aspects of spiritualism and especially his examination of the respective merits of sexual and spiritual love has not been fully explored. It is significant that Haggard's most probing considerations are to be found, not in the context of fabulous settings and characters in popular romances such as *King Solomon's Mines* (1885), *She* (1887) and *The World's Desire* (1890), but in two of his less well-known novels. There is no documentary evidence to explain why this is the case. However, since Haggard states in author's notes to these books that he wrote *Stella Fregelius* and *The Way of the Spirit* because their themes interested him, it seems likely that he judged that issues that appeared to him serious should be presented, in order to best scrutinize them, in 'realistic' novels of English life without the distractions of colourful and exotic scenes, characters and plots. Certainly, there were contemporary readers who recognized, and welcomed, Haggard's interest in aspects of spiritualism. Christine Ferguson observes that Victorian spiritualists were eager to draw attention to Haggard's concern with spiritualism amidst his overwhelming reputation as a writer of adventures: 'Popular authors such as Haggard and Caine may have posed as proud, primal romancers, but spiritualistically attuned readers knew better.'[27] While Haggard could hardly be labelled as a spiritualist writer, his interest in spiritualism was genuine and personal as was his preoccupation with the respective merits of spiritual and sexual love.

Haggard offers no precise definition of what he understood by spirituality, but as defined by his consideration of spiritual love in his fictional writings it indicates concern with things outside the material, with determining the meaning of life and death, with an ability to have an instructive communication with a like-minded lover, to feel an ongoing rapport with dead loved ones and to have an implicit confidence in the reunion of lovers in an afterlife. His treatment of these subjects can be seen in relation to that of near contemporary novelists such as Robert Buchanan in *The Moment After* (1890), Theodore Watts-Dunton in *Aylwin* (1898) and Marie Corelli in *The Life Everlasting* (1911), all of whom handled aspects of the same theme. And it is instructive to observe some of the close similarities between Haggard's consideration of sexual love in an afterlife, spiritual communication between lovers, the divine attributes of spiritual women and communication with the dead, and consideration of the same themes in the writings of contemporary spiritualists, particularly the poet and writer George Barlow and the writer Laurence Oliphant, who deal directly with these issues, and the way in which Dante Gabriel Rossetti had earlier presented them in 'The House of Life' (1870). Haggard seems to have been wary of the writings of Swedenborg and other, unspecified, philosophers, opining in his autobiography that it was not wise to 'rely too much upon the revelations of seers such as Swedenborg, for these may be and doubtless are self-deceived or victims of hallucinations'.[28] Nevertheless, his attitudes to spiritualism appear to derive in some measure from Swedenborg.

Haggard believed in the possibility 'of the communion of the individual soul still resident on earth with other souls that have passed from us [...] without the intervention of any medium'.[29] Morton Cohen records that 'Haggard [...] was always fascinated by the supernatural [...] even [...] after rejecting spiritualism, he kept a careful eye on psychical research [...] he leaned toward reincarnation' and linked 'true love with the eternal spirit', believing that 'Both the spirit and the love it manifests would never cease to be.'[30] Haggard maintained an extensive correspondence with William T. Horton, who illustrated some of his books but who was also, in Haggard's words 'a mystic of the first water',[31] and in a letter to Horton in February 1899 he refers to his interest in 'mysticism which by appointed and wholesome paths seeks a closer and more daily union with all the surrounding spiritual'.[32] While Haggard firmly rejected spiritualism of the discreditable table-tapping variety, he clearly found it a psychological imperative to embrace spiritualist theory on the reunion of spirits in an afterlife, especially since he was able to reconcile it with established Christian teaching on the subject. He makes plain in his autobiography the importance with which he invests the Christian assurance of this reunion of souls when he writes in his final chapter, 'A Note on Religion': 'He will lead us to our lost ones [...] in the home He has prepared for us [...] from Eternity to Eternity'.[33] Both *Stella Fregelius* and *The Way of the Spirit*, and later *Love Eternal* (1918), engage with the subject.

Stella Fregelius and Its Biographical Resonances

Stella Fregelius, like its predecessor novels *Jess* (1887), *Beatrice* (1890) and *Joan Haste* (1895), concerns a young man who is deeply attracted to one woman while being committed to another. But the key difference is that the attraction is of an entirely spiritual nature;

there is no physical contact between the lovers. The focus of the book is threefold. It presents a love that is spiritual rather than sexual, and, as Haggard points out in an author's note, it depicts the conflict 'between earthly duty and spiritual desire'. It emphatically asserts a reunion of lovers in an afterlife. It also illustrates how an obsessive spiritual desire can lead to an involvement in the destructive aspects of spiritualism. Haggard was pleased with the book at a personal level and refers to it in a letter to his literary agent A. P. Watt as a 'work by which I set some store'.[34] But he was aware that it might disappoint his readers and in an author's note apologizes that it was 'in no sense a romance of the character that perhaps they expect from him' (Haggard's syntax is unfortunate but he is not of course suggesting that the book is a romance) and, perhaps anticipating its tepid critical reception, explained that he wrote it 'purely to please himself'. The contemporary critics were indeed unenthusiastic. The *Times Literary Supplement* reviewer, apparently concerned that the book would encourage spiritualist practices of a harmful sort, warned that it 'makes too insidious an approach to the foolishness that breeds mischief'.[35]

Norman Etherington has asserted, without offering any detail, that *Stella Fregelius* is 'an exercise in veiled autobiography'.[36] There are certainly significant autobiographical resonances in the book. Morris's overbearing father and his manoeuvrings both to press Morris into an engagement with the financially secure Mary and to separate him from Stella are reminiscent of Haggard's own father having placed obstacles in the way of his pursuit of Lilly and of his wholehearted approval of the heiress Louisa. Mary's love and loyalty towards Morris and her forbearance towards his obsession with Stella probably derive from Haggard's own appreciation for Louisa's understanding of his ineradicable feelings for Lilly and for the fact that, according to Lilias, she was 'unwaveringly kind' to Lilly when she returned to England.[37]

Higgins has suggested that Haggard's dedication of the book to Agnes Barber (in her pen-name of John Berwick) was in gratitude for her reassuring advice on his concerns 'about its clear autobiographical account of Lilly's influence on him'.[38] While it is possible to argue that Haggard's depiction of Morris's dilemma derives from the tension he himself experienced between his duty to Louisa and his feelings for Lilly, there is also something of Agnes in the deep spirituality of Stella. If it is probable that Haggard's first fully-drawn spiritual woman, Jess, owes a significant amount to Agnes, then it seems likely that his subsequent spiritual women owe a similar debt. It is also noteworthy that Mary in *Stella Fregelius* has much in common with Bessie in *Jess*. Both are sexually attractive, if emotionally unimaginative, women and as such have stronger overtones of Lilly than of Louisa. It seems probable that in *Stella Fregelius*, while Haggard may at one level have been agonizing over the way his continuing devotion to Lilly cut across his duty to Louisa, he was also comparing the predominantly sexual woman with the predominantly spiritual as he had in *Jess*, and that he had Agnes in mind in this latter context. This probability is enhanced by consideration of his earlier heroine Stella Carson in *Allan's Wife* (1889), who relates back to Jess and forward to Stella Fregelius. Like Jess she is an English girl brought up in remote, rural Africa. Like Jess and Stella Fregelius she is 'radiant [...] with a wild, spiritual beauty'.[39] Like them she dies to await her lover in an afterlife. Like them, and unusually for Haggard's heroines, but like Agnes, she is dark-haired. Moreover, Stella Carson becomes the wife of Allan Quatermain who, Haggard wrote, 'is only myself set in a variety of imagined situations, thinking my thoughts and looking at life through my eyes'.[40] Just as it seems likely that in *Jess* Haggard was giving expression to his feelings for Agnes and wondering, through the mouth of John, whether he ought not to have married her rather than Louisa, the same autobiographical reflections are discernible in *Allan's Wife* and *Stella Fregelius*.

The Way of the Spirit and Its Biographical Resonances

In *The Way of the Spirit* Haggard once again considers the dilemma of a young man who falls in love with one woman when committed to another. Like Geoffrey in *Beatrice*, Rupert Ullershaw is married to an unworthy woman. He attempts to find a way out of the moral impasse and act fairly to both women by renouncing sexual relations with the one he loves in favour of a purely spiritual love. The nub of the book, Haggard claims, is the question 'should or should not circumstances be allowed to alter moral cases'.[41] More accurately, it is an examination of the merits of sexual renunciation. As he had done in *Stella Fregelius*, Haggard prefaced the book with an author's note apologizing for it to his readers and offering the same justification: 'I should ask forgiveness for my deviation from the familiar trodden pathway of adventure.' He explains that: 'I have ventured on the history of Rupert Ullershaw's great, and to all appearances successful Platonic experiment chiefly because this problem interested me.' Haggard showed the manuscript to Rudyard Kipling and records that the subject also 'interested him very much'.[42] When Haggard discovered that its original title *Renunciation* had been used before, they agreed together on the new title, which, according to Cohen, 'they found [...] in Ecclesiastes'.[43] The verse in question reads:

> Rejoice, O young man, in thy youth [...] and walk in the ways of thine heart, and in the sight of thine eyes; but know thou that for all these things God will bring thee into judgement. Therefore remove sorrow from thy heart, and put away evil from thy flesh; for childhood and youth are vanity.[44]

The origin of the title makes clear that, for Haggard, the theme was serious and personal. He refers to the book of Ecclesiastes as 'One immortal work that moves me [...] a work that utters all the world's yearning anguish and disillusionment in one [...] bitter cry'.[45] Of the book's reception, Lilias comments that 'It was not [...] particularly popular. Few books upon the subject of platonic relationships between men and women are.'[46] Charles Longman declined to serialize it on the grounds that the basis of the book was sexual relationship and its renunciation 'which I think it better not to discuss in magazines'.[47] However, Haggard's literary agent A. P. Watt wrote to him, saying 'it is perhaps one of your best and finest books'.[48] The reviews were mixed, but the *Times Literary Supplement* called it 'a strong, straightforward and well told story which deserves respect',[49] and the *Saturday Review* perceptively commented that 'the evident earnestness of the author rescues it from the ever-ready dangers of the commonplace'.[50]

There are fewer, and less obvious, autobiographical traces in the book than are apparent in *Stella Fregelius* and in most of Haggard's earlier novels. But in Rupert's youthful affair with the married Clara it is difficult not to detect resonances of Haggard's own youthful affair. Higgins proposes that 'It was almost certainly while he was writing *The Way of the Spirit*'[51] that Haggard learned Lilly's husband was dying of syphilis, and that Lilly, suffering from the same disease, was to return to England. If Higgins's assertion is correct, then the tension Haggard depicts in the book between Rupert's strong sexual urges and the practical need for sexual renunciation in the situation in which he finds himself may well have reference to what was surely Haggard's personal realization that, while his strong, sexually originated passion for Lilly persisted, his marital situation, not to mention Lilly's own illness, dictated absolutely that he should conceive that passion exclusively in spiritual terms.

The Question of Celibacy

Implicit in the majority of Haggard's considerations of spiritual love in his fiction written between 1899 and 1908 there remains the underlying and unchallenged assumption that the lovers involved eventually enjoy a sexual relationship. Suzanne and Ralph in *Swallow* (1899) and Rachel and Richard in *The Ghost Kings* (1908) marry. Miriam in *Pearl Maiden* (1903) stipulates that she will not marry Marcus (and by definition consummate their love) unless he converts to Christianity, but he does so, and they do marry. The pious Godwin's relationship with Masouda in *The Brethren* (1904) is exclusively a spiritual one but it is evident that in an afterlife their relationship will have a sexual dimension. It is only in *Stella Fregelius* and *The Way of the Spirit* that Haggard addresses the difficult question of celibacy, although the two books stand at opposing ends of the spectrum in the debate.

Celibacy was a topic that concerned novelists, especially the New Woman writers, in the later years of the nineteenth century. Sally Ledger notes Sue's wish for a 'comradely' relationship with Jude in *Jude the Obscure* (1895), Angelica's adoption of male clothes in order to conduct a friendship of equals with a boy in *The Heavenly Twins* (1893), and Lyndall's friendship with Waldo in *The Story of an African Farm* (1883), which she tells him is based not on gender but upon their common intellectual curiosity.[52] This novelistic concern was a response both to the perceived negatives for women of the Victorian marriage equation and to the contemporary demographics which, in the form of the English Census for 1861, recorded a steadily increasing surplus of unmarried women.[53] The journalist William Greg records that they were compelled to 'lead an independent and incomplete existence of their own'.[54] Elaine Showalter opines: '*Fin-de-siecle* feminists interpreted [...] the surplus of unmarried women to prove that women's traditional domestic roles were outmoded'. And she proposes two further literary considerations of the subject. Olive Chancellor, a Boston feminist vying with Basil Ransom for the affections of Verena Tallant in Henry James's *The Bostonians* (1886), loses the battle but in doing so gains an articulacy to argue for the feminist movement. Later writers depicted celibacy as altogether less empowering. Rhoda Nunn in George Gissing's *The Odd Women* (1891) is a militant feminist strongly opposed to marriage and deeply suspicious of men. Despite herself, and much to her chagrin, she falls in love with Everard Barfoot. She finally refuses to marry him, but finds that she is profoundly changed by her self-discovery.[55] Evadne

Frayling in Sarah Grand's *The Heavenly Twins* (1893) marries Colonel Colquhoun on the understanding that their marriage will not be consummated. However, the strain of sexual abstinence results in depression and her attempted suicide.

Referring to these preoccupations of some New Women writers, Showalter comments that 'advanced late nineteenth century thinkers acknowledged women's capacity for sexual pleasure and discussed the psychological and biological harmfulness of celibacy'.[56] Haggard aligns himself with this position when he comes to consider the question of celibacy in *Stella Fregelius* and *The Way of the Spirit*. But the two novels differ fundamentally in their representations. In the former, Haggard attributes to Stella a feminist, New Woman view of marriage: 'I have my own ideas about matrimony, and the conditions under which I would undertake it are not at all likely ever to be within my reach' (168), although no biographical or ideological reasons are offered as substantiating background to her assertion. And Stella, unlike the New Woman heroines of Gissing's and Grand's novels, encounters no moment of self-revelation or debilitation in her insistence upon celibacy. Its result and the focus of Haggard's apparent interest in the book is the negative impact upon Morris. In *The Way of the Spirit* too the focus is primarily on the male protagonist. Rupert may insist upon a sexual renunciation in the form of a purely celibate relationship with Mea: 'there must be no more of this love-talk between us' (197). But this is as a response to solely practical considerations; his sad experience with Clara, his mother's plea that he 'follow the way of the Spirit, not that of the Flesh' (20), and the fact that he is already married.

Although *Stella Fregelius* considers a celibate relationship, this does not represent an exacting sexual renunciation. Morris may find Stella a striking and compelling woman, a 'strange, new star [...] to shine upon his life and direct his destiny' (102), but there is no representation of any truly sexual response to her on his part. From the start Stella dictates the spiritual nature of their relationship, telling him unequivocally, 'with your flesh I have nothing to do' (237), and Morris accepts this diktat without any resistance. But he *is* faced with the duty to make a spiritual renunciation. It is clear that his obsession with the dead Stella threatens his marriage, including perhaps his marital sexual relations, and while his feelings for her may be valid, and involuntary, the book makes it plain that, with the assurance of a reunion with her in an afterlife, it is Morris's duty, until death, not to allow her to interfere with the harmony of his marriage and the happiness of his wife. There seems to be a similar sentiment in the subtext to a phrase in a letter Haggard wrote to Louisa shortly before their marriage in which he tells her 'till [...] death separates us, will I be your true and faithful lover and husband'.[57] The narrator comments on Morris's attempts to communicate with the dead Stella: 'In their practice these arts are as superlatively unwholesome as in their result, successful or not, they are unnatural' (335). The impact is to distort his feelings for Mary and to obscure his duty to her: 'fair and gracious as she was [she] became almost repulsive to him' (358). Despite the warning in Stella's diary 'do not search, but wait' (327), Morris is unable to exercise restraint and patience, even though he himself realizes that he has only to wait for death, 'the great immortal waking, when from the twilight he passed out to light' (357). Morris is no more capable of making a spiritual renunciation than Leo in *Ayesha* (1905) is capable of making a sexual one. Leo's overwhelming desire for sexual relations with Ayesha prompts him repeatedly to pressurize her to marry him, even though both are aware he should first bathe in the Fount of Life. This, however, is far away, and Leo is insistent that he cannot wait. They marry, and he dies, 'withered in Ayesha's kiss, slain by the fire of her love'.[58] Both Ayesha and Mary are understanding of the imperatives acting upon the men they love. Ayesha recognizes the inevitability of the outcome given that Leo's unsatisfied passion would have caused him to die had she forced him to wait; passion satisfied and passion thwarted have the same result. There is something of the same sense with Morris. Mary, 'remembering [...] the dust whereof he was made' (361), forgives him his human weakness.

The imperatives, and outcomes, of spiritual and sexual passion are not so very different. Morris's spiritual desire for Stella has all the insistency and impatience of its sexual equivalent. And while Haggard makes an attempt to establish Stella as a woman for whom sexual renunciation has a significance, he fails to convince. After her spiritual 'marriage' with Morris, the narrator reflects 'she was but [...] a woman with a very human heart [...] she was [...] weighed down by the flesh over which she triumphed' (239). In a scene that so closely resembles the conclusion of *Dawn* (1884) – where Mildred, having surrendered Arthur to Angela, throws herself onto the floor of her Egyptian museum 'and sobbed till the darkness of the night covered her' (371) – that it seems merely a reprise, Stella 'cast herself down there upon the cold stones before the altar, and wept till her senses left her' (239). But these images evaporate before that of Stella's stark, pre-emptive and unattractive rejection of Morris's 'flesh'. Both she and Morris are largely devoid of humanizing sexual feelings; their sexual renunciation is almost entirely involuntary and without real significance, and their spirituality is poor compensation.

In *The Way of the Spirit* Haggard presents, with equal scepticism, a sexual renunciation that is infinitely more meaningful and dramatically convincing. There is a dual aspect to his consideration of it. Although he presents the issue in his author's note as a practical one that considers 'should or should not circumstances be allowed to alter moral cases?' (10), Rupert's mother, who first recommends sexual renunciation to him, addresses it as a question of principle. After Rupert has made a full confession to her of his affair with Clara, his mother advises:

Conquer yourself and the weakness which comes of your blood [...] Life is not long [...] but remorse may be a perpetual agony. (20)

It is difficult to avoid making a strong autobiographical connection. There is no documentary evidence to suggest that Haggard confided in his mother about his affair with Johanna and that she gave him advice on sexual continence, but in the light of their close relationship it seems not unlikely, and if it did not occur, it is hard to believe that Haggard did not have in mind an exchange he would like to have had with her. There are clear autobiographical resonances in what Mrs Ullershaw has to say. The reference to the inherited weakness is suggestive of a passage in Lilias's biography in which she speaks of an hereditary tendency to waywardness and wildness in a branch of the Haggard family, including their 'far from reputable love affairs'.[59] A similar reference in *Swallow* emphasizes how difficult it is to overcome such family traits: 'how good is that man who can conquer the natural promptings of his blood!'[60] And Mrs Ullershaw's warning that 'remorse may be a perpetual agony' is closely related to Haggard's autobiographical reference to his own deep regrets for the sexual sins of his youth: 'remorse rises in the after years and stands over us at night'.[61] It is clear that the burden of Mrs Ullershaw's advice to Rupert, extolling the virtues of adopting sexual renunciation as a way of life, must be interpreted as something Haggard had entertained seriously as a valid practical alternative to the sexual relations that his experience had proved could be so damaging.

Although initially Rupert does not elect to shun women and avoid sexual relations entirely, he later becomes a kind of holy man, and in his transformation Haggard examines the merits of such total asceticism, adopted as it is as a practical response to the complications of relationships with women rather than out of a conviction. Rupert makes two sexual renunciations, both prompted by what he sees as his duty. Both, ironically, involve neglecting his sexual duty. He fails to consummate his marriage with Edith, whom he finds sexually attractive, because he sees it as his duty to go away on a mission immediately after their marriage. The result of his decision is the humiliating failure of the mission, the loss of his reputation and his mutilation and, indirectly, the breakdown of his marriage. But it also results in his meeting with Mea. The second renunciation involves his refusal to consummate his relationship with Mea, whom he loves and who loves him, on the grounds that he is married to Edith, who has cruelly and disloyally rejected him. The question of Rupert's motivation for his second renunciation is further complicated by his mutilation. Haggard explicitly states that this involves the loss of a foot and an eye but, bearing in mind that Ibrahim lusts after Mea and that Rupert is her protector and, in Ibrahim's eyes, his sexual rival, it is difficult not to interpret his mutilation as including castration. This has overtones of a punishment for his youthful sexual sins, as well, of course, as throwing a new light on the reasons for his renunciation of sexual relations with Mea. The result of their renunciation is that both Rupert and Mea undergo a serious emotional trial. Unlike Morris, Rupert initially finds sexual renunciation difficult and begs Mea not to tempt him to break his resolve, asking her to 'have pity on my weakness' (256). Mea readily agrees but, like Rupert, finds the task 'not without difficulty, backward looks and struggling' (258).

Haggard is suggesting that sexual renunciation is a complicated business that involves uncertain outcomes. Despite his reference in his author's note to Rupert's 'great, and to all appearances, successful Platonic experiment', the book also suggests that it is not entirely admirable. The cynical and worldly-wise Bakhita regards Rupert and Mea's spiritual, but not sexual, relationship as unnatural. She considers Rupert a 'fool' for declining sexual relations, and sympathizes with 'Poor Mea, who has fallen in love with a holy man' (253). (The reference to a holy man appears to draw upon Kipling's *Kim*, published five years earlier in 1901.) But while it is of course possible to view Bakhita's comments as adumbrating the admirable spirituality of Rupert and Mea, the sense that there is some truth in her observation is more persuasive. Rupert is, after all, far removed from the context, obligations and pressures of English polite society and expects never to see Edith again.

Similarly, when he has renounced sexual relations with Mea, he turns his attention to improving the lot of her people and instructing them in Christianity. He becomes a paragon of virtue and Christian charity. 'He had no vices that could be discovered' (292) and he 'greatly improved in looks' (291). His renunciation may eventually be morally and physically uplifting for Rupert. While Mea, however, accepts their 'strange life' (291), it exacts a certain toll on her. Her face grows thinner and 'the rich, full lips had a little wistful droop' (291). Worthy and morally irreproachable though Rupert may have become, his decision inflicts pain on Mea. She is reduced in the same way as Leo is reduced in *Ayesha*. He declines physically and mentally because, although he stands in an 'intimate relationship' with Ayesha, he is not 'allowed so much as to touch her lips' (290) since she refuses to marry him and thereby to have sexual relations, until he has bathed in the Flame of Life.

Edith's reappearance and her plea for Rupert to return to her pose some incisive questions about how far his renunciation has been a self-serving device to avoid his duty to return to a wife with whom he is unwilling, and perhaps unable, to have sexual relations. It is also clear that if he embraces his duty and returns to Edith his convenient sexual renunciation will be at an end, since that duty will include the consummation of their marriage. But Haggard sidesteps the need to depict the price Rupert must pay. Once he has firmly decided to return to Edith, Haggard relieves him of the necessity of carrying out his resolution through the dramatic device of his death.

Despite the author's note it seems plain, above all in the final note of the book, which is represented by Mea's triumphant assertion that her reunion with Rupert in the afterlife will have a sexual dimension, that Haggard's conclusion is that while temporary sexual renunciation may sometimes be a practical necessity, celibacy is not a valid response for a man wounded by sexual and emotional entanglements, involving as it does emotionally damaging complications. And that sexual passion must, albeit when it is combined with a significant degree of spirituality, rightly prevail. Although *Stella Fregelius* and *The Way of the Spirit* have, apart from the brief and unsubstantiated labelling about Stella, little in common with many of the concerns of the New Woman novels, they emphatically concur with those of them, such as *The Odd Women* and *The Heavenly Twins*, and separately and rather later Joseph Conrad's *Chance* (1914), which propose that a celibate relationship is damaging. Their conclusions about the essential nature of a sexual ingredient in a loving relationship, both in life and in an afterlife, coincide with those of contemporary novelists and spiritualist writers alike.

The Capacities and Limitations of Spirituality and Spiritual Intimacy

Haggard's focus is not only to demonstrate that a loving relationship between a man and a woman that does not include a sexual element is arid and emotionally damaging, but to explore the limitations and enabling capacities of a profound spiritual intimacy. His insistence in *Stella Fregelius* and *The Way of the Spirit* about the limitations of a love that chooses to exclude a sexual element marches with a certain ambivalence in his presentation of spirituality and its outcomes. While he draws it as a humanizing quality and as a balancing element to the potential destructiveness of a love that is purely passionate, and while he associates it with established religious belief, he also suggests that in a relationship between lovers that does not include a sexual element it is connected with a weak, unrealistic, obsessive other-worldliness; in a man with unmanliness, in a woman with a rarefied and selfish view of life that is damaging to her male partner. He associates these negative attributes of spirituality with an underdeveloped sexuality most emphatically in *Stella Fregelius*.

Morris and Stella and Rupert and Mea may be equally spiritually inclined, but in terms of sexual passion they are polar opposites. Morris is by nature sexually timid. He 'was afraid of women' (4) and only reluctantly decides to marry Mary under pressure from his father and because he sees it as his duty. He embraces her almost by accident, the first woman he has kissed, and is immediately 'abashed at what he had done' (63). He finds this new, sexual, experience embarrassing rather than exciting. There is nothing to suggest that Mary elicits a truly sexual response from him. Although he finds her attractive, Mary's main recommendation for Morris seems to be that she is reassuringly familiar; they have known each other since childhood. Similarly, his response to Stella is predominantly spiritual. He sees her as 'without being lovely, breathing a curious power and personality' (105). She awakens in his mind 'a sympathy' (141) that denotes a spiritual intimacy. John and Geoffrey feel exactly the same sympathy with Jess and Beatrice, respectively, however, unlike their feelings for the women they love, there is no tangible sexual dimension to Morris's feelings for Stella. Morris's withdrawn, introspective, personality and his apparent low sexuality may constitute ground propitious to spirituality, but he is not depicted as the more admirable for these attributes. If he is weak and unmanly in allowing his father to bully him, his response to the loving, loyal and sexually attractive Mary is even more contemptible. As his father puts it, 'It isn't natural' (16). His eventual proposal to her is prosaic: 'Dear, will you take me?' (64). He finds his spiritual love for Stella more compelling than his physical love for Mary and as a result neglects her and fails in his marital duty towards her despite the fact that she remains unremittingly loving towards him. There is of course a strong autobiographical resonance here. Although Morris feels he was over-hasty in proposing to Mary, and – in echoes of John's feelings about his engagement to Bessie in *Jess* – tells his father 'I should have done better to have waited till I felt some real impulse towards marriage' (229), he is keenly aware that in undergoing his spiritual and private 'marriage' to Stella he has acted disloyally to Mary, and he confesses to her: 'I have done you a dreadful wrong' (266). His ultimate act of betrayal and ultimate humiliation comes when Mary discovers him, pleading with the dead Stella to appear to him, and the depth of his obsession is finally revealed to her. She sees him 'in his madness most unfaithful' (360). Mary, 'the kind and gentle wife who was so good to him' (360) voices some telling doubts about the kind of excessive spirituality in which Morris indulges, and speaks with a common sense that is difficult to resist: 'I detest all this spiritual hocus-pocus to which you have always had a leaning' (270).

Rupert, on the other hand, is a sexually passionate and sexually experienced man. He has had a youthful affair with Clara. He finds Edith 'beautiful' (51), falls unreservedly in love with her and marries her; his sexual passion for her blinding him to the fact that she does not love him or even reciprocate his attraction to her. His first impression of Mea is of a woman who is deeply sexually alluring: 'She wore thin draperies – so thin that her rounded shape and limbs were visible through them, and so white that they gleamed like snow' (153). Rupert is so affected by her beauty that his judgement is swayed into allowing her to accompany his party, thus attracting the hostile attention of the malevolent

Sheik of the Sweet Wells, who desires her, and ultimately precipitating the failure of his mission. While Morris is impervious to female charms, Rupert is fatally vulnerable to them.

The same contrast is observable between Stella and Mea. Stella's response to Morris is expressed in purely spiritual terms. She loves him, but there is no physical contact between them. Although they 'marry' alone together in the abandoned Dead Church, aptly since their union will be in an afterlife, it is made clear that this is, and will remain, solely a spiritual union. Stella says as much, telling Morris that she is marrying him, 'Not in the flesh [...] – but in the spirit' (237). Although Mea and Rupert also promise themselves to each other in an equally spiritual, and equally private, marriage, it is clear that Mea, like Rupert, is sexually passionate. Like Billali in *She*, who has preserved the foot of the beautiful female mummy with which he fell in love in his youth, Mea, in a gesture of similar sexual passion, has preserved Rupert's severed foot, cut off by the Sheik's men in a vengeful act of mutilation. While Stella, on the point of death, emphasizes her lack of interest in Morris's 'flesh', Mea, when both she and Rupert are about to die, sinks into his arms and 'for the first time their lips met. It was their kiss of farewell and of greeting' (342). In final, triumphant, words she asserts that in death they will be sexually united: 'Way now, make way for Tama [Mea] who comes to her lord's bed' (344). There is no mistaking the unequivocally positive nature of her assertion. Haggard may have had doubts about Swedenborg's revelations, but that here they are exactly in step is evidenced in Swedenborg's *Conjugial Love* (1768), where he writes, 'With those who come into heaven, who are those who become spiritual on earth, conjugial [sic] love remains.'[62] The main protagonists of *Stella Fregelius* and *The Way of the Spirit* may be equally spiritual but their sexual passions are of an entirely different order. Moreover, the distinctiveness of these two conceptions is apparent not simply in the chief protagonists. While the one novel barely considers sexual passion, the other is saturated with it.

An identical dichotomy can be found in Haggard's romances of the period. Like *Stella Fregelius*, *Swallow* and *The Ghost Kings* depict a pair of first-time lovers who fall immediately and instinctively in love. But this love is characterized by a profound spiritual union and by the lack of any representation of sexual passion on the part of the lovers. In *Pearl Maiden* sexual passion is subordinated to religious spirituality. Miriam prefers that Marcus should die rather than that she should compromise her religious principles because, as she tells him, 'my faith is more than my love'[63] and their marriage and consequent physical union is enabled only by his conversion to Christianity. The spiritual response is conceived as a means of avoiding the difficulties involved in the sexual. In *Stella Fregelius*, *Swallow* and *The Ghost Kings* the lovers meet in, and as a consequence of, a fierce natural and life-threatening storm. This imagery, which Haggard used in *Jess* and *Beatrice* to denote the ignition of sexual passion, here depicts the lovers, in surviving the storm, as escaping from its ultimately destructive demands. Sexual passion in these books is reserved exclusively for morally deficient characters. While Layard's, albeit tepid, thwarted passion for Stella, causes his malevolent sister to spread malicious and damaging rumours about Stella and Morris, Swart Piet in *Swallow* and Ishmael in *The Ghost Kings*, the one a half-caste Boer, the other a Jew, are men of violent passions whose lust for the heroine causes them to attempt to murder the hero. Stella's contemplation of marriage, and consequent physical relations, with Layard causes her to experience an acute physical distaste: 'her blood shrank back to her heart at the very thought, and then rushed to her neck and bosom in a flood of shame' (183). It is significant that the only image of sexual response in the book represents sexual relations as physically loathsome. This is also the case in *Swallow* and *The Ghost Kings*. Suzanne, forced by Piet to kiss her, tells him, 'I wish to God that my lips were poison' (79). Rachel is horrified by the touch of Ishmael's hand on her skirt and calls on her African subjects to help her: 'suffer not that I be thus defiled'.[64] And to reinforce the moral criminality of their sexual passion, Piet and Ishmael both undergo violent punishments. Piet falls over an abyss, his body shattered on the rocks beneath. Ishmael throws himself over a cliff to escape being burned to death in a fire.

By contrast, in *The Way of the Spirit*, *The Brethren* and *Ayesha*, sexual passion is presented in a less polarized fashion. Rather than being the preserve of melodramatic villains, it is attributed more evenly. Although it is depicted as potentially damaging, it is also recognized as an integral part of the human experience, which can cause almost anyone to behave in a destructive and self-destructive manner, but which, legitimized by a corresponding degree of spiritual intimacy, can be a positive force in the lives and afterlives of lovers. *The Way of the Spirit* reverberates with depictions of sexual passion and its capacity to warp judgements and wreck lives. But there is also an overriding sense of humans caught in the sexual bind by circumstances and by a determination that is beyond their control. Clara's sexual appetite causes her to seduce the youthful Rupert; the same kind of impulsiveness and lack of imagination ensures that they are found out. But she was forced into marriage with Devene 'whom she cordially disliked' (13) and there is therefore a degree of justification, or at the least rational explanation, for her behaviour. Devene pushes Clara into suicide and thereafter hates Rupert. Sympathy for his sexual jealousy is tempered by the fact that he himself had had affairs but it is unclear whether these were provoked by the knowledge that Clara disliked him. Edith cruelly rejects Rupert when he returns from Egypt to her, mutilated and disgraced. But she was forced into marrying him, and abandoning any thoughts of marrying Dick, by her mentor Devene, despite the fact that she loves Dick: 'the only man who does not make me shiver' (52). In an indication of a physical distaste for Rupert she notices 'how large and red' his hands are (93). Dick's desire for Edith prompts him to orchestrate Rupert's death. But Edith has 'always' (60) been in love with him and 'whilst in her teens' (113) made a conditional promise to marry him, and he genuinely loves her.

Rupert's mutilation occurs, dramatically, because of the Sheik's lust for Mea and his wish to be revenged on his rival for her affections. But there is also a sense that it is an appropriate sexually debilitating punishment for Rupert's youthful sexual sin of which he, like Haggard himself, is so conscious: 'Once […] I committed a great sin – a love affair – a married woman' (95). Haggard invites the reader to set Rupert's deep sense of guilt alongside the suggestion that the blame for the affair lay with Clara, who seduced him. Devene refers to her as a sinner 'who did not even shrink from the ruin of the boy she pretended to love' (286–87). Haggard is touching on a subject that has a profound autobiographical resonance for him and, at a dramatic level, offering an alternative reading of the reasons behind Rupert's renunciation of sexual relations. Tabitha attributes

Devene's inability to father living heirs to his 'sin' in tricking her into marriage by mendaciously claiming religious leanings: 'the sin of the father was wreaked upon the bodies of her children' (91). And yet Devene did so precisely because he longed for an heir. There is a real and sophisticated sense in the book of the inextricable tangle of human motivation and response, of moral cause and effect, especially in the sexual arena. The moral divide between admirable and less-admirable characters is blurred.

There is something of the same sense in *The Brethren* and *Ayesha*, which immediately precede *The Way of the Spirit*. Despite its apparent emphasis upon the spiritual and upon self-sacrifice, the former abounds with depictions of sexual passion and its outcomes. The entire dramatic action is triggered jointly by the worthy Sir Andrew's youthful passion for Saladin's daughter, which prompts him to abduct and marry her, and by the evil Lozelle's lust for Rosamund, which causes him to collaborate in her kidnapping on behalf of Saladin. Godwin may be pious and spiritual and able to contain his feelings for Rosamund, but when the exotic and highly sexually charged Masouda sits herself 'straddle-legged' behind him on an Arab stallion and tells him that she wishes 'for a gallop on the mountains with a good horse beneath me and a brave knight in front',[65] he finds himself 'leaning back against [her] breast' (118) in an exhilarating and dangerous ride that opens his eyes to a profound and new experience. As the horse is about to leap a chasm he notes 'the sharp, sheer lips of the cliff, the gulf between them, and the white foam of the stream a score of yards beneath' (119). Godwin has awoken to his own powerful, responsive, but previously sublimated, sexuality. *Ayesha*, too, although it lacks the spiritual emphasis of *The Way of the Spirit*, illustrates the life-changing, morality-distorting and instinctive effects of sexual passion. Like Godwin, the pious monk Kou-en discovers a new and permanent dimension to his own persona when he finds that the sight of Ayesha has 'lit a fire in my heart which will not burn out' (48). Atene, married to a husband whom she hates, falls in love with Leo with a passion that causes her to wage war on Ayesha. Leo finds that his sexual passion for Ayesha is greater than he can control and is destroyed by it. The morally admirable and the morally reprehensible alike are driven by the same imperative.

In *Stella Fregelius* and *The Way of the Spirit*, and in their corresponding romances, Haggard is postulating two separate dramatic scenarios, one in which sexual passion is relegated to a minor role in the relationship between lovers and portrayed as the preserve of the morally deficient, and another in which the universality of the imperative is recognized, and in which earthly lovers celebrate sexual union in an afterlife. Against the background of these two different scenarios he examines the merits of spirituality, especially the quasi-divine spirituality of the female and the relationship between spiritual and physical love. He also considers the associated question of the reunion of lovers in an afterlife and the nature of that reunion.

Haggard establishes the protagonists, Morris and Stella, and Rupert and Mea alike, as spiritual beings by means of straightforward narratorial labelling, by attribution to them of origins, qualities and talents associated with the contemplative life and, dramatically, through their actions and interactions. Morris believes the key element of marriage is a mutual spirituality. He reflects: 'Without a union of the spirit was there […] any marriage as it should be understood?' (23), acknowledging to himself that he needs to find a woman 'who spoke [...] to the core within him' (22). Morris's spirituality marches, from the outset, with his low sexuality. Rupert's, on the other hand, is less obviously semaphored and is observed through the prism of his unquestionable sexuality. But, in fact, his sexuality is compromised by his spirituality. Despite being a handsome man, he fails to attract Edith apparently because he has about him a spiritual delicacy, which she finds uncomfortable. She reflects: ' "I don't think that I care for him" and she shivered a little' (52). Both experience visions. Morris's are triggered by his overwhelming desire to communicate with the dead Stella. Rupert's is occasioned by an unconscious uncertainty about the outcome of his engagement to Edith, and in it he sees 'the waters of the Nile red as though with blood' (98). Both Morris and Rupert share attributes that define them as reflective, tentative, conformist and vulnerable. There is an other-worldliness about them. Morris is an introverted boffin, 'an inventor who dreamed dreams' (2). He is obsessed with the scientific perfection of his aerophone to the exclusion of material and emotional considerations. Rupert is naïve and uncalculating. He fails to foresee the end result of his affair with Clara as he fails to perceive that Edith cannot find him attractive and does not love him and that Dick is plotting against him. Both are dutiful to the point of damaging their own interests. Morris agrees to marry Mary, not because he really loves her, but because he sees it as his duty. Rupert's sense of duty causes him to abandon Edith after a few hours of unconsummated marriage in order to involve himself in a mission that will cause him physical, psychological and reputational damage. Both also display weakness. Morris allows himself to be bullied by his overbearing father in a way very similar to Devil's bullying of Philip in *Dawn* and, at an autobiographical level, to Haggard's own experience. Higgins has pointed out that Haggard's father had 'a belligerent manner and a violent temper'.[66] The fact that Morris, at thirty-three years old, is prepared to tolerate it suggests a very passive aspect to his character. Rupert's weakness is his vulnerability to feminine charms. He allows himself to be taken in by the exploitative Edith. And not only does he display weakness in allowing Mea's beauty to distort his judgement in permitting her to accompany his mission, he later attempts transparently and discreditably to convince himself and his companions that he did so for reasons of strategy. Both Morris and Rupert have a psychological predisposition to spirituality, which is allied to a certain weakness of character. But it properly overtakes them only when it is triggered by the woman they love; Morris, after the death of Stella; Rupert, on his return to Mea, after his rejection by Edith.

Stella and Mea, by contrast, are naturally spiritual. Haggard indicates as much by their origins. Both are foreigners, and both are exotic. Stella's parents were Danish, so she has a heritage of Norse myth and saga. Additionally, she reminds Morris of an Egyptian: 'in face she was somewhat Eastern' and she is 'tinged with the fatalism of the East, mingled with a certain contempt of death [...] and an active, pervading spirituality' (155). Given the prevalent contemporary association between the East and mysticism – as Janet Oppenheim points out, 'The East, ever exotic, mysterious, alien, was an escape from and an alternative to the shallow, externally-oriented culture of the West'[67] – it seems that Haggard apparently saw no need to be quite as explicit about Mea. As an 'Eastern' (154) she has a natural spirituality. Rupert first sees her in an Egyptian temple praying to the gods and looking like 'some sculptured Egyptian queen' (153). Haggard used similar foreign, half-foreign or overseas origins as a metaphor for spirituality in heroines like Jess and Benita in his eponymous books, and like Suzanne in *Swallow*, Rosamund in *The Brethren* and Rachel in *The Ghost Kings*.

Both Stella and Mea have spiritual attributes. Stella is clairvoyant, a woman 'to whom it was given to see before the due determined time of vision' (239). Mea, with the help of the witch-like Bakhita, foresees Rupert's return to her. Clairvoyance is also associated with spirituality in Haggard's contemporary romances. Suzanne foresees the coming of her eventual lover Ralph. Rosamund, who has a prescience that derives from her Eastern blood, believes 'we [...] can feel the shadow of the future before it lays its hand on us' (44). Benita is told: 'You have [...] the precious gift of clairvoyance'.[68] Rachel, like her mother, is 'fore-seeing' (7).

Both Mea and (especially) Stella project their spirituality through song, and at the same time captivate and inspire the men they love, in exactly the same way that Jess does to John. Morris, approaching the wrecked ship, hears Stella singing a Norse death song, 'strong, clear and thrilling' (100), in the belief that she is about to die. At the point of her death, in the Dead Church, she sings it once more. The song, like the venue, illustrates Stella's attitude to death. She has no fear of it, believing that it is the gate to real existence, and she writes in her diary: 'We do not live to die, we die to live' (298). Stella's song celebrates achieving a life through death; Mea's song to Rupert when he is 'in utter darkness of mind and body' (192) offers him life-enhancing comfort. Haggard invests these female protagonists with an ability to relate to what Barlow refers to as 'an unseen and suprasensual world',[69] making the same connection between the female and an enhanced form of spirituality that Watts-Dunton does in the character of Winifred in *Aylwin* and Barlow himself does in a later work, quoting Maeterlinck's article 'On Women' in *The Treasure of the Humble*, which contends that 'all women have communications with the unknown that are denied to us'.[70] Spirituality may be unmanly in Haggard's male protagonists, but in his women it is deeply empowering. However, while Mea's spirituality enables her, self-sacrificially, to support her male partner, Stella's produces an insensitive self-centeredness that proves destructive to hers.

Female Power and Female Divinity

If Haggard firmly establishes Stella and Mea's spiritual attributes, he also makes plain their considerable feminine power, spiritual and sexual in varying degrees, and in this creates parallels with other sexually powerful women of his fiction, not simply the particularly spiritual Jess and Beatrice, but Joan Haste, Ayesha, Helen and Nyleptha in *Allan Quatermain* (1887), women who are on occasion prepared to exercise this power over the men they love. Morris recognizes Stella as 'a woman of strange and impressive power' (140). It is a power she uses, with success, by singing to him a song 'unearthly, spiritualised' (190) when she wishes to prevent him from going away. But it is also a power she is prepared to set aside in the interests of moral behaviour. She refuses to take him from Mary. Mea has a similar power that is illustrated by the potentially destructive effect her beauty has on Rupert. But she becomes aware of that power, is angry with herself for having put into his mind the possibility of leaving his wife and readily agrees not to tempt him into sexual relations.

Both Stella and Mea exercise their feminine power benignly, but they still assume a kind of spiritual divinity for the men who love them. Morris first sees Stella in a moment of quasi-religious awakening: 'out of the darkness [...] did this woman arise upon his sight' (102). In reading her diaries he experiences the same religious fervour: 'He was like the neophyte of some veiled religion, who [...] is at length conducted to the doors of its holy of holies' (293). When she finally appears to him he sees her as 'beyond all imagining, divine' (354) and, for the first and only time, his devotion takes on a sexual edge: 'oh! to die at those glittering feet, with that perfumed breath stirring in his hair' (357). Rupert first sees Mea as resembling 'some sculptured Egyptian queen' (153) and later, in her fury at Ibrahim's mutilation of Rupert, she looks 'more like a goddess of vengeance than a woman' (184). Both Stella and Mea have the capacity to touch a sexual nerve in men; their spirituality does not prevent them from being as potent as Haggard's dominating women of his romances, such as Ayesha and Cleopatra. In fact Mea's spirituality incubates and throws into sharper relief her sexual passion for Rupert as her final triumphant assertion of a sexual union with him in death illustrates. Rhoda Broughton makes a similar connection in her depiction of Nell in *Cometh Up As A Flower* (1867). Laurie Garrison observes that 'spiritualism [...] offers Broughton a method of intensifying the forms of passion her heroine experiences and it posited a set of theories of spiritual connections between lovers on earth and beyond'.[71]

The sense of female divinity resonates through Haggard's fiction and draws its strength, both from the idea that women have the innate ability, through their sexuality, to dominate, and to inspire, men, and from the implication that this power has a spiritual and religious origin and validity. Rossetti had made the same assertion of the power of a sexual union that has a significant spiritual dimension to inspire a comprehension in a man of a link between the female and the divine in 'The House of Life' in 1870:

> I was ...
> A spirit when her spirit looked through me,–
> A god when all our love-breath met to fan
> Our life-blood, till love's emulous ardours ran,
> Fire within fire, desire in deity. (Sonnet VI, 'The Kiss', 9–14)[72]

Making a related association in a more prosaic fashion, Oliphant argues that 'the great work of Christ was to bring the Divine Feminine within reach of every human being'.[73] And Barlow later expressed the idea still more explicitly and emphatically in *The Higher Love* (1895):

> If [...] we are to hold that the tenderest and purest love-current can only be communicated through the spiritually refined and delicate atomic structure of woman, she is to be lifted to a place in creation hitherto undreamed of, and becomes a being potentially of angelic importance and angelic attributes.[74]

While Haggard's most persuasive concept of female divinity finds expression in a physicality, a sexuality, similar to Rossetti's, he, like Barlow and Oliphant, also holds a belief in woman's spiritual capacity to morally elevate and ennoble men.

Spiritual Communication between Lovers

In both *Stella Fregelius* and *The Way of the Spirit* Haggard represents the spiritual intimacy of the lovers as profoundly enabling, as he had in *Jess* and *Beatrice*. Their love empowers them to communicate spiritually in ways similar to Beatrice and Geoffrey. This is made especially evident in *Stella Fregelius*, in which Haggard uses the aerophone, a telephone-like device invented by Morris, which functions only between those with a strong spiritual affiliation, first Morris and Mary and later Morris and Stella, as a metaphor for this enhanced, spiritual, communication. Corelli makes a similar connection between the scientific channelling of personal spiritual attributes and the achievement of a deeply enabling spiritual and divine love in *A Romance of Two Worlds* (1886). As Anne Stiles points out: 'In Corelli's unusual cosmology [...] light, heat and electricity are equated with God's love'.[75] About to die in the Dead Church, Stella 'threw out' her mind to Morris to prompt him to go to the aerophone for their final conversation (241). Rupert, on the point of suicide, after having been rejected by Edith, sees Mea's face on the surface of the river into which he is about to throw himself and recalls his promise to return to her if things went wrong between himself and Edith.

Haggard also depicts this enhanced communication between predominantly spiritual lovers in his contemporary romances. In *Swallow*, Suzanne has a dream in which she is able to go to Ralph and assure him that she is safe. At the same time Ralph hears her assurance in a similar dream. In *The Ghost Kings* Richard sees Rachel, in a dream, guiding him towards her. This enhanced spiritual communication between lovers, signalling a profound union between them is expressed succinctly in Shelley's 'Epipsychidion' (1821): 'we shall be one/Spirit within two frames'[76] – and rather more clinically by the anonymous heroine of Corelli's *The Life Everlasting*:

> No one can fulfil the higher possibilities of his or her nature, till each individual unit is conjoined with that only other portion of itself which is as one with it in thought and in the intuitive comprehension of its higher needs.[77]

In Haggard's fiction this spiritual communication is primarily enabled by the spirituality of the female partner. Oliphant depicts it in *Scientific Religion* (1888) in terms of the descent of the 'pneuma [...] the spirit which conveys to man the consciousness of the Divine Feminine', but he establishes that it is also a reciprocal process that fulfils the woman as 'her completion consists in union with her male counterpart'.[78]

The Reunion of Lovers in an Afterlife

Haggard's lovers are not only able to communicate spiritually in this life, but they have the assurance of a reunion in an afterlife. Morris dreams of a transfiguring life after death. Stella has 'a contempt of death' (155) and tells him, as she is about to die, 'I go to wait for you […] I will […] be near you always – till you die, and afterwards will be with you always' (242). Her spirituality enables her to disregard death in exactly the same way as Florence Marryat when she writes in *There Is No Death* (1891): 'the greatest good Spiritualism does is to remove the fear of one's own death […] *I have no fear of death whatsoever*'.[79] Rupert confides in his mother his belief in an afterlife: 'the world will pass from beneath our feet, and then […] the true life begins' (143). And Mea, about to die, looks forward to reunion with Rupert: 'very soon we two shall have done with separations and with griefs' (343). There is an unyielding assertion in both books of the certainty of an afterlife in which earthly life continues, and of a reunion in this afterlife of spiritually intimate lovers, which seems to find at least part of its origin in Haggard's personal preoccupations at that time. But it is also reminiscent of similar absolute assertions in contemporary writing. The evanescence of life and the corresponding psychological need for the reassurance of an afterlife where loving souls are reunited was of substantial concern to the Victorians. Wheeler notes that 'In the Victorian age […] consolatory Christian literature emphasized the continuance between this life and the next, and particularly the idea of heaven as continuity'.[80] In *The Moment After* Buchanan presents his protagonist, Maurizio Modena, as undergoing, through his harrowing experience of death, a complete conversion from a scepticism about an afterlife to an unshakeable belief in it. Buchanan's narrator records in an epilogue a dream of his own death from which he awakes to state 'I knew then that Divine Death was the one thing certain, and that Death is only the heavenly name for that Love which is Eternal Life.'[81] Barlow's narrator in his poem 'To Gertrude in the Spirit World' in *The Marriage Before Death and Other Poems* (1878) addresses his dead lover:

> Shall not our music sound beside the sea
> Of Life, long after we are no more twain,
> But one in death's inseparable domain. ('Shall Not The Future?')[82]

And Nell Lestrange in Broughton's *Cometh Up As A Flower* has the same assurance as she contemplates her imminent death from consumption and reflects that 'through the grave and gate of death I should pass to my beloved'.[83]

Haggard goes out of his way to establish a connection between spirituality, and particularly the spiritualist belief in the reunion of lovers in an afterlife, and Christian teaching. He makes a cast-iron connection between the quality of Stella's thought, her spirituality, and the teachings of Christianity as they appear 'in the pages of the Gospel' (322) in Morris's reflection that

> Stella believed in nothing which our religion […] does not promise its votaries […] immortality of the personal soul […] A heaven where there is no earthly marriage, but where each may consort with the souls most loved and most desired. (321–22)

There is something in this insistence of the self-serving tone that is apparent in *The Witch's Head*, where the narrator depicts Eva's remorse at having deserted Ernest, and it suggests the same imperative for self-persuasion. It seems that, at this juncture in his life, Haggard had an overwhelming need to be convinced of the reunion of souls in an afterlife. He labours the conventionality of Stella's beliefs. Morris realizes that 'In Stella he beheld an example of the doctrines of Christianity really inspiring the daily life of the believer' (322). Her faith embraces 'nothing exotic; no combination of mysticism and mummery' (323). The same close association of spirituality and Christianity appears in *Pearl Maiden* and *The Brethren*. Miriam, in the former romance, declines a physical as opposed to a spiritual relationship with her lover until he converts to Christianity. In the latter the entire plot, including the spirituality of the chief protagonists, is set against the backdrop of the Crusades. Haggard is emphatically endorsing spirituality as morally mainstream. Barlow makes a similar absolute assertion in *The Higher Love*: 'The spiritualism of the actual senses is an idea involved in the very structure of Christianity.'[84] Swedenborg too expresses conjugal love (which he defines as the highest form of love), spirituality and religion as one unity. Conjugal love, he asserts is 'celestial, spiritual, holy, pure and clean, above every other love'.[85] In Haggard's case there is a transparent degree of over-protest, which seems to suggest a strong wish to convince himself.

Communication with the Dead

It is when Morris's self-indulgent over-spirituality spills over into a compulsion to communicate with the dead Stella that his behaviour becomes truly self-destructive and reprehensible. Haggard, in his lifelong passion for the unattainable Lilly, inevitably has a ready comprehension of, and an element of sympathy for, Morris's obsession for Stella, for the sentiment that F. W. H. Myers suggests in *Fragments of Inner Life* (1904) that 'love in its highest – in its most spiritual form […] can only be defined, as Plato says, as "a desire for the eternal possession" of the beloved object'.[86] As Watts-Dunton expressed in *Aylwin* in the words of Aylwin's father concerning his dead wife:

> Should you ever come to love as I have loved […] you will find that you dare not leave untried any creed, howsoever wild, that offers the heart a ray of hope.[87]

Catherine Maxwell has pointed out of the key male characters in *Aylwin* that:

> Each man suffers because of the loss of a beloved woman with that loss defining his character and subsequent actions. In each case the bereaved man will turn to mystical belief to allay his grief.[88]

But while Haggard clearly believed his assertion in *Stella Fregelius* that 'a passion for the dead' was a strong, natural and 'holy' human response to bereavement (282), he is plainly critical of Morris's attempts to conjure the spirit of Stella. And he documents Morris's decline as a result of his obsession in a way similar to Barlow in 'To Gertrude in the Spirit World', who depicts what John Holmes describes as 'the impact of a man's obsessive love for a spirit on that man's grasp of reality'.[89] Etherington argues that 'the exaggerated emphasis on the purity of Morris's love for Stella evades the sexual issue'.[90] This seems to miss the point. Far from evading the issue, Haggard is advancing an alternative to sexual passion – an alternative that proves profoundly unconvincing as much, apparently, to himself as to his reader.

Although the narrator in *Stella Fregelius* states of Morris's passion for the dead Stella that 'there was nothing carnal about this desire, since the passions of the flesh perish with the flesh' (282), there is in Morris's secretive, solitary and obsessive attempts to invoke her spirit something undeniably and disreputably physical, something deeply shameful and degrading, a kind of sexual displacement. Haggard is suggesting that when spirituality becomes excessive and self-indulgent it takes on the characteristics of sexual lust. Morris himself is aware that he may be too weak to control these harmful impulses. Haggard conceives the practical culmination of Morris's repeated attempts to communicate with Stella in physical imagery as a gratifying but ultimately unsatisfactory experience: 'soft, sweet pulses of impression beat upon him' (339), and 'Again and again those sweet, yet sickening waves flowed over him, to leave him shaken and unnerved' (340). It is plain that the sexually unconfident Morris has neglected the loving and desirable Mary for the pursuit of a quasi-sexual fantasy in an unrewarding and humiliating act equivalent to masturbation and, in the process, has achieved a self-disintegration from which he never recovers. He is found by his wife, having died in an identical act. Haggard's conclusion on Morris's behaviour is indisputably bleak. It seems that at a personal level he is contemplating that his own obsession for the lost Lilly might constitute a betrayal of his loyal wife.

While Haggard writes unequivocally in his autobiography that 'Spiritualism should be left to the expert [...] investigator [...] To most people that door should be sealed, for beyond it they will find only what is harmful and unwholesome',[91] he nevertheless remained concerned with the question of communication with dead loved ones. In *The Ghost Kings* Rachel travels to the land of the dead in what is presented as an entirely valid search for Richard. But they are first-time lovers uncommitted to anyone else. It seems as though Haggard's own personal emotional imperatives are prompting him to entertain the idea of a quality of earthly love that has the ability to project itself beyond death, what Barlow refers to in *The Higher Love* as 'The love that so purifies the soul that it becomes capable of mingling with the purified spirit that has passed the gates of death.'[92] In later fiction Haggard is more equivocal. In *She and Allan* (1921) Allan Quatermain is criticized by Ayesha for making the same journey to seek his dead wives. In *Finished* (1917) and *Moon of Israel* (1918), while the dead appear to the living, the living do not visit the afterlife. In none of these later works, however, is the subject of communication with dead loved ones portrayed as negatively as it is in *Stella Fregelius*. Haggard's concern is not that the search itself is unacceptable. Stella's diary records the 'awful joy' with which she had earlier communicated with her dead sister (301). The problem lies in obsession taking over, and in the damage it causes to others. Stella records: 'I will stop while there is yet time' (301). Unlike Stella, Morris, a weak male, cannot control his desire and, in the process, commits the cardinal sin of disloyalty to Mary.

Conclusions

Unlike the authors of *Jude the Obscure*, *The Odd Women* and *The Heavenly Twins*, Haggard touches only lightly on the effects of celibacy upon his heroines. In *Stella Fregelius*, although it is Stella who dictates that her relationship with Morris should be a celibate one, the book makes no real attempt to explore her motives, nor does it depict this relationship as having any impact on her. In *The Way of the Spirit* it is Rupert who dictates sexual renunciation, and there is only the briefest account of Mea's decline as a result. Haggard's focus in both books is almost exclusively the impact upon the male protagonist.

It is clear, though, that Haggard is asking serious questions about the harmful effects in a relationship between a man and a woman of an over-spirituality that is divorced from a normal and healthy sexual element. If Morris's spirituality is discredited by being divorced from a sexual element, Rupert's sexuality is compromised by his spirituality. The balance between sexuality and spirituality is even more clearly drawn in the female protagonists. Stella's spirituality conceives of no sexual passion, either in this world or in an afterlife, but it is still damaging. She may claim, self-righteously, that she has no intention of stealing Morris from Mary but, in emotional terms, that is exactly what she does. She is, in many respects, a femme fatale, a dangerous, mystical siren (a suggestion reinforced by the fact that, in the first instance, her spiritual magnetism lures Morris to the dangerous, sinking wreck) who, after having enticed Morris through her feminine power, coldly dismisses any notion that their relationship will ever be more than platonic and spiritual. If their relationship is somehow abnormal in lacking a sexual element, it is wholly Stella who dictates that it should be so. Mea, on the other hand, is a woman of considerable sexual passion that is modified by her spirituality, and not only does she consciously decline to tempt Rupert into sexual relations but she nobly encourages him to return to Edith. But her self-sacrifice is no more persuasive than Beatrice's. It is equally counter-intuitive and misguided. Haggard seems to be suggesting that over-spirituality, and a spiritual love that is divorced from a sexual element can produce rarefied, self-indulgent, self-deluded and destructive responses. The same implication is evident in his contemporary romances, which depict an intimacy between lovers that is largely devoid of a sexual element. The protagonists of *Swallow* and *The Ghost Kings* triumph over adversity and achieve marital happiness, but their unmodulated spirituality takes the books they inhabit onto the borders of fantasy and deprives them of any close claim to reality. In this recognition of the necessary interweaving of the spiritual and the sexual in the highest form of love between men and women, Haggard is echoing Barlow, Oliphant and Swedenborg.

Haggard has moved from an anger, in his early novels and romances, at the potentially destructive nature of sexual passion, through a consideration in *Jess* and *Beatrice* of passionate, sexually oriented and illicit relationships that include a high degree of spiritual intimacy, to an examination of whether it is feasible to avoid the potentially wounding nature of sexual passion by a sexual renunciation in favour of a love that is purely spiritual and, implicitly to a consideration of the respective merits, in the context of a loving relationship, of the sexual and the spiritual. In doing so he tests, through his fiction, a number of propositions that have a strong autobiographical resonance. He suggests, in *Stella Fregelius* and in romances like *The Ghost Kings*, that a love between a man and a woman that is entirely spiritual in nature and which excludes any significant sexual element, runs somehow across the grain of the way in which humans are inescapably psychologically framed, and that those who can feel satisfied with such a love are narrow, unimaginative, self-indulgent and susceptible to obsessive behaviour. In *The Way of the Spirit* and contemporaneous romances such as *The Brethren*, he proposes, as he had in *Jess* and *Beatrice*, that while a high degree of mutual spirituality is an essential ingredient in the highest form of human love, a lack of sexual relations between a genuinely loving couple is profoundly disabling, and that sexual and spiritual intimacy are indivisible in the highest and purest form of love, which is itself both eternal and divine.

The doubts Haggard voices about the validity of purely spiritual love and sexual renunciation are reinforced by the sense these books project that human beings are irretrievably susceptible to passions – sexual and also spiritual – that are overwhelming and totally irresistible. Mary forgives Morris his obsession with Stella on the grounds that he is only human and consequently helpless before his spiritual passion. Haggard illustrates the involuntary nature of the submission in Rupert's helpless response to Edith's feminine power: 'For one moment he resisted her as sometimes a moth appears to resist the splendour of the flame' (94). The narrator reflects on the human enslavement to the sexual imperative: 'Driven by impulses that we did not create, but which are necessary to our creation, we follow after the flesh' and tentatively concludes, 'perhaps […] the flesh was meant to be our master, to rule us, as the spirit shall in its appointed kingdom' (257). But even this suggestion of the sexual finally giving place to the spiritual in an afterlife is overturned in Mea's final assertion of the eternal validity of sexual passion. Just as in his earlier novels, Haggard finds himself forced to recognize that the pull of the sexual imperative is quite simply an integral part of being human. This is a position that he reiterates in his later fiction.

Chapter Six

THE FINAL FICTION: SPIRITUAL CONSOLATION AND THE DICTATES OF THE SEXUAL IMPERATIVE (1909–30)

The distance between Haggard's two final novels, *Love Eternal* (1918) and *Mary of Marion Isle* (1929), illustrates a distinct sea change in his fictional writing. While the former, driven by contemporary events, constitutes a reversion to a consideration of the merits of aspects of spiritualism, the latter offers a reflection, albeit a cautious and conservative one, of the literary modernity apparent at the beginning of the twentieth century. Haggard's fiction published in the period 1909 to 1930 falls in fact into three distinct categories. The romances published between 1909 and 1914, turning away from a consideration of the virtues of a love that is predominantly spiritual, as exemplified by *Stella Fregelius* (1904) and *The Way of the Spirit* (1906), and by romances such as *Swallow* (1899) and *The Ghost Kings* (1908), depict strong, powerful, sexually predatory but sexually vulnerable women who, unlike their counterparts in Haggard's earlier fiction, such as Ayesha and Cleopatra, fail to entrap the male protagonists. These books continue to propose that the sexual nexus has the capacity to disrupt lives but also present a male capability to resist sexual temptation, either when a genuine love is available or when the male is emotionally mature. The fiction published in the period 1917 to 1921 and influenced by the Great War, while continuing to acknowledge the often-damaging consequences of sexual passion, is self-consciously tentative about representing such passion, emphasizing instead the consolatory aspects of liaisons that are predominantly spiritual and, above all, is unswervingly insistent upon an afterlife in which earthly lovers are reunited. There is, however, a strong underlying recognition that sex plays a valid and inevitable role in relations between men and women. The books published between 1921 and 1930 reaffirm the overwhelming nature of sexual passion and illustrate the inescapable imperatives of the human situation, representing and celebrating the triumph of true passionate love between men and women over the hollow and emotionally disabling moral caveats of society and asking difficult questions about marriage and the representatives of the established church.

Haggard's final fiction illustrates that, although he retained a keen and personal sense of the capacity of sexual betrayal to inflict deep and lifelong wounds, he had arrived at an acceptance, which was at least partly driven by personal psychological imperatives, of the emotional parameters within which humans perforce operate and at a recognition that genuine love, which embraces both sexual and spiritual elements, has a profound moral validity, and that the individual human right to self-fulfilment transcends civil and religious laws.

Haggard's Contemporary Biography

The early years of the twentieth century saw Haggard suffer two major bereavements. In April 1909 Lilly died. Both Haggard and his wife visited her regularly until her death:

> The ravaged shadow of the woman Rider had loved when they were both young and whom, as Louie well knew, he still loved with an affection which transcends all earthly passion and stretches out hands beyond the grave.[1]

Lilias's florid assertion about Haggard's belief in an eternal reunion with Lilly in an afterlife has to be considered in the context of her close and apparently confiding relationship with her father and in the light of the fact that it finds echo in *The Witch's Head* (1884) in which Haggard clearly gives expression to his feelings for Lilly, and in which the protagonist, Ernest, tells Eva, who has betrayed him as Lilly betrayed Haggard: 'my love for you [...] is of the spirit, unending and [...] when this hateful existence is done with I shall in some way reap its fruits with you'.[2]

In July 1912 Haggard learned of the death of Andrew Lang, a close friend and a valued literary advisor with whom he had co-authored *The World's Desire* (1890). Haggard devotes a chapter of his autobiography to Lang, writing that he was

> among men my best friend, perhaps, and the one with whom I was most entirely in tune [...] the world is poorer and greyer for the loss of a pure and noble nature. For myself I am more lonely, since of those men, not my kin, whom I knew and loved while I was still young, now Charles Longman and Arthur Cochrane alone are left.[3]

Lang and Longman were important figures in advancing Haggard's early literary career and were key sponsors of his work. Lang particularly was a strident and influential advocate for the revival of adventure romance. There is in Haggard's grief at his death a sense of the passing of a literary movement that underpinned his own work, and of the end of his writing career.

These losses came at a time when Haggard was experiencing frustration about what he had thus far achieved in his life. It was his ambition to make a contribution to public service, but he felt he was making little progress. D. S. Higgins records: 'Disturbed that he seemed fated not to be able to spend his latter years in some worthwhile service Haggard grew [...] depressed'.[4] In his autobiography, which he commenced in August 1911, he records of fictional writing that he does not find it 'altogether congenial', confessing that 'at the bottom of my heart' he has a 'contempt for the craft of story-writing'.[5] It is noteworthy that he considers the writing of fiction as 'craft' rather than art, and in doing so he brings to mind Lang's observation that he is no 'master of style' but 'writes like a sportsman of genius'.[6] At any event he is clearly recording a dissatisfaction with what he had achieved. As Higgins comments, 'It was [...] with a feeling of failure and unfulfilment [...] that Haggard began to write the story of his life'.[7] It was also with a sense that he was growing old. In his introduction to his autobiography, he writes, 'the day must come, when [...] my place will know me no more'.[8] This sense intensified with the passing years. On his sixtieth birthday on 22 June 1916 he writes in his diary, 'Today I have definitely entered upon old age [...] of my friends but two remain [...] For me the world is largely peopled with the dead.'[9] Lilias records that from 1917 'Rider commenced to set his affairs in order, as if he felt that the time left to him was perhaps not very long.'[10] In September 1918 he presented all but two of his manuscripts to the Norwich Castle Museum and put his beloved cattle up for sale.[11]

For all Haggard's frustration about making his mark in public service, the reality was that it was beginning to be recognized that he had a contribution to make in this context. He was appointed to a Royal Commission on Erosion and Afforestation, and as a commissioner to inspect Salvation Army Labour Colonies in the United States, and in 1912 he was appointed as one of six British commissioners reporting on the colonies. He was knighted in the 1912 New Year Honours. In 1914 he visited South Africa in his capacity as Dominions commissioner, and made a trip to Pretoria Cemetery, during which he visited the graves of his former mistress and their child. On his departure from this, his final visit to South Africa, he wrote in his diary that the country was 'the dominant word in my life [...] Then life was before me, I had hopes and ambitions. Now life is practically behind me, with its many failures and its few successes'.[12] The Great War brought its bereavements for Haggard. Two of his nephews and the sons of his close friends Rudyard Kipling and Charles Longman were killed in action. But if the years of the war and those immediately preceding them were ones in which Haggard experienced the loss of close friends and family, and in which he suffered both from self-doubt concerning his life's achievements and from a sense of his impending death, his post-war years were happy, according to his daughter. She writes: 'it seemed [...] that he [...] whose spirit was shadowed with a certain inescapable melancholy [...] had reached some haven of inner peace'.[13] The differences in tone between *Love Eternal* and *Mary of Marion Isle* and their associated romances illustrates this shift in Haggard's state of mind.

Love Eternal and Its Biographical Resonances

Love Eternal concerns a pair of lovers, Godfrey and Isobel, who have been, instinctively, in love since their early youth, who have a sense of having been lovers in previous incarnations, and between whom there is a profound spiritual bond that enables them to communicate in extrasensory ways. In this respect they resemble Richard and Rachel in *The Ghost Kings*. Like Arthur and Angela in *Dawn* (1884) they are prevented from marrying and forced to separate by overbearing, selfish, bigoted and materialistic fathers. When, after many years, they eventually marry and enjoy a brief sexual union, they are once more separated by the Great War, in which both are killed. The book is emphatic about their happy and eternal reunion in an afterlife. While it focusses on spiritual rather than sexual passion and recognizes, like Haggard's earlier novels, the destructiveness implicit in the sexual equation, it also points up the appropriateness, indeed the inescapability, of a powerful sexual content in the love of a man and a woman. There is a strong underlying sense of humans as victims of circumstances beyond their control. The book, published in 1918, was undeniably topical. The *Times Literary Supplement* reviewer observes that it 'will bring comfort and consolation to many who in these days need it' and calls it 'a story peculiarly suited to these present times'.[14] Haggard recorded in his diary: 'if what

I have said [...] does bring any comfort to bruised and sorrowing hearts, well, I have my reward'.[15]

The book has clear autobiographical overtones and in many respects represents a threading by Haggard of formative personal experiences onto a thin and tenuous narrative cord. The narrator's description of the adolescent Godfrey seems to tally with Haggard's description of himself at a similar age, at least in respect of the first attributes:

> In some ways he was clever [...] in others [...] stupid, or as his father called him, idle. In company he was apt to be shy and dull [...] By nature intensely proud; the one thing he never forgot was a rebuff, or forgave, was an insult.[16]

He records: 'I was rather a quiet youth [...] I believe I was considered the dull boy of the family'.[17] Haggard makes no personal claim to Godfrey's latter attributes but his 'imaginative and apprehensive temperament'[18] suggests that he probably shared them as well. Isobel, like Jess, and unusually for one of Haggard's heroines, is not a woman of striking personal appearance. Her eyes are her only beauty. She is, however, 'an individual of character' (6–7) and like Jess and Beatrice she has a sharp and original mind. Her reflections take her 'on the road of rebellion against the Existing and Acknowledged' (8). It seems likely that in creating Isobel as a physically undistinguished but thoughtful and compelling woman, Haggard had in mind Agnes Barber as he had when he created Jess.

Godfrey's first separation from Isobel is caused when his father attempts to discourage their association by sending him off to Switzerland to improve his French, with the injunction that he is not to communicate with her. For what may have been similar reasons, Haggard's father caused his separation from Lilly when he insisted upon him visiting Tours for an identical purpose. Higgins suggests: 'Perhaps because he feared the seriousness of his son's romantic intentions, William Haggard [...] ordered Rider to join the family at Tours'.[19] On the eve of Godfrey's departure he goes to get a final glimpse of Isobel, who is attending a ball in London, and sees her flirting with 'a fine, tall young man' (55). Haggard first encountered Lilly at 'a ball at Richmond'.[20] Godfrey's stay in Switzerland and his brief love affair there with 'the fresh and charming Juliette' (177) almost certainly owes something to Haggard's own youthful experiences. He records in his autobiography that during a holiday in Switzerland he and his brother Andrew 'made friends with a pretty Swiss chambermaid'.[21] While in Switzerland Godfrey attends seances as Haggard himself had done while a youth in London. Godfrey's mentor, Miss Ogilvy, implores him to discontinue the habit, saying 'now I am sure that it is dangerous for the young' (100). Haggard himself came to the same conclusion and writes of seances in adjacent terms in his autobiography: 'men and women, especially if they be young, will do well to leave them quite alone'.[22] Godfrey attends Scoone's crammer in London to prepare himself for the army entrance examinations. Haggard notes that he too attended 'Scoones, the great crammer' to prepare for 'the Foreign Office examination'.[23] Godfrey's friend Arthur Thorburn, with whom he serves in India, is almost certainly modelled on Haggard's close lifelong friend Arthur Cochrane, with whom he shared a house in Pretoria at the time of his affair with Johanna Ford, and when Cochrane was romantically involved with Johanna's sister. Finally, the refusal of the lovers' fathers to countenance their marriage and their construction of obstacles to separate them almost certainly derives from the letter Haggard's own father wrote refusing to permit him to return from South Africa to England after he had persuaded his superior to agree that he could make the trip carrying despatches provided he was privately funded. Haggard's personal motive for wishing to make the trip was to formalize his engagement to Lilly and, according to Lilias, he took his father's refusal hard, having 'a certain super-sensitiveness to harsh criticism, especially from those he loved'.[24] Certainly the savage portrayal of Godfrey's father suggests an animus against his own. It is clear that in *Love Eternal* Haggard is drawing repeatedly on episodes from his own youth. In a dramatic sense this serves to invest the book with a disjointed, staccato aspect. But it also illustrates Haggard's emotional proximity to its issues.

Mary of Marion Isle and Its Biographical Resonances

Mary of Marion Isle is the story of Andrew, an idealistic and emotionally naïve young man, who is betrayed by Rose, his first love who, like Rupert in *The Way of the Spirit*, marries a cold and calculating wife, Clara, and who eventually falls in love with, and takes as his common-law wife Mary, a fellow castaway on a remote island. The book reflects elements of *The Witch's Head* in its depiction of sexual betrayal, and of *Beatrice* (1890) and *The Way of the Spirit* in its consideration of the moral legitimacy of an extramarital relationship. It represents in undiluted form the searingly wounding nature of emotional betrayal and concludes that the human right to self-fulfilment overshadows the individual's duty to society. It amplifies the sense projected in *Love Eternal* of humans caught in a situation that is none of their making and beyond their capacity to influence. With its, albeit caveated, endorsement of a socially unsanctioned ménage, it constitutes a striking departure from the surface moral tone of Haggard's earlier novels.

The book is unquestionably autobiographical in its representation of Andrew's betrayal by Rose and its aftermath. As he had done in *The Witch's Head*, Haggard gives fictional vent, often through the judgemental voice of the narrator, to his own experience of betrayal by Lilly. Rose tells Andrew when he proposes to her that they should wait at least a year before marrying and meanwhile should 'say nothing as to an engagement'.[25] Eva says much the same to Ernest in *The Witch's Head*. And it seems that Lilly also wrote to Haggard when he was in South Africa giving him to understand that they were unofficially engaged. Lilias asserts: 'Rider had great hopes that if he went home he might bring the whole matter to a formal engagement.'[26] The narrator is unequivocal about the effect on Andrew of Rose's subsequent behaviour, referring to her as

> his first love, the woman whom he adored with all the blind passion of an ardent nature and who was destined to deal him the deadliest blow a man can receive in his youth. (88)

Like Rupert in *The Way of the Spirit*, Andrew contemplates suicide. Lilias, presumably drawing upon what Haggard had told her, records of her father's response to the news of Lilly's engagement to another man that 'he knew the desolation of loneliness, the grey days which lacked all interest, the occupation from which all meaning had fled'.[27]

It seems that Haggard may also have been attracted by the idea of death since he writes in his autobiography, 'It was a crushing blow, so crushing that at the time I should not have been sorry if I could have departed from the world.'[28] While this assertion may represent post facto self-dramatization, it is clear that in dealing once more, in his final novel, with the subject of sexual betrayal, some forty years after he first gave full expression to it in *The Witch's Head*, he remains personally and painfully involved. And equally personal and painful is his depiction of the impact upon Andrew of the death of his daughter by his wife Clara. The narrator records: 'What he suffered was known to God and himself alone, for of it he said no word to any human creature' (158). Haggard's response to the death of his own son appears to have been virtually identical. Haggard never spoke of Jock again within his family, and later told his daughter 'I did not know then what a man can endure and live.'[29] The narrator offers an element of comfort for Andrew:

> Night by night he would find himself in closer communion with this departed spirit which had left his arms unstained by any earthly vileness, than could possibly have chanced had it remained in this world. (159)

Haggard makes an adjacent observation in his autobiography,[30] where in a passage about his son's death he quotes from his romance *Montezuma's Daughter* (1893), in which Thomas says of the death of his young son:

> When we bend our heads before the shrouded shape of some lost child, then it is that for the first time we learn how terrible grief can be [...] there is no comfort save in the truth that love which might have withered on the earth grows fastest in the tomb, to flower gloriously in heaven.[31]

In the narrator's observation of Andrew that, 'In addition to his mother he had loved but two creatures in his life, the woman who had betrayed him and the child who had been taken away from him' (181), Haggard is assuredly writing about himself.

The Sexual Potency of Women: Representations of Female Sexuality in Haggard's Late Fiction

The chief catalyst of the action in Haggard's final two novels, and indeed in all of his later fiction, remains the sexual potency of women. This is especially vigorously depicted in four of the romances published between 1909 and 1914. Asika in *The Yellow God* (1909), Tua in *Morning Star* (1910), Mameena in *Child of Storm* (1913) and Iduna in *The Wanderer's Necklace* (1914) are all, in varying degrees, dominating and sexually exploitative women. They are also sexually vulnerable. Asika, a despotic ruler, takes a new husband every year, consigning the old one to death because she can never find the right man. Sexually unsatisfied, her frustration turns to violence. When she loses Alan, the only man she truly loves, her face expresses 'the rage of betrayal, the agony of loss'.[32] The predatory woman has become the victim of her own passion. The Empress Iduna, still beautiful but past her best years, exploits her position by trying to force Olaf, the chief of her bodyguards, into marrying her, and when he refuses she has him blinded. Haggard is once again expressing frustrated sexual passion in this blinding metaphor, as he had with Ernest in *The Witch's Head* and elsewhere in his fiction, but in this case the victim projects the violence onto the cause of her frustration. Tua's Double, or alter ego, vents her fury against Abi, whom she hates and whom she is forced to marry, by using her sexual allure to tyrannize him. Mameena exploits her sexual power to forge marriages with men in order to enhance her social position but loves only Allan Quatermain, who refuses to reciprocate her love unreservedly. In a rare confession of vulnerability, she tells him: 'I love you […] as you will never be loved till you die, and I shall never love any other man, however many I may marry'.[33] It seems likely that Haggard had Lilly in mind and that in Mameena's assurances he is offering himself personally flattering consolation. And the proof of Mameena's devotion is that at the point of her death her final act is to beg Allan to kiss her.

Female sexuality, although central to their plots, is depicted in Haggard's late novels more conservatively and cautiously than in their predecessors. Isobel in *Love Eternal* apprehends a spiritual intimacy with Godfrey, which precipitates in her a physical response. Overhearing him confess that he thinks of her often, she 'flushed in the flesh and rejoiced in her innermost being' (229). After he kisses her hands, she reflects on her newly discovered sexuality: 'When she sat down […] she was still a girl and virginal; when she rose […] she was a developed, loving woman' (236). Mary in *Mary of Marion Isle*, in whom Andrew elicits a similar sexual awakening, feels that 'The full tide of Nature was swelling in her young heart' (243). Neither Isobel nor Mary is represented as experiencing the strong sexual responses of the heroines of the earlier novels. In *Dawn* Angela's awakening to sexual passion is compared by the narrator to 'an ice-bound river' to which 'presently the spring comes, the prisoned waters burst their fetters, and we see a glad torrent sparkling in the sunlight' (139). The late novels have nothing to equal this evocation of the female orgasm. It might have been expected that they would be equally adventurous in this respect in the light of the pertaining more liberal moral climate. But *Love Eternal* is constrained by the imperatives of the Great War. And it may be that in portraying Mary as an ingénue, a half-child, Haggard considered it inappropriate to detail her sexual responses. He may well also have felt that the book was already adventurous enough in terms of plot to make explicit imagery undesirable.

This restraint in the depiction of female sexuality is, in general, echoed in the late romances. Laleela in *Allan and the Ice Gods* (1927), for example, contemplates Wi in terms that may be fundamentally sexual, but which are undeniably prosaic, as 'a perfect shape of developed manhood'.[34] The exception is *Wisdom's Daughter* (1923), in which Ayesha, shown the Flame by its guardian Noot the hermit, finds that to her eyes it assumes 'the shape of a mighty man' with 'blood-red splendid arms that stretched themselves towards me as though to clasp me to that burning breast […] Never until I saw it had I known beauty.' When she hears the music of the advancing Flame, she recalls: 'It swelled and grew and now I had entered on to womanhood and in my heart were strange, uncomprehended longings.'[35] Not only did Haggard need in his third depiction of Ayesha to maintain a consistency with his preceding portrayals, but he regarded *Wisdom's Daughter* as a seminal work, recording in his diary that Kipling described the book 'as "a philosophy of life" and an epitome of all the deeper part of my work',[36] and arguably therefore as one in which he should be free of constraints.

Female Self-Sacrifice

While the sexuality of the heroines of Haggard's later novels is depicted in restrained, cautious terms, they are emphatically self-sacrificial women like the eponymous heroines of *Jess* (1887), *Beatrice* and *Joan Haste* (1895). But Isobel and Mary make, or have the intention of making, their self-sacrifice for entirely different reasons. And this difference is illustrative of the substantial contrast between *Love Eternal* and *Mary of Marion Isle*.

Arthur Conan Doyle writes of the Great War period:

> The deaths occurring in almost every family in the land brought a sudden and concentrated interest in the life after death [...] People [...] eagerly sought to know if communication was possible with the dear ones they had lost.[37]

Joseph McCabe adds that 'Spiritualism [...] hoped and aimed to give the consolation of its message to these people'.[38] Randall Stevenson explores the impact upon fiction of the period of this pressing psychological imperative. While he asserts that 'sexual relations in their extramarital forms [...] figured with new explicitness in fiction at the time', he also identifies 'a widespread disposition during and after the war, to replace straightforward accounts of terrible events with consolatory, mystic or mendacious versions of them, through spiritualism for example'.[39] It is this latter, consolatory spiritual tendency Haggard follows in *Love Eternal*. *Mary of Marion Isle*, on the other hand, is a freer, franker and patently conscious representation of his final view of the overwhelming significance of sexual passion. These differences are reflected in the self-sacrifices of the heroines. Andrew's wife Clara, who has discovered him on Marion Isle after organizing an expedition to search for him, urges Mary not to cause his ruin by agreeing to continue to live with him on the island as his common-law wife. Mary resolves to drown herself rather than contribute to his disgrace. In the event, she survives, and it is Clara who drowns. Mary's intended sacrifice therefore closely replicates that of Joan Haste, to whom Henry's mother appeals in terms similar to Clara, and of Beatrice, both of whom die to save their lovers' careers, and that of Jess who dies to save her sister from grief. Isobel, on the other hand, becomes a nurse during the Great War and dies in a hospital ward, the victim of a German bomb, shielding an injured soldier with her own body. Hers too is a sacrifice of love, but of a love for her fellow man and, ultimately, for her country. She is a casualty of the war, dying in an act of heroism comparable to that of a volunteer soldier. The sense of giving of herself is reinforced by the image of her lying on top of the soldier to protect him from the blast. Yva performs a similar sacrifice in *When the World Shook* (1919) which, despite being a romance set in the South Seas, quite explicitly takes place during the war. Yva's father, the malevolent Oro, intends to destroy half the world by diverting the trajectory of the great Flame of Life. Yva prevents this by standing in the path of the Flame but is herself killed. Effectively she saves the world from the threatened destructive violence. Her sacrifice is Isobel's writ large. Both die with complete confidence in a reunion with their lovers in an afterlife. It is made explicit that Yva's sacrifice will lead to her glorification. In an image that clearly evokes violent, but glorious, death on the battlefield, one of the explorers, Bastin, comments that 'She had exactly the appearance of a person going up to Heaven in a vehicle of fire.'[40]

The parallels with *She* (1887) and *Ayesha* (1905) in the depiction of the Flame of Life are obvious, the contrasts less so. Not only does the Flame in *When the World Shook* denote violence, it also denotes sexual passion, just as does the image of Isobel using her body to protect the soldier from the bomb blast. But while Ayesha stands in the flame to enhance her sexuality and perpetuate her life so that she may remain attractive to her lover, Isobel and Yva do so to counter its intensity with the spiritual, selfless nature of their sacrifice. In the process they terminate their own lives on earth, but enter an eternal afterlife in which they are eventually reunited with their lovers. In equating the violence and destructiveness of war with the fierce, potentially destructive and evanescent nature of sexual passion, and asserting that spiritually driven self-sacrifice culminates in eternal happiness and a reunion with loved ones in an afterlife, Haggard is plainly offering comfort to the many who were suffering bereavement because of the Great War.

The Influence of the Great War upon *Love Eternal* and Certain of Haggard's Contemporary Romances

Love Eternal and *When the World Shook*, together with *Finished* (1917), *Moon of Israel* (1918) and *She and Allan* (1921), make a striking contrast to the romances written between 1909 and 1914 in their emphatic reversion to the themes of spiritual love, reincarnation, communication with the dead and above all of an afterlife in which lovers separated by death are reunited. The former books were written between 1915 and 1919, years in which the British public had come to view the war as an unmitigated, and very often personal, tragedy rather than as an heroic enterprise. Haggard's reflection of the general anxieties and concerns of the war years was part of the response of British writers across the board. Philip Waller has observed that 'It was natural that [...] many authors should be drawn into propaganda'. Much of it, he adds 'carried weight by being unofficial although surreptitiously commissioned' by Charles Masterman, a Cabinet colleague of Prime Minister Lloyd George, who 'urged [this cause] upon him'. According to Waller, in September 1914 a 'conference of eminent authors' was convened for this purpose in London. Those present included Barrie, Bennett, Binyon, Bridges, Hall Caine, Chesterton, Conan Doyle, Galsworthy, Hardy, Anthony Hope, Masefield and Wells.[41] Haggard does not seem to have been present, possibly because a few days earlier he had arrived back in England from Canada, which he had been visiting in the context of his position as one of the royal commissioners reporting on the colonies.[42]

Naturally enough, writers were not unaware of the opportunity for self-promotion. And the public were eager for new books. According to Jane Potter, 'wartime not only served to perpetuate existing reading habits but appeared to encourage new readers'.[43] But authors had to strike the right note. George Bernard Shaw's initial anti-war position 'arrested his previously rising literary reputation [...] Newspapers turned down [his] essays and epistles [...] his books went unsold'.[44] Haggard realized the possible prejudice to his interests if he misjudged the situation. In his diary entry for 17 October 1914 he records a lunch with Sir Ian Hamilton, the general who led the Gallipoli expedition in 1915:

> [We] talked about Censorship and generally of the methods of supplying war information to the public [...] I told him that I would gladly help in the matter if I could be of any use [...] On reflection I rather hope I shall hear no more of it, as what between red tape and the public it would be putting one's head into a hornet's nest.[45]

Haggard was also critical of the concept of charity books, which some authors were coerced into writing through direct requests from the king or other royalty, and writes in his diary for 23 April 1915 that 'they compete most seriously with the work of those who live by writing, including that of their own authors'.[46] Haggard's war contribution took other forms. He joined his local Volunteer Corps, recording in his diary for 28 June 1915:

> I can shoot and am still man enough to fight Germans from ditch to ditch until knocked out. I would sooner die in putting up a fight against them than in any other way [...] How I envy all my nephews who can go to the front.[47]

However sceptically we may regard Haggard's assertion, he certainly set off in February 1916 on what could only have been a hazardous sea voyage to South Africa, Australia, New Zealand and Canada in his capacity as honorary representative of the Royal Colonial Institute, charged with ascertaining the possibilities for the post-war resettlement of soldiers in the colonies. He regarded the responsibility as his 'war offering'.[48]

Direct references to the war in Haggard's fiction are limited. This may be explained by his diary entry for 22 June 1915, in which he writes:

> I have received a letter from Watt [his literary agent A. P. Watt] enclosing one from Cassell's in which the latter request that any authors writing fiction for them will avoid all mention of the war [...] the public is 'sick of war' I suppose.[49]

Curiously, the two books in which he does, directly but briefly, refer to the war were both published by Cassell's. But *Love Eternal* and *When the World Shook* adopt significantly different tones. In the former, Godfrey's regiment share in the 'glory' of the retreat from Mons in 1914, 'that retreat that saved France and Civilisation' (292). Godfrey's mind is filled with

> horror at the deeds to which men can sink and [...] wonder at the heights to which they can rise when lifted by the inspiration of a great ideal and a holy cause. Death, he reflected could not after all mean so very much to men, seeing how bravely it was met every minute of the day and night. (293)

Love Eternal depicts a war which, despite its cruelties, brings out the best in man, and illustrates the inconsequentiality of death. *When the World Shook*, written later in the same year, speaks only of the brutality of war, albeit exclusively German brutality, and of its futility. Oro takes Arbuthnot, through the medium of sleep, on a journey, in the course of which they view several scenes of German atrocities, including one in which a colonial soldier is crucified, prompting Oro to ask: 'Did you not tell me […] that the Germans are of your Christian faith?'(253).

Haggard's Emphasis in His Fiction upon Spirituality and the Spiritual Union of Lovers

If Haggard limited direct references to the war, his consideration in *Love Eternal* and its associated romances of spiritual love, reincarnation, communication with the dead and the reuniting of lovers in an afterlife offers clear and purposed consolation at a time when the public were emotionally vulnerable. Potter has pointed out that

> there was a continuing demand for stories that brought order where there was chaos […] such novels, in providing encouragement in the face of loss and uncertainty were, in effect, vehicles for the dissemination of patriotic ideals and models of appropriate wartime behaviour.[50]

McCabe avers succinctly that 'Bereavement turned the minds of thousands to spiritualism.'[51] *Love Eternal* certainly resounds with spirituality. Although the book centrally concerns two lovers, sexual passion is scarcely on the agenda. There is a repeated insistence on the spiritual and eternal nature of the lovers' relationship, of its divine aspect and of the spiritual communication between them that it generates. The opening establishes the tone of the book:

> Two atoms of the eternal Energy sped forth from the heart of it which we call God, and incarnated themselves in the human shapes that were destined to hold them for a while. (1)

The narrator surmises that these atoms 'having no end, could have no beginning' (1). Haggard is asserting the continuity of human life and of spiritual love and that they both have their origins in the divine; proposing the reassuring doctrine of reincarnation at a time when it had especial attraction. In doing so he echoes George Barlow's concept in *The Higher Love* (1895) of the conversion of atoms into soul atoms that betoken spiritual love, and his contention that passion of the higher kind 'involves and implies the resurrection of the body, the transformation and transfiguration of matter'.[52]

In *When the World Shook* Haggard makes an identical proposition to that in *Love Eternal*. The explorers discover Yva in the glass coffin in which she has been lying in a state of suspended animation for the last two hundred and fifty thousand years. She is so perfectly preserved that she exhibits the same quality of life in death that Charles Dickens depicted in the dead Little Nell in *The Old Curiosity Shop* (1841): 'She seemed a creature fresh from the hand of God and waiting for the breath of life.'[53] They succeed in reanimating her, and she proves to be an earlier incarnation of Arbuthnot's dead wife, just as he proves to be a reincarnation of Yva's former lover, the Prince of the World. Arbuthnot's conviction that this is the case has overtones of the narrator of D. G. Rossetti's 'The House of Life' (1870) in *Collected Poetry and Prose*, who tells his lover, 'You have been mine before.'[54]

Yva observes that 'one spirit may be clothed in different garments of the flesh' (267). She tells Arbuthnot that when she dies, a further reunion with him in an afterlife is assured. Haggard pursues the theme of reincarnation, albeit with less insistence, in *Mary of Marion Isle*. Mary, having given birth to a daughter by Andrew, tells him that the child is Janet, his daughter by Clara, who died in infancy. The subject of a dead child was a deeply personal one for Haggard and one that punctuates his fiction, and it seems that his reiteration of it in his valedictory novel and the offer of reassurance through the medium of reincarnation was a further instance of self-solace.

Haggard establishes the spirituality of the protagonists in *Love Eternal* through the voice of the narrator in the same way as he does with Morris and Stella in *Stella Fregelius*. The result is equally uncomfortable. Not only are Godfrey and Isobel first-time lovers, they are also lovers through an instinctive, spiritual imperative. When Isobel first sees him, Godfrey is asleep:

> A strange affinity for him came home to her [...] it was as if she knew that her spirit was intimate with his, yes and always had been, and always would be intimate. (20)

The voice of the narrator reinforces the spiritual bond between the lovers: 'A strange and uncommon intimacy existed between these young creatures, almost it might have been called a friendship of the spirit' (26–27).

Haggard had depicted this mutual realization by lovers of a profound and eternal spiritual union in *Stella Fregelius*, where Stella tells Morris that they have loved 'from the beginning [...] and – perhaps [...] before',[55] and in *The Ghost Kings* where Rachel, looking at the sleeping Richard 'knew that her life and this lad's were interwoven'.[56]

Reticence about Sex but Subtle Assertions of the Pull of the Sexual Imperative

Although Godfrey and Isobel, unlike Stella and Morris, eventually marry formally and consummate their sexual relationship, the sexual element is referenced only perfunctorily. By means of the narrator's comment on Isobel, Haggard goes out of his way to emphasize that sex is incidental in their relationship:

> She knew [...] that this great mutual attraction did not depend on sex, though by the influence of sex it might be quickened and accentuated. It was something much more deep and wide [...] The sex element was accidental [...] but the perfect friendship between their souls was permanent and without shadow of change [...] theirs was the Love Eternal. (113)

Haggard's repeated and awkward use of the word sex lends it pejorative overtones further emphasized by its location at the opposite end of the spectrum from 'Love Eternal'. He is driving home the point of the book, but with an excessive insistence that leaves a seed of doubt in the reader's mind.

Haggard makes it equally plain that sex will also not be on the agenda in an afterlife. The narrator comments that 'Perhaps the best thing of the little we have been told about heaven [presumably by Christian teaching] is that in it there will be no sex' (181). This proposition is reiterated in Haggard's next book, *Moon of Israel*, where Seti, thinking about his marriage with the now dead Merapi, looks forward to a reunion with her 'when we reach a land where sex with its walls and fires are forgotten, and love alone survives'.[57] And in *When the World Shook*, published immediately afterwards, Arbuthnot discovers his dead wife reincarnated as Yva only to lose her again when Yva dies, their relationship unconsummated, with the assurance of a reunion in an afterlife. But this, too, it appears, will be an entirely spiritual relationship. Yva tells him:

> Nor earth, nor heaven, nor hell have any bars through which love cannot burst its way toward reunion and completeness. Only there must be love [...] ever striving to its end, which is not of the flesh. (268)

It seems that Haggard is responding to the authorial imperatives of the war by emphasizing the merits of the eternal and spiritual rather than the immediate and sexual. It may be, from the vigour of his assertions, that at a personal level he is expressing a revulsion against the sexual imperative on the grounds of the emotional destruction it can cause. But, at the same time, he acknowledges its inevitability. And his insistent representations of a sexless union are unappealing and unconvincing. It appears as if Haggard is deliberately undercutting his authorial assertions in order to indicate his own views. Godfrey's lack of obvious sexual passion for Isobel may invite superficial comparisons with Morris in *Stella Fregelius*. But Godfrey and Isobel marry, and Haggard makes it clear, in the scene in which Godfrey awakes the morning after the wedding and contemplates Isobel lying at his side, and she awaking 'stretched out her arms to receive him' (319), that they have sexual relations. Similarly, the narrator records that while in India Godfrey 'had his flirtations [...] being a man of susceptibility who was popular with women [...] For above all things Godfrey was a man, not a hermit or a saint or an aesthete' (287). The language is uncompromising and the intent plain. Haggard is establishing a point, but one which he does not wish to assume prominence. Writing of *Love Eternal* to his sister Ella, he observes: 'In such a narrative the sexual element must be taken as a symbol and no more.'[58] Despite the confusing syntax he appears to be saying that sexuality must be represented only by inference or imagery. He was not alone at this period in exercising such self-censorship. In 'The Spirit of Man' by the poet laureate Robert Bridges, which was dedicated to the king and published in 1916, Bridges's purpose, according to Waller, was to emphasize that 'spirituality is the basis and foundation of human life. Sexual passion is therefore excluded'.[59] Haggard's contemporary romances demonstrate the same coyness. Representations of sexual passion do not feature in *Finished* but, in an acknowledgement that it remains a powerful undertow, the spirit of Mameena, which appears to Allan, tells him that she is the true physical Mameena 'whose kiss thrills your lips and soul'.[60] Yva in *When the World Shook* is primarily represented as a profoundly spiritual woman, but her sexual allure still causes all three explorers to fall helplessly in love with her. Although Yva is a benign version of Ayesha in that she lets her admirers down gently and makes no attempt to exploit her feminine power, she remains a sexually potent woman. It seems clear that Haggard's representation in *Love Eternal* and its associated romances of liaisons from which sex is virtually excluded has to do primarily with the contemporary constraints of the Great War, under which he recognized he had to work, rather than any significant personal inclination to once more entertain the possibility. His subtle and discreet but plain assertion of the sexual imperative makes this evident.

Mutual Spirituality and the Divine and Eternal Aspects of Spiritual Love

Having focussed predominantly on the spiritual aspects of his lovers' unions, Haggard associates their mutual spirituality with the same enabling, divine and eternal qualities that he had attributed to the spiritual aspects of the love of the protagonists of his earlier fiction. In the context of the war this had, of course, a particular appeal. He invests Godfrey and Isobel with an ability to communicate with each other, which derives from their mutual spirituality. Godfrey, thinking about her in her absence, feels 'that she was uncommonly near to him in soul if not in body' (239). When he is wounded he dreams of Isobel who, although he does not know it, is already dead. Her voice 'appeared to speak within him in his consciousness, not without to his ears' (333). She tells him that until his death 'You will always feel me near, and I shall be with you' (334). Haggard had represented the same enhanced communication between lovers through dreams and spontaneous thought sensation in his earlier novels, *Jess*, *Beatrice* and *Stella Fregelius*, and in earlier romances such as *Swallow* and *The Ghost Kings*. In *Love Eternal* the comfort offered to lovers separated by circumstances and by death, in the form of the assurance of their ability, if their love is sufficiently spiritual, to continue to communicate, is surely driven by contemporary events. Haggard makes the same proposition in *Finished*, in which Allan Quatermain is constantly aware of the presence and the protection of the spirit of the dead Mameena and in *When the World Shook*, where Arbuthnot hears his dead wife telling him in a dream that she and Yva are one and the same and that she and their dead child are awaiting him in an afterlife. Other authors writing at the time depicted the same consoling sense of the spiritual proximity of dead loved ones. In Janet Laing's *Before the Wind* (1918) in which Ann Charteris loses her mother and her brother, both Ann and her father have this strong sense in moments of repose: 'The spirit world would seem very near them, and the things unseen were the only things that mattered.' And, later, when Ann's father too has died, she feels that her dead family are endorsing her engagement: 'The spirits of the dead seemed to greet her [...] and to be glad that she was the promised bride of him whom they had known and trusted'.[61]

Haggard also proposes, as he had in his earlier novels, that profound spiritual love is closely associated with the love of God, and that it invests its participants with an element of the divine. The narrator comments of Isobel's love for Godfrey: 'He was at once her divinity and her other self, the segment that completed her life's circle' (306). Haggard had previously depicted a woman regarding her lover as a form of divinity in his first novel *Dawn*, where Angela kneels to Arthur and tells him 'it is the attitude of adoration, and I have found – my divinity'.[62] Jess too feels that she and John are 'knit up in a divine identity'.[63] Haggard's male protagonists see the women they love in the same divine context. Godfrey contemplates Isobel and sees her as 'a very Fire of spiritual love incarnate in a veil of flesh' (318). Haggard is re-enforcing this divinity and Isobel's spirituality by referencing the Creed in which it is stated that Christ 'was incarnate by the Holy Ghost of the Virgin Mary'.[64] Arthur in *Dawn* sees Angela in a spiritual as well as physical light and observes in her 'a reflection of God's own light that tinged the worship her loveliness commanded with a touch of reverential awe' (105). Geoffrey in *Beatrice* trembles 'at the sight of the conquering glory of the woman whom he worshipped'.[65] Isobel, like Angela and Beatrice, formerly sceptical about accepted Christian beliefs, arrives at a sense of the love of God through the spiritual intensity of her love for Godfrey. The narrator records:

> As the cruelties and the narrow bitterness of the world had bred unfaith in her, so did supreme love breed faith [...] since she learned that without the faith her love must die, and the love she knew to be immortal [...] Also this love of hers was so profound and beautiful that she felt its true origin and ultimate home must be elsewhere than on earth. (307)

Haggard refers to Isobel in his dedication to *Love Eternal* as 'one whose human love led her from darkness into light and on to the gates of the Love Eternal'. Beatrice, too, contemplating her love for Geoffrey, begins to consider whether 'the cruel paths of earthly love may yet lead the feet which tread them to the ivory gates of heaven' (76). Haggard's insistence in *Love Eternal* that the highest form of human love, which is spiritual love, both leads ultimately to the love of God and derives from it, seems to find its origin in the emotional imperatives of a period when even the most spiritually intimate of earthly loves was likely to be severed peremptorily. But it is also the case that, in a personal context, Haggard had a profound, and biographically self-interested, belief in the divine nature of human love. He writes in 'A Note on Religion' in his autobiography that 'all love is immortal. It is God's light permeating the universe, and therefore incapable of diminution or decay.'[66]

The Reunion of Lovers in an Afterlife

The most emphatic voice in *Love Eternal* and its associated romances is that which insists upon an afterlife in which lovers are reunited. The subject resonates throughout the book. Isobel's mother, cajoled into marrying her brutal and unloving husband, cherishes the belief that in an afterlife she will be reunited with her true lover from whom she was forced to separate. Godfrey's patron, Miss Ogilvy, tells him that her dead lover 'still lives elsewhere and awaits me' (94–95) and on her deathbed bids Godfrey 'goodbye till the dawn' (102). Haggard deploys the dawn as a symbol of the spiritual renewal of entering into a better world throughout his fiction, commencing with the title of his first fictional book, his novel *Dawn*. Isobel appears to Godfrey on his deathbed, and he understands her to say:

> Our lives seem to have been short and sad, but these are not the real life [...] Do not be afraid then of the blackness of the passage, for beyond it shines the immortal light in that land, where there is understanding and all forgiveness. (343)

Haggard could hardly have constructed a more reassuring assertion about death, or one that had greater relevance to the time. Mrs Humphry Ward makes a similar assertion in *Missing* (1917), in which the heroine Nelly, whose husband George is believed killed in action, feels that 'She seemed to have been walking with George "on the other side" and to have left him there – for a while'.⁶⁷ Haggard forces home the message by concluding *Love Eternal* with the statement that 'Godfrey slept awhile to wake elsewhere in the land of that Love Eternal which the soul of Isobel foreknew' (344). He offers the same emphatic consolation, in deeply personal terms, at the conclusion of *Moon of Israel*, when Seti sees a vision of his dead wife Merapi and their dead child, which Merapi holds out to him, and Seti sees that it is alive. Shortly after, Seti, on the point of his own death cries triumphantly: 'We have seen the dead [...] and [...] *the dead still live*' (327). Haggard replays this scene in his immediately succeeding book *When the World Shook*, in which Arbuthnot sees his dead wife in a dream and she says to him: 'behold all that I am making ready for you where we shall dwell in a day to come' (225). Arbuthnot and Yva, who is a reincarnation of his wife, promise themselves to each other 'not for time but for eternity' (273). Haggard's insistence is unequivocal.

It seems likely that in Yva, in *When the World Shook*, Haggard had in mind Eva in *The Witch's Head*, who was undoubtedly a portrayal of Lilly, and that, in representing a deep and genuine love permanently lost in life but recuperable for eternity in an afterlife, he is again offering himself a measure of comfort. Like *Love Eternal* and *Moon of Israel*, *When the World Shook* concludes on an absolute assertion of an afterlife. Arbuthnot dies immediately after having written of his dead wife in his journal 'I have seen her' (346). While Haggard's other novels, and most of his romances, insist on the reunion of lovers in an afterlife, none do so with the unassailable, unconditional conviction of *Love Eternal* and his contemporary romances. Haggard is clearly responding to the emotional imperatives of the period. But he is also voicing a Christian conviction that offered him, at a personal level, consolation for his own bereavements: the belief that: 'He will lead us to our lost ones [...] in the home He has prepared for us [...] from Eternity to Eternity'.⁶⁸

The Dangers of Aspects of Spiritualism

If Haggard's fiction that was driven by the social and personal trauma of the Great War lays huge emphasis upon the importance of the spiritual aspects of love, it largely reiterates what *Stella Fregelius* has to say about the dangers of some of the practices of spiritualism. *Love Eternal* offers his most thorough and personally derived demolition of the more extravagant and less reputable of its aspects. Godfrey's youthful experiences draw in significant measure upon Haggard's own. Haggard, while studying in London, attended seances, as he records in his autobiography, at the residence of Lady Paulet, 'a great spiritualist'.⁶⁹ Morton Cohen points out that Haggard's Lady Paulet is in fact almost certainly Lady Poulett née Charlotte Fanny Portman, wife of the fifth Earl of Poulett, and a charter member of the Spiritual Athenaeum.⁷⁰ Similarly Godfrey is introduced to seances in Switzerland by his mentor, Miss Ogilvy. It is not recorded whether the young Haggard found Lady Poulett attractive, but there is certainly an undertow of sexual attraction between Miss Ogilvy who, although she is 'over forty' is described as 'very charming and gracious' (51), and the young Godfrey. The suggestion of a sexual connection in Godfrey's introduction into the world of spiritualism is enhanced by the narrator's comment on him that 'having once given way to' Madame Riennes – a clairvoyant, possibly based on Madame Blavatsky – who is the chief architect of the seances, 'who was to him a kind of sin incarnate, he had become her servant' (135). This evocation of a quasi-sexual obsession is reminiscent of the sexual overtones of Morris's obsessive desire to see the dead Stella. Moreover, during the seances, Godfrey encounters Eleanor, a beautiful young spirit, just as Haggard had encountered attractive female spirits during a séance. Haggard's linking of youthful experiences of the more colourful aspects of spiritualism with early sexual feelings both underlines the obsessive nature of the former and, at a personal level offers a self-exculpatory rationalization of a young man's sexual susceptibility, in the context of new and exciting circumstances, to an older woman. At any event *Love Eternal*, like Haggard himself in his autobiography, is unreservedly critical of these aspects of spiritualism. In a similar way, J. M. Barrie is critical of séances in *A Well-Remembered Voice* (1918) in which Dick, killed in the war, appears privately to his father and denies sending messages to those in the world of the living or receiving messages from them. Haggard also touches on the subject in *When the World Shook* in which Jacobsen, the Danish sailor, holds seances on board the explorers' ship. Although the table-tapping aspects of these seances are held up to ridicule, Jacobsen is informed by a spirit of an impending hurricane. While he warns 'It is an awful thing to know the future. Never try to learn that' (71), the book tacitly acknowledges the existence of the occult. This was Haggard's personal conclusion from his own experiences and he attributes the phenomena he had himself observed to 'some existent but unknown force'.[71]

Attempts to Communicate with the Dead

Haggard had addressed the question of direct communication with the dead without the intervention of a medium in his earlier fiction, most fully and notably in *Stella Fregelius*, where Morris's obsessive desire to communicate with the dead Stella is presented as weak, self-indulgent and self-damaging. On the other hand, Rachel in *The Ghost Kings* is permitted to visit the land of the dead in order to establish whether her lover Richard has died. The difference appears to lie partly in the romance permissions of *The Ghost Kings* but also in Morris's marital status and his selfish impatience. In *Love Eternal* and in the romances *Finished*, *Moon of Israel* and *When the World Shook*, all of which were written between 1914 and 1918, the dead appear, through dreams and visions, to the living, in order to offer them consolation and reassurance. But in *She and Allan*, completed in 1919, after the end of the Great War, Haggard again questions the appropriateness of seeking communication with the dead, at least in an active sense. Allan Quatermain and Umslopogaas, earlier the hero of *Nada the Lily* (1892), visit the land of the dead, with the assistance of Ayesha, in order to establish whether those we have loved in life 'still care for us after they have left the earth'. Allan sees his two dead wives, 'the women who had been mine upon the earth'. It is clear that they represent Lilly and Johanna. One comes 'shining like a star',[72] recalling the description of Eva, a thinly veiled portrayal of Lilly, in *The Witch's Head*, from whose eyes shines a light 'like the light of a star' (45). The other is accompanied by her daughter in a plain reference to Johanna and her daughter Ethel. Allan discovers they have apparently forgotten him and that it is only Mameena, whose love he never fully returned, who greets him passionately. Umslopogaas sees Nada arm in arm with his best friend. Although they conveniently agree that what they have seen was confected by Ayesha, and was, in the first place, the result of their own folly in wishing to see the dead, the outcome is uncomfortable, particularly in comparison to the reassurances of *Love Eternal* and its associated romances. Haggard directly questions the validity of attempting to communicate with the dead in his autobiography where, in the final chapter, 'A Note on Religion,' he comments on those seekers after truth, who

> start out on wild searches of their own [...] they bring themselves, or so they imagine, into some faint and uncertain touch with the dead [...] only to return unsatisfied, unsettled, hungry – frightened also at times – and doubtful of the true source of their vision.[73]

In autobiographical terms it seems probable that an aspect of Haggard's dislike of direct attempts to communicate with the dead is that they risk revealing things that might contradict his psychologically necessary faith in love after death.

The Newness of *Love Eternal*

Haggard's representation, in *Love Eternal* and its associated romances, of a love that is almost exclusively spiritual and his unqualified entertainment of the consolatory theme of an afterlife in which lovers are reunited was, it seems, primarily a response to the emotionally harrowing times. But, in the margins, he discreetly demolishes the feasibility of excluding a sexual element from the relationship between a man and a woman. *The Way of the Spirit* had evidently, for Haggard, appended a final period to any serious consideration of sexual renunciation. While the earlier book had given it serious examination and had even commended aspects of it, *Love Eternal*, primarily through its savage criticism of the mean-minded and emotionally stunted Reverend Knight, dismisses the notion. On the other hand, Haggard's unqualified entertainment of the consolatory themes of the divine attributes of the spiritual aspects of love, of reincarnation and especially of the eternal reunion of lovers in afterlife, while they were evidently partly driven by contemporary circumstances, are also themes he had considered in his earliest fiction, and in which he had a personal belief. *Love Eternal* has little that is new to offer about the spiritual. But while it continues to recognize the potential of sexual passion to wound, Haggard offers in it the first truly substantive sense in his novels, and romances, of that same passion being an integral, ineradicable, and unblameworthy part of being human. And, in this respect, it represents the first page in the closing debate of his final fiction.

Male Ability to Survive Emotional Betrayals by Females

Haggard's scepticism in *She and Allan* about a subject that underpins much of his earlier fiction, that of the dead patiently and faithfully awaiting their lovers in an afterlife, is unmistakable evidence of a clearly discernible shift. This is characterized by an increasing sense of the inescapability of life's realities and imperatives and begins to be apparent in his 1909 to 1914 romances before the Great War cut in and, for the period obscured but did not entirely suppress, that tendency in his fictional writing. While *Love Eternal* and its corresponding romances are obliged to tiptoe around the question of sexual passion, *Mary of Marion Isle* and *The Virgin of the Sun* (1922) offer searing portrayals of the impact upon men of betrayed sexual passion. But the outcomes differ significantly from those Haggard depicted in his early novels, such as *Dawn* and *The Witch's Head*, in that the male protagonists rise above the emotional setback. Haggard began to present this more robust vision in the romances he published between 1909 and 1914. Asika's beauty causes a succession of husbands to marry her and suffer death at her orders in *The Yellow God* but the protagonist, Alan, is able to resist her. He is conscious of the dangers of her 'evil loveliness' (183) and aware that in her palace 'the atmosphere seemed heavy with secret sin' (207). But he remains faithful to the loving but only moderately attractive Barbara, whom he marries. Olaf in *The Wanderer's Necklace* is deeply attracted by Irene's 'dazzling bosom' and her 'low cut garment of white silk' but he too resists her blatant and insistent sexual overtures and remains faithful to Heliodore, his eventual wife.[74] Mameena, in *Child of Storm*, seduces a succession of men to advance herself but Allan Quatermain, although he is quite aware of her attraction, does not respond to her advances. In contrast to Leo in *Ayesha* and Harmachis in *Cleopatra* (1899), who are destroyed by their passion, Alan, Olaf and Allan are able to resist their particular sirens.

Haggard continues to represent this male survival in *Mary of Marion Isle* and *The Virgin of the Sun*, in which there are deeply personal resonances in his treatment of the subject of female betrayal. If Rose in the former book bears the name of a flower like Lilly Jackson, albeit a more dangerous one, Blanche in the latter shares with Lilly the same suggestion of white purity and is described by her lover Hubert as 'stately as a lily bloom'. Like Hardy's Tess, Blanche confesses to him after their marriage that she was seduced in her youth, in her case by the feckless Deleroy who, according to Blanche's father, 'wasted all my substance' just as Lilly's husband Archer speculated irresponsibly with, and ultimately lost, her family fortune. Hubert reflects on the lifelong, ineradicable, impact of lost first love:

> If we love her [...] the touch of a beautiful woman's lips, felt for the first time, affects us in our youth. Whatever else we forget that we always remember, however false those lips afterwards be proved. For then the wax is soft and the die sinks [...] so deep that no after- heats can melt its stamp and no fretting wear it out while we live beneath the sun.[75]

But both Andrew and Hubert are able to put their betrayals behind them in their love for another woman.

It is instructive to observe how Haggard in his final fiction reiterates the theme of the impact upon a man of sexual betrayal, which he had last expressed in the same undeniably personal and direct fashion in his second novel, and second work of fiction, *The Witch's Head*. It is also interesting to note, as further evidence that Haggard reverted in his final fiction to the predominant theme of his earlier writing, that, according to Higgins, he originally devised the plot for *The Virgin of the Sun* in 1891 as an alternative to the one he actually used for *Montezuma's Daughter*.[76] In many respects Haggard's handling of the theme in *Mary of Marion Isle* replicates that of *The Witch's Head*. But there are also some significant differences. Both Ernest and Andrew experience an intense response to the physical beauty of the women they love. The narrator relates Ernest's first sight of Eva:

> The dress was cut low, and her splendid neck and arms were entirely without ornament. In the masses of dark hair [...] there glistened a diamond star [...] From those dark eyes there shone a light that few men could look upon and forget. (45)

When her eyes meet Ernest's, 'something passed from them into his heart that remained there all his life' (45). Rose's impact upon Andrew is similar:

> the grace of her form, the scent that rose from her rippling hair, the loveliness of her eyes [...] in their sum intoxicated him who for the first time passed beneath the yoke of passion. (37)

And 'he lost his reason, his judgement' (30). While both descriptions are suggestive of a personal subtext, Ernest's experience is genuine, reasonable and permanent, while Andrew's results from a confusion of the senses. A kind of moral inebriation causes him to act irrationally, and the narrator makes it clear that he has entered an undesirable state of emotional servitude. When Ernest learns of Eva's betrayal, the narrator records that 'all the bloom and beauty had gone from his life [...] for many years he was handed over to a long-drawn-out pain' (200). When Andrew apprehends that, in his absence abroad, Rose has married Dr Black, 'his senses seemed to be shrivelled in a flame of agony' (113). Ernest's pain is lifelong, while Andrew's, although apparently more intense, is shorter-lived and his injury capable of recovery. In both books Haggard permits his male protagonist to speak directly to his betrayer in what may be interpreted as a personal catharsis. The terms are almost identical. Ernest tells Eva 'You have wrecked my life [...] you have taken that from me which I can never have to give again' (298), while Andrew says to Rose 'You are a traitress [...] you have betrayed me. You have broken my heart and ruined my life, and never again shall I be able to believe in any woman' (113). In an apparent piece of self-soothing, Haggard also depicts in both books the remorse of the woman. The narrator, in an intervention that is both judgmental and gloating, says of Eva 'she realised how great, how bitter, how complete was the mistake she had made' (293). And Rose says to Andrew 'I have been a wicked and foolish girl' (128). But although the general sentiment is the same, the intensity clearly differs.

While the tone of *The Witch's Head* is angry and wounded in terms of its representation of sexual betrayal, that of *Mary of Marion Isle*, although an equally personal statement by Haggard, is clearly less visceral. And the outcomes are significantly different. Ernest can never forget Eva. Although he finds a degree of comfort in his marriage to the loving and faithful Dorothy, he is permanently scarred by his loss. Andrew, on the other hand, although he is initially devastated by Rose's betrayal, experiences what is essentially another first love in Mary and settles down happily with her. Although his love for her has a spiritual content that is absent from his youthful passion for Rose, he also has a strong sexual response to her and finds himself unable to resist her 'overmastering beauty' and 'her snowy arms and breast' (247). Hubert too, gets over the loss of Blanche and falls in love again with Quilla with whom he lives for the rest of his life. Their love, also, has spiritual and sexual content. The youthful Ramose in *Belshazzar* (1930) is seduced by the beauty of an older woman, Atyra, and his overwhelming desire for her warps his judgement. He tells her: 'at your touch my purpose melts like wax in the midday sun'.[77] But he survives her untimely death to fall in love again with the spiritual but sexually attractive Myra. Haggard is implying strongly that the spiritual and the sexual are indivisible in genuine passionate love. Women may provoke fierce sexual passion in men, but they have the spiritual capacity to inspire as well as to disrupt the lives of the men they love. Men may always be susceptible to feminine charms, but they do have the ability to discriminate between the enabling and the disabling, and once betrayed, they can love fully again. Haggard is suggesting that literal first love may not be the final word in the male emotional lexicon. But he is also of course offering – in *Mary of Marion Isle*, in which Andrew rediscovers both a first love and his dead daughter, and in *The Virgin of the Sun*, where Hubert's loss of Blanche is fully compensated by his love for Quilla – the ultimate happy ending in a new kind of reality and a comfortable reassurance, both of which suggest a consciousness on Haggard's part that he was playing out his literary endgame.

Criticism of the Established Church

This sense of the final word is also apparent in some of the severe, unexpected, even subversive things Haggard has to say about the established Church, marriage, duty to society and above all about personal sexual and emotional fulfilment. While these find expression most strikingly in *Mary of Marion Isle* and his romances published from 1921 onwards, Haggard in many ways opens the debate in *Love Eternal*. He had presented unflattering portrayals of clergymen in *The Witch's Head*, *Beatrice* and *Stella Fregelius*, but his depiction of Godfrey's father, the Reverend Knight, in *Love Eternal* is particularly savage. Knight is narrow, Calvinistic, emotionally underdeveloped, misogynistic and uncharitable. He is bullying towards Godfrey and resentful of Isobel's questioning intelligence. Suspecting that Godfrey has been 'infected by that pernicious girl, Isobel' (38), he sends him off to Switzerland and forbids him to communicate with her, just as Haggard's father had sent him for the same reason to France and thereby separated him from Lilly. Godfrey's father destroys correspondence between them that falls into his hands, and when they are reunited he encourages Isobel's own father's objection to their marriage and collaborates in separating them. He dies without a reconciliation with his son, and the narrator comments that 'Notwithstanding his continual profession of the highest Christian principles he could never forget or forgive' (284). He is even despised by Isobel's vulgar and materialistic father, who regards him as a 'vicious little viper' (273). Haggard's demolition of Knight is total. He effectively ruins Godfrey's life as another clergyman, Plowden – in autobiographical terms representing Lilly's husband Archer – collaborates with Eva's sister in *The Witch's Head* in order to force Eva to marry him and hence to ruin her life and Ernest's. But whereas Plowden acts out of a selfish sexual desire for Eva, Knight acts out of a meanness of spirit and out of a profoundly unnatural view of emotional and sexual relations. The narrator comments that 'sex and everything to do with it were repellent to him' (249). It is striking that in his two most evidently autobiographical novels, both of which deal centrally with the loss of, or separation from, a first love, Haggard attributes a substantial part of the blame to clergymen who are driven by a perverted attitude towards sex. There is no conclusive clue available in his letters or autobiography to explain this connection. However, his daughter Lilias records that the rector of Louisa's parish dragged his feet over the publishing of the banns of her marriage to Haggard, under pressure from her guardian, and that Haggard 'wrote telling him that if further obstructions were thrown in the way of the wedding taking place he must be prepared to accept the legal consequences'.[78] At any rate he also offers portrayals of morally deficient, hypocritical clergymen in the materialistic fathers of Beatrice and Stella, and in Bastin, one of the explorers in *When the World Shook*, he depicts a clergyman who, if sincere, is slow-witted, narrow-minded and unimaginative.

But if Haggard is critical of the representatives of the established Church, he ensures that his protagonists, at least those of his novels and those of his romances set within a Western context, believe in, or come to believe in, the tenets of the Christian faith. Isobel, like Beatrice, moves from a position of unbelief, through her passion for her lover, to an appreciation of a Christian divinity. Stella, the narrator points out, is 'an example of the doctrines of Christianity really inspiring the daily life of the believer' (322). Mary, despite having lived as a castaway on an uninhabited island since her childhood, remains a Christian. Mea in *The Way of the Spirit* is, as she tells Rupert, half Christian, although not baptized. In *The Virgin of the Sun* Quilla, an Inca princess, renounces her religion to marry Hubert. Yva in *When the World Shook* converts to Christianity on the morning of her death. In *Montezuma's Daughter* where the hero marries the eponymous heroine, Haggard employs the device of her suicide, on the grounds that she realizes that her pagan attitudes will always constitute a barrier between herself and her husband, which permits him to return to England and his first love. Haggard does not allow his male protagonists to fall truly and permanently in love with women who are not in some measure Christian. Gertrude Himmelfarb claims of the late Victorians that if they had 'no dogmatic social ideology, no binding religious faith, they did have a compelling, almost obsessive faith in morality'.[79] But Haggard clearly seems to be concerned with Christianity rather than morality. He apparently had a firm Christian faith. He records in his autobiography that he read the Bible daily and states: 'I believe in the simple and unadulterated doctrines of Christianity as these appear within [...] the New Testament'.[80] If Haggard's refusal to permit the protagonists of his novels to persevere in a lack of Christian faith sprung from his own beliefs, it seems reasonable to suppose that his depiction of Christian ministers, particularly in *Love Eternal*, derives from his own experience. But he is very clear that his doubts about the sincerity of its clergy do not extend to Christianity itself.

Scrutiny of Marital Relationships

While in *Love Eternal* Haggard continues to look sceptically at the representatives of the established Church, he depicts the institution of marriage, in his final novels, in a more variegated and scrutinizing light than he had done hitherto. Before the publication of *Love Eternal*, he had represented in his novels and their associated romances four kinds of marriage. First, as the eventual, triumphant culmination of true love, as depicted in *Dawn* and in *Montezuma's Daughter*. Second, marriage with a good and faithful woman as a consolation for the loss of a true love who can never be forgotten, as depicted in *Jess*, *Joan Haste* and in *The People of the Mist* (1894) where the hero Leonard, although happily married to Juanna, can never forget his first love Jane. Third, an unfortunate and unhappy marriage with a morally deficient woman, as depicted in *Dawn*, *Colonel Quaritch*, *Beatrice* and *The Way of the Spirit*. Fourth, an expedient and unhappy marriage contracted as the result of pressure from family, as depicted in *Dawn* and *The Witch's Head*. In *Love Eternal* Haggard represents something rather more complicated. Godfrey and Isobel are first-time lovers who eventually prevail over adverse circumstances and marry. But, unlike the protagonists of *Dawn* and *Colonel Quaritch*, they do not live happily ever after, at least not on earth. The celebration of their union is, for the most part, in an afterlife, where it is entirely spiritual. It seems that Haggard is, in an autobiographical sense, considering both Lilly and Louisa, in respect of the former offering himself the consolation that a relationship that perforce had little or no sexual content on earth will enjoy an eternal reunion in an afterlife, and in respect of the latter reflecting upon whether sex is really more important than a close mutual affection.

In *Mary of Marion Isle* and *Allan and the Ice-Gods*, he presents marriage in a way similar to *Beatrice* and *The Way of the Spirit*, but is drawn to reflections adjacent to those in *Love Eternal*. Clara only partially subscribes to Haggard's previous representations of unworthy and unloving wives. Significantly, the reader is told more about her than her predecessors. She is no seductress. Her attraction lies in the fact that she is pretty and neat and tastefully dressed. She is purposed and focussed, and the narrator considers her to be a 'cool and very level-headed young lady' (136), but if she is prepared to scheme for what she wants it is not in an offensive way. Andrew reflects that she 'isn't at all bad [...] Her transparency is quite delightful' (20). When he is disinherited in favour of Clara by their uncle she generously offers to divide her wealth with him, ashamed that she originally put the idea of disinheriting Andrew into her uncle's mind. She schemes and dissembles in order to persuade Andrew to propose to her but no more so, it seems implicitly suggested, than another woman would have done at a time when an advantageous marriage was the pinnacle of many women's aspirations. That there is a measure of justification for Clara's energetic pursuit of her own interests is proposed by the fact that she is an orphan. Moreover, she has genuine feelings for Andrew and appears to be sexually squeamish, thinking to herself, 'I like him better than I ever did anyone else. He is the only male creature who does not actively repel me, and very nice-looking too, in his way' (109). Although she also has failings – she is unmaternal, like Geoffrey's wife Honoria in *Beatrice* and, like Edith in *The Way of the Spirit*, she hopes her missing husband will not materialize – Clara engages a measure of the reader's sympathy.

Haggard's depiction of an unsatisfactory wife is significantly more modulated than in his earlier novels. He pursues the same question more insistently in *Allan and the Ice-Gods*, in which Allan Quatermain, after smoking a narcotic, enters the spirit of a much earlier incarnation of himself in the person of Wi, a dweller in the ice age. Wi's relationship with his wife Aaka is a difficult one, and he falls in love with the beautiful and exotic Laleela, who arrives in his land from overseas. Given that Haggard tells us Allan Quatermain is himself set in imagined situations,[81] and that Laleela's name resembles Lilly's, the autobiographical resonances of the book seem to be plain. Despite the familiar framework, Haggard deviates from his earlier plot lines in which a new love is consolation for an unhappy marriage, in that despite their differences Aaka is fiercely loyal to Wi and rushes to his side when he is threatened with death by his own people, saying, 'Kill me also [...] Shall we who have slept together for so many years lie in different beds at last?' In the final scene of the book Wi, Aaka, Laleela and others board a canoe intending to escape the destruction caused by a rapidly melting glacier. Finding the canoe dangerously overloaded, Wi and his faithful male servant heroically remain behind, and just as the mist is about to enclose the canoe, they see 'a tall woman's shape stand up in the boat and plunge from it into the water' (253, 276). Allan awakes from his stupor before it is clear whether it is Aaka or Laleela who refuses to desert Wi.

Haggard, in his final fiction, is looking with a more scrutinizing and sympathetic eye at the question of marital relationships that are difficult or tired or have never inspired in the male partner a real passion as opposed to a comfortable affection. At an autobiographical level he almost certainly has in mind his own faithful and devoted wife. It seems likely that he was reflecting on his affection for her and, in his own mind, setting her tested loyalty against the documented fickleness of the woman he really loved. And in *Wisdom's Daughter* he gestures self-interestedly towards a reconciliation of this duality when Ayesha observes:

> A man may love two women and at the same time; one with his spirit and the other with his flesh since through all things runs this war between the spirit and the flesh. (141)

The Sexual Imperative and Sex Outside Marriage

Haggard's final novels also look, in what is an equally new way for him, at the relevance and significance of marriage, and at the associated question of sex outside marriage, when viewed in the light of the imperatives of sexual passion and the realities of being human. There is a real sense in Haggard's observations of an urgency on his part, at what he must have recognized as the end of his writing career, to express alternatives to some of the stereotypes he had propagated. He was of course writing in a different literary climate. Chris Baldick observes that 'Literature in the years after 1910 defined its own modernity most obviously by its stance of anti-Victorianism' and that this was exemplified by a new frankness in discussing sexual relations: 'The abandonment of "Victorian" reticence and euphemism in sexual matters was at the heart of the fully modern experience.'[82] Peter Keating asserts that 'The general reaction against Victorianism [...] pointed to the overthrow of mid-Victorian fictional stereotypes',[83] one of which in the novel was of course the conventional ending of a happy marriage. Although Haggard could not, by any stretch of the imagination, be classified as a modernist, his examination in his final novels of marriage and sex outside marriage is in step with the times.

For all its insistence upon the spiritual as opposed to the sexual, it is in *Love Eternal* that Haggard begins this examination. There is an ambivalence about the book's attitude to sex. The strident voice of the narrator records that, when a sexual element enters the relations between Godfrey and Isobel,

> these were half-spoiled […] this was the eternal complication of sex which curses more than it blesses in the world; of sex the eating fire that is so beautiful but burns. (181)

Haggard once again employs the fire imagery of his earlier novels to indicate the exhilarating and intense, but destructive, nature of the sexual imperative, but, in his reiteration of one of the book's title words in 'eternal', he makes the point that the sexual urge is as indestructible as the spiritual. The narrator, while acknowledging the 'beautiful' aspect of sex, concludes that its negative attributes outweigh its positive ones. And the Reverend Knight articulates an even less accommodating view of sex. He tells the young Godfrey: 'Woman […] is a painted snare' (47). But Knight is effectively and profoundly undermined and discredited both by the transparently bigoted tone of his own utterances and by the narrator's comments about him. His misogyny springs from his lack of emotional intelligence. The narrator opines: 'Matrimony was not a state which appealed to his somewhat shrunken nature' (12). And Knight is self-deluded. Although he has no inclination towards matrimony, he marries out of a bizarre sense of obligation, and regards himself as morally laudable for having done so. The narrator comments:

> he set down to virtue […] a sacrifice of the things of earth and of the flesh to the things of heaven, and of the spirit. In fact it was […] only the outcome of individual physical and mental conditions. (12)

Renunciation is only a reflex determined by innate psychological imperatives. The inescapable ambivalence surrounding the sexual imperative is apparent again in *Wisdom's Daughter*, a book steeped in representations of the outcomes of sexual passion. Isis, the goddess of spiritual love, tells Aphrodite, the goddess of fleshly love, that

> thou turnest men to beasts and makest a mock of them. Thy flowers fade, thy joys fill the mouth with ashes and those who drink of thy cup suck up poison in their souls. (18)

To this Aphrodite responds, 'without me would no children be born […] I am eternal and all life is my slave' (19). Haggard is offering a view of the sexual imperative that is far from simplistic; acknowledging its destructive potential, but also its beauty and above all its fundamental and irresistible nature. He is also offering a view of man caught in the toils of his own unalterable self, of the inescapable human bind.

Haggard takes this view a significant step further in his final novel. In *Mary of Marion Isle* Andrew and Mary live together and produce a child despite not having been through any form of marriage ceremony. And even at the conclusion of the book, although it is made clear that they will stay together, there is no mention of an intended marriage. Haggard had never before permitted the lovers of his novels to flout the institution of marriage, nor indeed those of his romances to live together without some formal ceremony, albeit often a pagan one. Andrew fights against his sexual desire for Mary on the grounds that he is already married. Haggard makes it clear that this is both an uphill and an unrealistic struggle. Having, with difficulty, restrained himself from embracing Mary, Andrew, the narrator relates, 'rushed off and indulged in an hour's hard manual labour' (238). It is difficult to believe that Haggard was innocent of the overtones, particularly since this episode is succeeded by one in which Mary experiments, for the first time, with underclothing, on which she consults Andrew to his 'intense embarrassment' (242), before finally deciding to revert to going without, to which Andrew tells her 'you are very nice as you are' (242). It is sincerely to be hoped that Haggard enjoyed this uncharacteristic interlude. Despite his best and noblest efforts, Andrew's self-control finally deserts him and, conquered by Mary's 'overmastering beauty' (247), he throws his arms around her and 'kissed her everywhere' (248). The narrator intercedes for him, commenting that 'Human nature has its breaking strain and this he had reached' (248). Although he is a man with a pronounced sense of duty, Andrew is vulnerable 'when his reason was overborne by the primary forces of nature' (248). And he finally capitulates to the inevitable, telling Mary 'either we must stop apart, which seems unnatural and also wrong, or we must go back to the caves – together' (257). Haggard is recasting the effects of sexual passion, which he had depicted in his earlier fiction as overwhelming and reason-warping, as reasonable and irreproachable, if equally overwhelming. He is legitimizing Andrew's cohabitation with Mary which, under the circumstances, he is saying, is both natural and right. He makes the same point more directly in *Wisdom's Daughter* where Noot, the guardian of the Flame, asks: 'Do we not all war upon ourselves?' (52). Haggard is arguing the futility of harbouring guilt for what is an integral part of being human. And he reinforces the assertion that self-fulfilment is more important than perceived social duty in the exchange between Clara and Mary in which the former accuses Mary of living in sin with Andrew, and Mary replies: 'My heart does not tell me that' (274).

Andrew's proposal to Mary that they accept the inevitable and live together is of course a great distance from Geoffrey's response to Beatrice after their putative sexual encounter when he asks her, in obvious moral bewilderment: 'What have we done? What can be the end of all of this? It is wrong' (211). It is an equally great distance from Jess's analysis to John, in similar circumstances: 'Ours is a position that only death can set straight' (229). Although it is evident that Haggard had sympathy for the lovers in *Jess* and *Beatrice*, he still felt constrained in 1894 to make revisions to the tone of the latter book in respect of their behaviour, including the narrator's unequivocal comment that 'Beatrice and Geoffrey are not held up to admiration' (225), and to write an advertisement in which he characterized anyone indulging in extramarital relations as 'a sinner and a fool'. In *Mary of Marion Isle* the narrator's voice is supportive of the lovers, and although at the book's conclusion Andrew says to Mary, 'I suppose that we are both sinners' (285), the tone of the book avers that they are nothing of the sort.

Haggard as Modernist

Mary of Marion Isle was written between 1921 and 1924[84] and published posthumously in 1929, some eleven years after Haggard's preceding novel in what Lindy Stiebel observes was a 'less sexually repressed age'.[85] Diana Wallace asserts that in the inter-war years 'Gender identity was a site of special conflict and anxiety.'[86] Baldick too specifies that 'this period witnessed an extraordinary dissemination of sexual discourses – medical, legal, popular and literary' and evidences 'the tendency of modern literature – especially in the novel – towards fuller and broader engagement with sexuality'.[87] Such engagement was, however, by no means afforded free rein. Celia Marshik makes reference to the 'scope of the censorship apparatus and the range of repressive measures at its disposal' that was 'active through the first three decades of the twentieth century'.[88] In *Mary of Marion Isle* the representation of a happy and permanent sexual union outside marriage seems, however, to derive in greater measure from Haggard's personal emotional journey rather than in imitation of a more permissive literary convention. The awkward depictions of Andrew's self-consciousness and initial sense of guilt, and the narrator's intrusive, justificatory comments taken together with Haggard's own unswerving morally conservative attitude toward sexual relations, strongly suggest a personal tentativeness on his part about his depiction of an irreproachable sexual ménage outside marriage. At a practical level he may well have allowed himself greater moral width in *Mary of Marion Isle* and in other late fiction because he realized that not only was he near the end of his career but that he had already ensured his literary market, making, in the latter respect, a similar calculation to Thomas Hardy, of whom Keating writes: 'The scandalous success of *Tess* and *Jude*, together with the growing public interest in his earlier novels, made him wealthy enough to devote the rest of his long life to poetry.'[89]

It seems unlikely, on the evidence of both his moral conservatism and his other fiction, that Haggard would ever have permitted himself to depict a pair of English lovers living together in England as common-law man and wife. The fact that Andrew and Mary live, and so far as the reader can tell intend to continue living, on a remote island in the South Indian Ocean permits a course of conduct not open to those in England. Geoffrey and Beatrice, too, briefly consider running off together to America to start a new life. And, of course, Mary, although British, is a sort of female Robinson Crusoe. Haggard invokes romance conventions to give himself moral elbow room, as had H. De Vere Stacpoole in *The Blue Lagoon* (1908), which was also set on a desert island, and concerns two children who grow to sexual awareness and eventually to parenthood, and about which Keating has observed that it was 'in some respects the ultimate sex novel […] illustrating the natural sexuality that had become merely a dream in corrupt modern society'.[90] While Haggard may conceivably have drawn upon *The Blue Lagoon* when he came to write *Mary of Marion Isle*, the two books have a limited amount in common, Haggard's having none of the intensity or sexual frankness of Stacpoole's.

Referring to women writers who wrote quite openly about sexuality in the years following the Great War, Nicola Beauman records that to avoid censorship 'they set their sexual adventures in remote surroundings and used a vocabulary imbued with moral overtones'.[91] Haggard of course does both of these things. But, nevertheless, Mary is Christian, and spiritually as well as sexually desirable, and Andrew is sincere, cultured and an aristocrat. And Haggard permits them to live happily in their unmarried state. Despite the setting and despite the fact that he seems to have felt the need to introduce various caveats into the book's proposition, it remains a notable statement viewed in the light of his previous fiction.

Haggard's adventurous proposal in *Mary of Marion Isle* that love is more important than duty to social convention, and his implicit questioning of the significance of marriage, finds echo in two of his contemporary romances. In *She and Allan*, the hero, visiting the land of the dead, discovers that his two wives have forgotten him while the exotic and wilful native woman Mameena can never forget him. And if Haggard allows Andrew and Mary to live happily in what, in the period, passed for sin, he permits Ramose in *Belshazzar*, his final published book, to marry Myra, his adopted child whom he brought up from infancy. The daring nature of this plot echoes that of Hubert Wales's *The Yoke* (1908), in which a female guardian sleeps with her young ward in order to save him from the dangers of syphilis implicit in casual sexual liaisons, and then hands him over in marriage to a younger woman. So morally scandalized was the National Vigilance Society that it took legal action against the book's publisher John Long, who 'agreed to withdraw the novel from circulation and publish no future editions of it'.[92] But *Belshazzar* was not only written significantly later than *The Yoke*, in fact between 1921 and 1924,[93] but it is a romance and shares none of the realistic attributes of the earlier book.

Baldick has drawn attention to 'the noticeable sexualisation of literature after the Great War',[94] and Martin Hipsky has observed the rise in the early twentieth century 'of what literary journalists and moral reformers censoriously dubbed "the sex novel", a label that referred to [...] the preoccupations of certain twentieth-century writers with questions of sexual psychology'.[95] Writers in the early twentieth century treated the sexual theme with differing, but growing, degrees of explicitness and approbation. Arnold Bennett depicts a relatively happy outcome to such behaviour in *Sacred and Profane Love* (1905) but the lovers' cohabitation ends with the death of the female protagonist. Stacpoole asserts that the sexual relations of his protagonists in *The Blue Lagoon* constitute 'An affair absolutely natural, absolutely blameless, and without sin.'[96] For Ann Veronica in H. G. Wells's eponymous novel of 1909 an irregular sexual relationship leads ultimately to happiness but only through the gate of social convention. And in *The Woman Thou Gavest Me* (1913) Hall Caine allows his protagonists a triumphant sexual liaison, but thereafter both die tragically. Nicola Wilson records that 'public pressure for some kind of censorship of modern literature had been mounting throughout the first decade of the twentieth century'. She argues that the power of the circulating libraries and 'their influence on the writing and production of fiction increased and in fact tightened during the Edwardian period' in response to 'the new strains of sex and realism associated with modern fiction'. The outcome, she adds, included 'the widespread banning of *Ann Veronica*'. *The Woman Thou Gavest Me* was listed as 'doubtful' and 'unsuitable for general circulation'.[97] Such censorship may have hindered the period's fictional representation of extramarital sex, but it clearly could not suppress it as the frequency of such representations bears testament.

Haggard's later fiction exhibits little of the realism or daring of these novels. *Mary of Marion Isle* may endorse unsanctioned cohabitation less reservedly than they do, but its romance aspects and often fantastical plotting mean that it does not bear serious comparison to any of them in terms of moral adventurousness. It is instructive to consider that D. H. Lawrence had published both *Sons and Lovers* (1913) and *The Rainbow* (1915) ten years before Haggard's death, and that before the publication of *Mary of Marion Isle*

Virginia Woolf's *Mrs Dalloway* (1925) and *To the Lighthouse* (1927) had appeared in print. Conceptually and stylistically Haggard's later fiction is about as far removed from the English Modernism of Woolf as it is possible to be. And, similarly, his expression of the sexuality that runs between men and women exhibits none of the groundbreaking intensity and intimate exploratory nature of *Sons and Lovers* or *The Rainbow*. Mary and Andrew may, in an awkward, embarrassed, guilt-ridden fashion, embrace their decision to continue living in sin. But they experience nothing in common with Anna and Will's profound recognition of the deeply sensual nature of their fleshly love in *The Rainbow*: 'They accepted shame, and were one with it in their most unlicensed pleasures [...] It was a bud that blossomed into beauty and heavy, fundamental gratification'.[98]

Much less did Haggard's fiction reflect the realistic representations of same-sex love that appeared in *The Rainbow* and were offered in more concentrated form in Radclyffe Hall's *The Well of Loneliness* (1928), published in the same year as *Lady Chatterley's Lover* and, like both it and *The Rainbow*, suppressed. The self-confessedly emotionally uninformative nature of Haggard's autobiography, completed in 1912 and published posthumously in 1926, is illuminated by consideration that in 1913 E. M. Forster wrote an intimate autobiographical account of his own homosexuality in *Maurice*, which was not published until 1971, a year after his death.

It is clear that, by the close of the Great War, Haggard was, in literary terms, a dated figure, rooted in the attitudes of his Victorian past, whose work remained untouched by the modernism developing around him. Nevertheless, in his final fiction he does make an unambiguous statement about the moral rights of humans to self-fulfilment regardless of social convention. And although he continues to acknowledge the overwhelming and sometimes disruptive force of the sexual imperative, he increasingly entertains the idea that, since it is an innate and hence irresistible part of being human, men and women cannot be blamed for acting under its impulse and can legitimately seize and enjoy its positive aspects while they are able. When Noot in *Wisdom's Daughter* sums up the human condition in fatalistic terms, 'we [...] know not whence we come nor whither we go, nor what we have been, nor why we are' (53), Haggard is implicitly making the proposition that sexual relations are a definable positive on a clouded canvas and should be embraced as such. Despite its prevailingly spiritual tone it is in *Love Eternal* that this argument begins, with the demolition of Knight's uncharitable and unnatural views about sex and the narrator's observation that it is 'the origin of life' (181). It proves both the mainspring and the justification for Andrew and Mary's extraordinary, and extraordinarily rewarding, ménage in *Mary of Marion Isle*. The contemporary romances join the debate. *Wisdom's Daughter* powerfully develops the view that man, psychologically framed as he is, is simply not responsible for his susceptibility to the sexual imperative and thus should not be blamed for responding to its impulse. Ayesha says:

> From the flesh came my sins, because it was begotten of other flesh and the flesh is sin incarnate. Yet my soul sins not, because it comes from that which is sinless. (39)

And she later insists that 'for every sin there is forgiveness' (247). Haggard directly questions the concept of sexual sin in his autobiography, observing that it 'often enough seems to consist merely in giving obedience to the imperious demands of that body with which we have been clothed'.[99] He takes the argument, and his own self-exculpation for the sins of his youth, a step further in *Wisdom's Daughter*, where Amenartas tells her lover Kallikrates that 'the moment is ours to enjoy' (240), and Ayesha laters avers, 'my treasure lies in the red heart of yonder raging flame, and presently I go to pluck it thence' (257), and in doing so echoes Quilla's urging to Hubert in *The Virgin of the Sun*, published the preceding year: 'let us pluck the flowers before they wither' (304). The resulting sexual knowledge is elating and elevating. After having entered the Flame, Ayesha recalls:

> The blood of the gods flowed through my veins. The soul within me became as a lighted torch. The Fire possessed me; I was the Fire's and in a dread communion the Fire was mine. (260)

She is physically and spiritually enabled by an experience that is both intensely sensual and, in its 'dread communion', divine, but ultimately fathomable. Haggard is proposing that the sexual imperative is natural and, in its inescapability carries no blame, and that although it may involve consequences that cannot be anticipated, it has to be embraced as part of being human.

Not only did Haggard, in his last novels and romances, apparently finally feel a freedom to give life to issues that, in his earlier fiction, he had judged he needed to handle with restraint, he consciously addressed for the last time in his fiction subjects that had a deeply autobiographical resonance for him, making some closing remarks about his view of the human condition. There is clearly a deeply autobiographical aspect to both *Love Eternal* and *Mary of Marion Isle* in their rehearsal of many of the key, and often extremely painful, and enduring episodes of his formative years. This seems especially evident in his final novel, in which he depicts both Andrew, Rose's youthful lover, and Black, her aged husband, as emotionally devastated by her betrayal of both of them. Haggard is saying that wounds of that sort are permanent. When the same strong autobiographical strain is apparent in his final romances it lends them a conviction and a strength. *The Virgin of the Sun* represents a blighted first love. *Allan and the Ice Gods* reflects upon the virtues of a loyal wife. *Wisdom's Daughter* documents, with a striking intensity, the fierce imperatives of sexual passion and its location at the centre of being human. But a sense of the valedictory is most obviously, and movingly, apparent in *Moon of Israel* where the protagonist, Seti, looks back on his life and reflects futilely on how it might have been different: 'had I been more of a man [...] I should have stood up against my father' (326). Seti's father had prevented him from marrying the woman he loved. This was a viscerally personal subject for Haggard in that he felt that his own acceptance of his father's refusal to allow him to return from South Africa effectively opened the door for Lilly to marry another man and effectively blighted his life. Seti's words paraphrase those of Haggard's autobiography: 'It was a very foolish act on my part [...] I may say in excuse of this want of judgement that I was very young'.[100] In his final fiction Haggard is unquestionably looking back over his own life with an element of self-pity, and in his final acceptance of the inevitable nature of the sexual imperatives involved in being human, and of the blamelessness of responding to their dictates, he is offering himself a significant measure of reassurance.

Chapter Seven

SUMMATION: A PERSONAL ODYSSEY

The sexual imperative is overwhelmingly present in Haggard's novels, his consideration of various aspects of the theme developing as he grows older and as his writing career progresses. His two earliest, and most intensely autobiographical, novels, *Dawn* and *The Witch's Head*, speak of youthful male anger at sexually exploitative and sexually disloyal women and the power they have to lacerate men emotionally. *Colonel Quaritch V. C.* depicts the price to be paid for early sexual follies and the violently destructive power of sexual passion. *Joan Haste* documents how a father's sexual passion and moral weakness blight the life of his daughter. The anger and violence of these novels gives way to a more measured consideration in *Jess* and *Beatrice* of the intellectual aspirations, social position and sexual passions of a woman and especially of the validity of emotional, and sexual, relations outside marriage. While both books formally uphold the sanctity of the marriage contract, the compatibility and emotional relationship of the participants notwithstanding, they also leave little doubt as to the superior moral worth of genuine love. *Stella Fregelius* and *The Way of the Spirit* entertain the merits of a love that is prevailingly spiritual, but while endorsing a strong spiritual component to a loving relationship, insist, in an exploration and eventual dismissal of sexual renunciation, upon the innate primacy of the sexual. *Love Eternal*, reflecting the particular spiritual and religious climate of the Great War, is insistent upon the spiritual and eternal aspects of love, but is also emphatic about the inevitability of the pull of the sexual imperative. Haggard's final novel, *Mary of Marion Isle*, replays the capacity of sexual betrayal to wound the male but asserts an outcome that is unreservedly happy and sexually liberated.

Throughout these novels there is a repeated insistence upon the eternal nature of genuine love and upon the reunion of lovers and the fulfilment of their passion in an afterlife, which acts as an underlying consolation and represents a reassuring foundation of permanence against the emotionally excoriating experiences of life. Haggard's primarily male-oriented consideration of the complications and destructive nature of aspects of the sexual imperative matures as he grows older, from initial youthful anger, through an attempt to identify a solution, to eventual acceptance of its universality and to the endorsement of an instinctive, but morally irreproachable, response to it.

In his earlier novels Haggard modifies the literary genres on which he draws to give fictional consideration to these persistent concerns. He uses some of the tropes of the sensation novel to give his initial novels colour and offer familiarity to his readers, but he does not subject his heroines to the kind of emotional scrutiny exacted in books like *The Woman in White* or *East Lynne*, nor does he explore issues such as women's legal status within marriage. Similarly, his New Woman heroines are able to finesse the consequences of their adventurous sexual behaviour by means of their extraordinary spirituality and their capacity for self-sacrifice. In both sets of novels, as indeed in his later novels, Haggard shows very limited interest in the contemporary position of women. His almost overwhelming focus is on the emotional damage that female sexuality can do to men.

Identical Concerns in Haggard's Romances

The same preoccupations, and identical attempts to find a solution, are evident in Haggard's contemporary romances, although sometimes, because of their distant locations, exotic characters and colourful plots these are less immediately visible. The early romances, notably *King Solomon's Mines*, *She*, *Allan Quatermain*, *Cleopatra* and *The World's Desire*, depict dangerous, exploitative women whose irresistible sexual power leads men involuntarily to sexual betrayals, violence and moral disintegration. They represent male anger at these women and the desire to punish them. The romances published between 1899 and 1908, particularly *Swallow*, *Pearl Maiden*, *The Brethren*, *Ayesha* and *The Ghost Kings*, depict the spiritual aspects of love and consider, and dismiss, the feasibility of sexual renunciation and in affirming the inevitable triumph of the sexual over the spiritual, foreshadow the group of romances published between 1909 and 1914 – *The Yellow God*, *Morning Star*, *Child of Storm* and *The Wanderer's Necklace* – which reiterate the powerful grip of sexual passion. *Finished*, *Moon of Israel* and *When the World Shook* reflect the spiritual imperatives of the Great War. The final romances, represented by *Wisdom's Daughter*, *The Virgin of the Sun* and *Allan and the Ice-Gods*, offer a mature, perceptibly valedictory, vision, recognizing the overwhelming nature of the sexual imperative but at the same time giving thoughtful consideration to issues such as the merits of the faithful love of a tested and dependable wife against the passion of a new love.

In the novels the strongest, the most involuntary and the most destructive, sexual passion is the preserve of morally deficient characters such as George in *Dawn*, Quest in *Colonel Quaritch* and Dick in *The Way of the Spirit*. In the romances the same order of passion and its consequences affect morally admirable characters such as Leo in *She*, Harmachis in *Cleopatra*, Odysseus in *The World's Desire*, Eric in *Eric Brighteyes*, Kallikrates in *Wisdom's Daughter* and Wi in *Allan and the Ice-Gods*, all of whom are situated in locales far removed from England. Haggard clearly felt constrained by the respective conventions of novel and romance. But his romances as well as his novels repeatedly present the same fundamental aspects of the sexual imperative.

Women in Haggard's Fiction

Women are the unremitting surface focus of Haggard's fiction. All of his female protagonists are sexually compelling, most are charismatic, some are also politically powerful. In the novels they are middle-class, intelligent, articulate, cultured and generally English. In the romances they are goddesses, rulers and princesses, and frequently foreign. They all exude sexual desire as well as sexual allure. Many, especially in the novels, are constrained by legal restriction and social convention, and many are pressurized to make unloving unions. Some are markedly virtuous, some are calculating, manipulative and vindictive.

They tend to be either the one or the other. Haggard, in this respect, conforms to the tendency of Victorian novelists to polarize female identity. Nevertheless, he proposes that all women are threatening to men. And this is the real centre of gravity of his fiction. Haggard shows little real interest in the psyches of his heroines or in their emotional life. Neither is he concerned, beyond formal genuflections towards them, in contemporary women's issues. The vast majority of his fiction represents a male observer's record of women's, frequently destructive, sexually derived influence over men. The plots of 52 of his 55 full-length fictional works revolve, essentially, about the emotional damage caused to his male protagonists by female sexual allure. Nevertheless, many of his female characters are drawn with vigour and colour, as well as with a modicum of sympathy. Haggard represents their sexual vulnerability as well as their sexual potency. Ayesha may be a remorseless and cruel tyrant, but her love for Leo is none the less tender and genuine. Meriamun may be exploitative and unscrupulous, but she is caught in an unhappy marriage, and she truly believes that Odysseus is the long-awaited, and prophesied, love of her life. Haggard acknowledges that women too are victims of an irresistible sexual imperative.

Men in Haggard's Fiction

While Haggard's women are strong and strongly depicted, his male heroes are markedly less interesting. They are flat, formulaic, conventional late-Victorian gentlemen who are compelled to step outside their limited sphere of experience through their susceptibility to sexually potent women, and whose emotional lives are threatened with destruction by sexual betrayals and lost loves. Carolyn Dever observes that 'women offer a formidable, frequently insurmountable challenge to heterosexual male figures in Victorian fiction'.[1] Dever's contention is illustrated in novels such as George Du Maurier's *Trilby* (1894) and Bram Stoker's *Dracula* (1897), in which the female protagonists pose just such a challenge to their male counterparts. As an apparent extreme response to this threat, there runs the suggestion throughout Haggard's romances, detectable amongst his novels only in *The Witch's Head*, that relations with women are all too dangerous and that homosocial relations are more dependable. The depiction of bachelors and bachelor communities was of course a characteristic feature of late nineteenth-century literature and appears, for example, in Arthur Conan Doyle's Sherlock Holmes stories, Jerome K. Jerome's *Three Men in a Boat* (1889), J. M Barrie's *My Lady Nicotine* (1890) and R. L. Stevenson's *Strange Case of Dr Jekyll and Mr Hyde* (1886). It is a phenomenon discussed briefly by Eve Kosofsky Sedgwick in *Epistemology of the Closet* (2008) and more extensively in her book *Between Men* (1985). But in Haggard's fiction it remains an undeveloped sub-theme. If women are destructive for men, they are also compelling.

Personal Issues in Haggard's Fiction

The nature of the main themes and allusions in Haggard's fiction that correspond with his own personal emotional experiences with various women in his life, and the conviction and persistence with which he expresses them, suggest a conscious and purposed consideration of issues he found compellingly important. Depictions of the wounds inflicted upon a man by sexual betrayal feature strongly in *The Witch's Head*, *Mary of Marion Isle* and *The Way of the Spirit*. Representations of a lost first, and true, love recuperable in an afterlife appear in *The Witch's Head*, *Jess*, *Colonel Quaritch*, *Joan Haste*, *Stella Fregelius*, *The Way of the Spirit* and *Love Eternal* and, amongst Haggard's romances in *She*, *The World's Desire*, *Ayesha*, and *When the World Shook*. *Montezuma's Daughter* and *The People of the Mist* speak of the enduring power of first love. *Mary of Marion Isle* and *The Virgin of the Sun* depict a complete and satisfying replacement for a first love lost through female betrayal; in essence, a second first love. In his two most clearly autobiographical romances, *Montezuma's Daughter* and *The Virgin of the Sun*, the first love is named, respectively, Lily and Blanche. In the equally autobiographical *Mary of Marion Isle* she is named, in a probable, although of course more ambivalent, piece of floral transposition, Rose. It seems certain that Haggard's repeated portrayals of a lost first love derive from his own experience with Lilly Jackson and that the male anger and bitterness, the reassurances of reunion in an afterlife, upon which he insists, and the eventual assertion in the later books that first love can be replicated, are a form of catharsis and self-consolation.

In a similar manner he makes frequent fictional reference to his affair with Johanna Ford. The capacity of sexual passion to corrode character, to cause men to act, albeit involuntarily, outside accepted moral frameworks, to betray existing loves and to disregard the most committing obligations, together with the associated topic of the consequences for his children of a father's sexual sin, are depicted throughout both Haggard's novels and romances. In his earliest novel, *Dawn*, he portrays a man abandoning a woman to whom he is engaged because of his compelling sexual attraction to her beautiful friend, who is German, as was Johanna. The theme is powerfully replayed in *She*, where Ayesha's irresistible female allure twice causes the men she desires to desert the women they really love, and finds continued emphatic expression in *The World's Desire*, *Eric Brighteyes*, *Montezuma's Daughter* and, with particular force, in *Cleopatra*, where the protagonist's breaking of his oath to the highest principles of love results in his punishment by being buried alive. The power of sexual lust to deprave the male character is depicted in *Dawn*, *Jess*, *Colonel Quaritch*, *Joan Haste* and *The Way of the Spirit*, as well as in 11 of Haggard's romances, notably in *The World's Desire* and in *Lysbeth*. And the seduction of young men by older women is portrayed in *Dawn*, *Colonel Quaritch* and *The Way of the Spirit* as well as in three of Haggard's romances, most powerfully in *She*. The death of an infant appears in 21 of Haggard's fictional books, the death of a child as a consequence of its father's sexual sin figures in *Joan Haste* and, most emphatically, in *Montezuma's Daughter* and *The Heart of the World*, all three of which were written shortly after the death of his son Jock. Haggard's fictional response to his affair has three aspects. It reflects his apparent belief that it constituted a betrayal of his lifelong love for Lilly, a moral crime for which he was punished by the death of his son, and perhaps also by that of his daughter Ethel. It appears to constitute a self-exculpatory attempt to assert that the real blame lay largely with Johanna that, under assault from her sexual allure, he was unable to help himself. And it represents an insistent, and of course self-serving, strain of fatalism that proposes that man cannot be held responsible for what is beyond his capacity to influence or to resist.

Haggard's fictional depictions of marriage and of wives are generally negative. While with the exception of *Mary of Marion Isle*, all of his fictional works that portray a happy earthly outcome for the protagonists represent a final union in marriage, such marriages are the exception. Heroes and heroines pressed by members of their family to conclude unloving but materially advantageous unions appear in each of Haggard's novels with the exception of *Doctor Therne*. Depictions of women forced or pressed, generally for political or material reasons, to marry men they dislike appear in 10 of the romances. And portrayals of the outcomes of unhappy marriages are found in *Dawn*, *Colonel Quaritch*, *Joan Haste*, *The Way of the Spirit* and *Mary of Marion Isle* as well as in four of the romances. Representations of men who, while they are married to affectionate and dependable wives, can never entirely forget their first, and true, loves appear in *The Witch's Head*, *Joan Haste*, *Stella Fregelius* and *The People of the Mist*. It is not until his penultimate published romance, *Allan and the Ice Gods*, that Haggard, in offsetting the dependable virtues of Aaka against the allure of Laleela, reflects upon the merits of a caring and loyal wife. Haggard's portrayals of existing marriages may be almost universally negative, but he demonstrates no real interest in exploring the virtues of the types of marriage depicted in earlier Victorian fiction. As Talia Schaffer points out, 'by the twentieth century, marriage is supposed to be sexual [...] it is a story that entirely reverses the emphasis in Victorian fiction'.[2] Haggard's fiction proposes that the only valid kind of marriage is one of genuine love contracted for romantic reasons, and that any other kind is a second-rate marriage of convenience regardless of whether that convenience is financial or carnal. Similarly, while Haggard references the disadvantaged marital situation of women, he fails to pursue this theme. He depicts marriage primarily from a male point of view as variously the apogee of a genuine romantic love, a disillusioning second-best after the loss of a first love, or a justification for socially and morally unconventional behaviour. It is difficult to dissociate Haggard's jaundiced fictional portrayal of marriage from his view of his own.

While fictional reflections of Haggard's relationships with his first love, mistress and wife resonate through his novels and romances, his admiration for Agnes Barber features less frequently. Nevertheless, in his depictions of spiritual women who have an overwhelming, life-changing attraction for men in *Jess*, *Allan's Wife* and *Stella Fregelius*, there can be little doubt that he has Agnes in mind.

It is clear from the evidence of his texts that in his fiction Haggard pursues themes closely connected to his personal emotional history and preoccupations. Max Saunders comments that it is striking 'how many [...] writers around the turn of the century are displacing their autobiographies [...] into various forms of fiction'. And, separately, he points out that 'this results in a proliferation of partially fictionalized life-writings, which combine expression with concealment in different ways'.[3]

Haggard himself writes in his autobiography, published posthumously:

> It is of course impossible for anyone [...] to set down life's every detail for the world to stare at, unless indeed such a person were prepared to order the resulting book to be buried for – let us say – five hundred years.[4]

Fiction offered him an outlet of expression he could not find elsewhere. He makes no mention of Johanna in his autobiography. Lilly is referred to briefly without identification and without elaboration. Agnes barely features. He writes of his wife strictly in affectionate terms. Conversely, he feels quite able to refer to his mother. Perhaps as a consequence, or perhaps because he felt his mother was the one woman of whom it would be unthinkable to attempt a fictional representation, mothers of grown men do not feature with regularity in Haggard's fiction, although unmaternal mothers of infants constitute bad wives, such as Honoria in *Beatrice* and Clara in *Mary of Marion Isle*. Amongst Haggard's novels a mother appears only in *The Way of the Spirit*, where the protagonist's mother, in what can only be interpreted as a real or imagined autobiographical genuflection by Haggard, urges her son to adopt the path of sexual renunciation after his disastrous affair with a married woman. The same connection between a mother and her son's sexual sin occurs in *Cleopatra*, which Haggard dedicated to his mother, in which the hero swears lifelong fidelity to Isis, 'the universal mother',[5] only to break his oath in giving way to his sexual passion. There is a sense that in a similar act Haggard offended not only against his eternal love for Lilly but also against his mother. Other portrayals of mothers in the romances are infrequent but generally benign, although the matriarchal figure is of course referenced in Ayesha and in similar powerful women. Norman Etherington contends of *She* that 'there is a case to make for Ayesha as the disguised embodiment of an unfulfilled desire for a forbidden love, a son's incestuous longing for his mother',[6] and Shannon Young has suggested that Haggard uses his fiction, particularly *She*, 'to work through his specifically oedipal problems of identity'.[7] But the text, and context, of *She* suggest that Haggard's prevailing view of Ayesha is of a sexually manipulative woman who is punished for her disruption to men's lives; a creation that owes more to Lilly Jackson than to his mother.

Certainly, Haggard seems, in another late romance, *When the World Shook*, to consider the mother figure to lie at the very core of what it is to be human when he reflects on

> the wonder of a woman's heart, which is a microcosm of the hopes and fears and desires and despairs of this humanity of ours, whereof from age to age she is the mother.[8]

Haggard is asserting the fundamental significance of woman, not only to the maternal, the physical, side of generating life, but in any attempt to comprehend the inescapable imperatives of the human condition. And, in his fiction, he is drawing upon his own closest experiences and preoccupations to mobilize such an attempt.

His fictional renditions of what Haggard regards as emotionally key autobiographical experiences take the form of weaving these experiences into a background which, although it may not exactly replicate Haggard's history, is never more than lightly fictionalized. This form allows Haggard to revisualize and evaluate his experiences and to implicate his reader in making moral judgements on the behaviour of his protagonists. He is thus able not only to present personal issues he regarded as being of prime importance in any assessment of what is involved in being human, but to offer himself an element of self-exculpation. This is particularly observable in the conflicting, ambiguous arguments apparent in some of his books, where he appears to subvert the dramatic action by strong cross-currents. These can be seen in his depiction of comfortable consolatory marriages, which are nevertheless unconvincing, in *The Witch's Head, Colonel Quaritch, Joan Haste*, and *The People of the Mist*; of spiritual alliances that are undercut by considerations of the damaging, introspective aspects of such relationships in *Stella Fregelius, The Way of the Spirit, The Ghost Kings* and *The Brethren*; of reassuringly consolatory spiritual unions in an afterlife that are set against the insistent and natural demands of the present and the sexual in *Love Eternal* and *When the World Shook*; and of tentative and caveated assertions of the primacy of the fulfilment of the individual over the demands of society in *Beatrice, Jess, Mary of Marion Isle* and *Allan and the Ice-Gods*. This authorial veering, the adumbrating of his conclusions and his ironical depictions of unworkable moral alternatives, most clearly apparent in the judgement of Eva in *The Witch's Head*, is evidence not only of Haggard's personal emotional proximity to the major issues of his fiction, but of his use of the fictional form to consider alternative evaluations of his own behaviour and occasionally to distort the strictly autobiographical in order to assuage his own feelings of guilt.

The Close Similarities between Haggard's Novels and Romances

The autobiographical nature of Haggard's fiction functions in different ways in his novels and romances. The novels are related through the voice of an anonymous and omniscient narrator who frequently intervenes, commenting and passing moral judgement on the protagonists, and who can never be far divorced from the author. The romances use well-recognized narratorial devices that include fictitious editors publishing manuscripts that record the experiences of the protagonists and accounts told directly by the protagonists themselves. Because of these devices, because of romance convention and expectations, and because of their exotic characters and settings, the romances express themselves both more emphatically and, paradoxically, less directly. While the main preoccupation of all the novels is immediately apparent, the romances need to be read through the prism of the novels before they can be seen clearly to be concerned with the same issues.

Despite the prescriptive classification of his fiction Haggard offers, there is in reality significantly less distance between his novels and his romances than this division suggests. Wendy Katz has rightly observed of Haggard's fictional books that 'they all exhibit enough in common to obviate the necessity of being accorded special categories'.[9] The novels are hardly realistic. *Dawn, The Witch's Head, Colonel Quaritch* and *Joan Haste* have strong elements of melodrama. *Stella Fregelius* and *Love Eternal* at times border on the fantastical. *Jess, The Way of the Spirit* and *Mary of Marion Isle*, partly set in exotic locations, have pronounced aspects of the romance. And the romances largely concern typical English gentlemen with attitudes typical of their class, forced for one reason or another to go abroad and often to abandon the women they love, and who, although they encounter worlds and characters radically different from those they are used to, are measured by the moral standards of the country of their origin and generally return to England. Bruce Mazlish argues that this enhances *She*, of which he asserts that the power of the book 'lies in [the] mixture of realism and romanticism'.[10] Thomas in *Montezuma's Daughter*, Leonard in *The People of the Mist* and Hubert in *The Virgin of the Sun* have everything in common with Arthur in *Dawn*, Ernest in *The Witch's Head* and Andrew in *Mary of Marion Isle*. But, despite these obvious similarities, it has not been recognized that Haggard's novels and romances proceed to the same point, albeit by different routes, and that this point turns on the impact of the sexual imperative upon the male. Haggard is making the same proposition Thomas Hardy made in his General Preface to the Wessex edition of 1912, where he asserts that 'the domestic emotions have throbbed in Wessex nooks with as much intensity as in the palaces of Europe'.[11] While Haggard's novels depict men in polite English society – tortured, and often reduced, by their inability to exercise control over their innate desires – his romances seem to offer an alternative in a flight from women in the form of various sorts of male quests after wealth and geographical truth. But these seemingly material quests transform into journeys into the realities of being human with the emergence of exactly the same fundamental imperatives represented in the novels. Linda Dryden observes of Haggard's romance heroes: 'their civilized selves remain uncompromised and they easily revert to the ideal of English gentlemanly conduct that characterizes them. The fate of Kurtz is not an option for Haggard's heroes.'[12] While the male protagonists in Haggard's romances may not suffer psychological collapse in the manner of Kurtz in Joseph Conrad's *Heart of Darkness* (1902), and survive intact to return to England, they are nevertheless chastened, saddened and permanently reduced by their experiences in the same way as the male protagonists of the novels.

The female protagonists of Haggard's romances, although they are often more exotic, more powerful and less morally scrupulous than their counterparts in his novels, are in reality no more sexually alluring and no more irresistible. They simply represent the same proposition more colourfully and more exotically drawn. This consistency of purpose casts Haggard's romances in a clearer light, and certain of them which are not regularly considered emerge as more substantial than is generally allowed.

The dark intensity of the depictions of a man caught in the grip of a sexual vortex and obliged, involuntarily, to break his oath to the woman he loves, and his punishment for his betrayal in *Cleopatra*, *The World's Desire* and *Eric Brighteyes*; the tension represented in *The Brethren* between the spiritual and the sexual; and the valedictory vision of *Wisdom's Daughter* and *Allan and the Ice Gods*, when viewed through the prism of his novels, are seen to signpost Haggard's developing fictional consideration of the preoccupation that dominated his personal life. Critical concentration on the early romances has tended to encourage dismissal of the later ones as merely imitative in terms of plot, setting and characters – as exploiting their successful predecessors for commercial gain. But considered in the light of Haggard's pursuit in virtually all his romances of the same serious issues he explores in his novels, this apparent unoriginality can be seen to derive from his conviction that settings and characters familiar to him invest his work in the same way as issues that were overwhelmingly important to him personally, with an integrity, conviction and worth.

The Integrity of Haggard's Fiction

The consistency with which Haggard pursued these issues proposes a more concerted seriousness of purpose in his fictional works than has generally been recognized. For

Haggard, the power of the sexual imperative and its capacity to disrupt lives was not simply part of his personal history, but an integral part, perhaps indeed the essence, of being human. In his journal article 'About Fiction', written as early as 1887, he asserted: 'Sexual passion is the most powerful lever with which to stir the mind of man, for it lies at the root of all things human.'[13] And some twenty-four years later he expressed in his autobiography an emphatic sense of the lifelong outcome of, explicitly sexual, sin when he wrote: 'sin [...] dominates all our landscape [...] never can we escape the sight of it. Our virtues [...] are dwarfed and lost in the dark shadows thrown up by our towering crime'.[14] These powerful statements about the capacity of sexual passion to shape lives translate with emphasis into Haggard's fiction. Representations of sexual power and sexual susceptibility, and their outcomes, saturate, equally, his novels and his romances, from the violence of *Dawn*, *Colonel Quaritch*, *She*, *Cleopatra* and *The World's Desire* through the more reflective but equally sexually dominated *The Way of the Spirit* and *The Brethren*, to the final, philosophical renditions of *Wisdom's Daughter*, *Allan and the Ice-Gods* and *Mary of Marion Isle*. Etherington comments that Haggard 'explored a greater range of important questions concerning woman's sexuality [...] than almost any male author of his time'.[15] More accurately, it is male responses to women's sexuality that concern Haggard. While the responses Haggard entertains in his fiction to this aspect of the human predicament develop as he grows older, his authorial moral platform alters very little. Forty-one years separate the publication of his first work of fiction and his death in 1925, but Haggard remains a Victorian in moral outlook, his interpretation of the emotional landmarks of his own life substantially unmodified by the passage of time. His undiminished sense of personal guilt partly accounts for the striking reiteration of the theme of the sexual imperative in his fiction and for his unyielding moral viewpoint. But it is also clear that he considered that the theme dignified his books.

It is evident that Haggard was concerned, not only with making a good living from his fictional output, but also with his future reputation. He was clearly conscious that the critics did not regard most of his work highly. He expresses this concern in the introduction to his autobiography, where he claims, in a transparently self-interested way, that 'The history of literature and art goes to show that contemporary criticism seldom makes and never can destroy a reputation. Time is the only true critic', and he goes on to assert that 'although it may seem much to claim, my belief is that some of my tales *will* live'.[16] Francis O'Gorman has suggested persuasively that Haggard's 'ambivalent financial representations' in his decentred depictions of the search for treasure in *Colonel Quaritch*, *King Solomon's Mines*, *She* and *Allan Quatermain* illustrate the tension he recognized between writing for present financial benefit and future reputation, his 'authorial nervousness and sense of the problematic value of his work, commercial and cultural, and its chance of lasting'.[17] The significance of Haggard's novels to an identification of the issues he considered most worthwhile to express in his fiction appears to be twofold. He had lower financial expectations of them than of his romances, which almost certainly explains why he wrote novels so infrequently. And he seems to have felt that in them he had more personal space. He makes it plain in his introduction to two of them, *Stella Fregelius* and *The Way of the Spirit*, that he wrote them primarily to please himself, while of one of them, *Beatrice*, he wrote that he considered it 'one of the best bits of work I ever did'.[18]

An application to Haggard's romances of the thematic template of his novels reveals, less obviously visible beneath the exotic romance overlay, identical themes, equally insistently pursued. This scrupulous insistence argues absolution from charges that he was merely an opportunistic writer simply reiterating a saleable formula of colourful and distracting, but ultimately futile, adventure. It also argues that allied to an undoubtedly over-sensitive, self-indulgent tendency to allow his personal psychological preoccupations to bleed into his fiction in an attempt to derive personal solace and personal resolution, Haggard felt an authorial compulsion to entertain issues he perceived as lying at the root of being. That he entertained them in a way that – while insistently seeking – defies complacent conclusions and offers a sense of the fundamentally sad incompleteness and incomprehensibility of the human dilemma, suggests a generally uncredited element of weight to his fiction.

Appendix
PLOT SUMMARIES

Dawn (1884)

Philip Caresfoot resides with Devil, his father, and his manipulative cousin George. Philip's father wishes him to marry the heiress Maria Lee but, despite being fond of Maria, Philip falls in love with her friend, the beautiful German, Hilda. Philip becomes secretly engaged to Maria and then secretly marries Hilda. In order to force his hand, his father publicly announces Philip's engagement to Maria and threatens to disinherit him in favour of George should he not marry her. Having subsequently learned of Philip's marriage, Devil confronts him and, having told him that he has written him out of his will, dies of a heart attack when Philip withholds his medicine. Hilda gives birth to Angela and then dies.

Philip is desperate to buy back his father's estate from George, whose ward Arthur Heigham falls in love with the beautiful Angela. George too desires Angela and coerces Lady Bellamy, a former lover, to help him. At her suggestion that Angela's marriage to George might solve the estate question, Philip eventually agrees to insist that Angela and Arthur should part for a year.

Arthur travels to Madeira and on the voyage meets Mildred Carr, a rich widow who falls in love with him. Meanwhile, Angela resolutely refuses to consider marrying George. The Bellamys go to Madeira, where Arthur ill-advisedly confides in Lady Bellamy and allows her to persuade him to entrust to her a ring that she undertakes to pass to Angela in England as a token of Arthur's continuing love. Meanwhile, Arthur resists Mildred's advances, and they part.

Lady Bellamy tells Angela that Arthur is dead of fever in Madeira and shows her the ring as well as a forged farewell letter from Arthur and his forged death certificate. Believing Arthur is dead and that George is terminally ill, Angela, against all her inclinations, finally gives way to her father's urging and marries George. Arthur returns to England on the following day, learns of the marriage, denounces Angela and hurries off back to Mildred. Angela goes mad and George is mauled to death by Arthur's bulldog. Bellamy, in an act of revenge for his wife's infidelities, reveals her plot, and she takes poison but survives, paralyzed.

Angela recovers her sanity, writes to Arthur and sets off to Madeira to see him in person. Mildred reads her letter and nobly declines to marry him. Angela arrives, and she and Arthur are reunited in love.

The Witch's Head (1884)

Ernest Kershaw, an orphan, goes to stay in the country with his uncle Reginald Cardus, who acts as guardian to Dorothy and Jeremy, the children of Mary whom

Reginald loved in his youth and who, at the insistence of her materialistic father, married another man.

The Ceswick sisters, Florence and Eva, live locally. Florence and Dorothy are in love with Ernest. He impulsively kisses Florence, who immediately takes this very seriously. Soon afterwards he encounters Eva, and they fall in love, despite Florence having previously warned off her sister. Florence breathes vengeance.

Ernest sets off on a continental tour in order to escape Florence. By chance he encounters his cousin, who drunkenly insults Ernest's mother and provokes a duel in which Ernest kills him. Ernest flees to South Africa to escape justice. He writes to his family and to Eva but, on the malicious advice of the ill-intentioned Florence, Eva does not reply.

The Reverend Plowden arrives in the village. He is attracted by Eva and is abetted in his pursuit by Florence. Under pressure, Eva finally agrees to become engaged to him. Meanwhile, Jeremy has set off to South Africa to find Ernest. He tells Ernest that Eva still loves him, and Ernest writes to ask her to join him and marry him.

Despite making an ineffectual attempt to terminate her engagement, Eva gives in to further pressure and marries Plowden. She replies to Ernest, telling him; he is devastated by the news. He receives an amnesty for the killing of his cousin, remains in South Africa and is one of the few British survivors of the Zulu victory at Isandhlwana. Later, he is blinded by a lightning strike.

On the death of his uncle, Ernest becomes a baronet and returns to England. He encounters Eva and reproaches her for her betrayal, but tells her that he still loves her and that they will be together in an afterlife. He marries the faithful Dorothy, although she is aware of his continuing passion for Eva. They enjoy an affectionate and comfortable life, but Ernest can never forget Eva.

Jess (1887)

Captain John Niel becomes assistant to Transvaal farmer Silas Croft, who lives with his nieces Jess and Bessie. Frank Muller, an untrustworthy and ambitious half-English Boer, is in love with Bessie, but she rejects him and falls in love with John. So does her elder sister Jess, who learns that her sister also loves him.

In order to leave the field to Bessie, for whom she feels both sisterly love and responsibility, Jess decides to go to stay with a friend in Pretoria. In her absence, John and Bessie become engaged.

The Boer rebellion against the British government occurs, and John goes to Pretoria to try to extricate Jess, but they become trapped there. He falls in love with her and they enjoy an idyllic existence. Muller, now in a position of power amongst the Boers, gets them a pass to leave, but treacherously attempts to have them killed on the way.

Believing that his plan has been successful, Muller sets about persuading Bessie to marry him and, to put pressure on her, has Silas tried by the Boers as a traitor, telling Bessie that Silas will die unless she marries him. She initially refuses but, eventually, believing John and Jess dead and that it is the only way to save Silas, she reluctantly relents.

Meanwhile, John and Jess, attempting to return to the farm, are captured by the Boers. Jess is allowed to go, returns home to discover the situation and decides that the only way to save Bessie from marriage to Muller is to kill him. Failing to persuade the Hottentot Jantje to do the deed, she stabs Muller herself, then flees. John escapes and goes to a cave Jess and he knew in the past. Jess discovers him there asleep and dies with her head on his chest. He awakes to find her. Silas is freed and he, John and Bessie go to England, where John marries Bessie. Their marriage is a happy one, but John cannot forget Jess.

Colonel Quaritch V.C.: A Tale of Country Life (1888)

Quaritch is a retired soldier who goes to live in a house in East Anglia bequeathed to him by an aunt. He meets Squire de la Molle and his daughter Ida. The squire owns an ancestral pile in or near which, legend records, one of his ancestors buried a great treasure. Lawyer Quest, who is being blackmailed by his legal wife Edith from whom he is separated, is living with Belle, generally believed to be his wife, and who imagines he is unfaithful. Quest learns that Belle, in turn, is having an affair with Edward Cossey, the handsome heir to a banking empire.

The bank decides to foreclose on the mortgages on Squire de la Molle's property. Quest is instructed to inform the squire and sees the opportunity for revenge on Belle by suggesting to Ida that she should seek help from Cossey. She does so, and he agrees to take on the mortgages on condition that she consent to marry him if he should ask. Feeling it is her duty to redeem her father's financial position, Ida agrees.

Quaritch falls in love with Ida and asks her to marry him. She is well disposed towards him but declines because of her understanding with Cossey, who takes Ida up on her promise and their engagement is announced. Quest threatens Cossey that he will cite him as co-respondent in a divorce case unless Cossey gives him the squire's mortgages.

Belle learns from Ida that she and Cossey are engaged and, in her jealousy, Belle shoots Cossey, who is injured but survives. Quest, now the holder of the squire's mortgages, informs the squire that he intends to foreclose. Ida decides to cancel her engagement to Cossey because he no longer owns the mortgages. But when his father dies and he inherits a vast fortune, Cossey renews his assault on Ida through her father. She wavers between duty to her father and her love for Quaritch.

Meanwhile, the squire's faithful servant George, who has learned of the existence of Edith, is determined to exploit the knowledge to save the squire's estate. George goes to London and fetches her back to confront Quest. Edith denounces him publicly and then sets off to return to London. Quest boards the same train, intending to kill her and, in a struggle, they fall together out of the door into a deep river and drown.

Upon Quest's death the mortgages revert to Cossey, who calls them in with the hope of persuading Ida to marry him. She eventually resolves to do so. At the eleventh hour Quaritch unravels a coded paper documenting the whereabouts of the treasure and succeeds in locating it. The squire's estates are saved, and Ida marries Quaritch.

Beatrice (1890)

Beatrice Granger, the daughter of a vicar, is beautiful, gloomy and reflective. She finds herself marooned on a beach with Geoffrey Bingham, a barrister married to Honoria, a cold and materialistic woman, and they try to escape in a canoe only to encounter a fierce storm. Beatrice saves Geoffrey's life and they are pulled out of the sea and recover. They begin to fall in love.

Owen Davies, a rich and undemonstrative man, loves Beatrice and asks her to marry him. She declines. Beatrice's sister Elizabeth, who wants to marry Davies, primarily for his money, realizes that Beatrice loves Geoffrey and aims to exploit this to discredit her with Davies so that she can marry him herself.

Geoffrey returns to the bar in London, wins an important case and enhances his reputation and his financial standing. He becomes a member of Parliament. Beatrice's impoverished father, at the prompting of Elizabeth, borrows money from Geoffrey and invites him to stay for a few days.

Geoffrey and Beatrice admit to each other that they are in love. She sleepwalks into his bedroom, and he returns her to her own room, which is shared with Elizabeth, who sees what has transpired. Elizabeth writes an anonymous letter to Honoria describing these events, and Honoria writes to Beatrice threatening her and Geoffrey with scandal if she does not break off all communication with him. They part.

Geoffrey subsequently writes to Beatrice asking her to elope. She declines because she does not want him to ruin his reputation and career. Davies proposes to Beatrice in front of her family. Elizabeth denounces her for her visit to Geoffrey's room. Nevertheless, Davies still wants to marry her and threatens to ruin Geoffrey if she refuses. Beatrice prevaricates. She decides that the only way out is suicide.

She travels to London to see Geoffrey once more as he participates in a debate in the House of Commons, but she does not speak to him. Thereafter she drowns herself while canoeing. Geoffrey is devastated. Shortly afterwards he learns that he has become a rich baronet and been offered a senior post in the government. Honoria dies in a fire. But although Geoffrey is now both rich and free he has lost Beatrice.

Joan Haste (1895)

Joan Haste is a village girl with some education and a breadth of imagination and sensibility, and in this she is different from her fellows. Born of an unknown father and a mother who is now dead she has been brought up by a rough and unscrupulous aunt who runs the village public house. Mystery surrounds the funding of Joan's education in a modest boarding school. She is courted by Samuel Rock, a Dissenter for whom she has no feelings.

She encounters Captain Henry Graves by a ruined abbey. Henry gave up his naval career when called home to attend to the depressed state of the family fortune. It is expected of him that he will marry Emma, heiress and daughter of Mr Levinger, his father's mysterious friend, who holds the mortgages on the Graves family property.

Henry falls from a tower at the abbey and is badly injured. Joan saves his life, nurses him back to health, and falls in love with him. After they have had sexual relations, Henry promises to marry her. Emma Levinger, upset by Henry's accident, confesses that she loves him. Henry's sister Ellen takes the lead in pushing Henry to marry Emma to save the family fortune. At the urging of Levinger, who also wants Emma to marry Henry, Joan's aunt tries to coerce her into marrying Rock. She refuses. Henry's father tries on his deathbed to extract from him a promise that he will marry Emma; Henry declines and says that he is promised to Joan. His father dies, cursing them.

Joan realizes that to marry Henry will ruin him, and she determines to go away. She talks to Levinger, who administers a fund set up for her by her late father, and he assists her to start a new life as shop girl in London, where she lodges with the kindly Mrs Bird.

Joan finds herself pregnant, and falls dangerously ill after glimpsing Henry. Mrs Bird alerts Joan's aunt and Levinger about her illness. She also writes to Henry telling him of Joan's situation and including a letter that Joan wrote to him when she was delirious, expressing her love for him. Henry, who has been inclined towards marrying Emma, decides to marry Joan and writes to her to this effect. His mother goes to see Joan without his knowledge to persuade her to reject Henry in the interests of his family. Joan eventually agrees and writes in this vein to Henry. Rock travels to London to see Joan, and she agrees to marry him in order to choke off any temptation to marry Henry. When Henry learns of Joan's marriage, he feels shame and anger towards her, and marries Emma. Joan gives birth to a daughter, who dies shortly after.

Levinger, on his deathbed, sends for Joan and tells her that she is his only legitimate daughter, and that Emma is illegitimate. Joan meets Henry and tells him all. Rock has spied on the meeting and, mad with jealousy, announces that he intends to kill Henry. Joan decides to save Henry by impersonating him and drawing Rock's fire. Mistaking her for Henry, Rock shoots her, and she dies in Henry's arms.

Dr Therne (1898)

James Therne, the narrator, is from a family of doctors. When his parents die, he travels to Mexico where he meets his eventual wife, Emma. They narrowly escape death from bandits and flee to Emma's uncle's hacienda only to find it and the nearby village ravaged by smallpox. Therne persuades himself that he cannot be of any practical use, so they return to England and marry.

Therne sets up in practice at Dunchester and finds himself in competition with Sir John Bell, previously assistant to his father and now jealous of Therne's expertise. Bell tries to sabotage Therne's practice but makes a blunder in a case in which Therne's diagnosis is correct. Therne's wife, Emma, is attended in childbirth by Bell, contracts puerperal fever and dies. Therne unwittingly passes this fever on to Lady Colford, a rich patient who also dies. Her husband prosecutes Therne, and Bell gives false evidence to inculpate him.

A rich tradesman, Stephen Strong, a Radical and an anti-vaccinationist, goes bail for him. Therne is acquitted, but Colford threatens to bring a civil suit to ruin him. Therne decides to commit suicide and prepares poison, but Strong dissuades him. Therne becomes associated with the anti-vaccinationists and accepts money from them. He privately believes in vaccination but declines to say so publicly, since to do so would be to lose his livelihood.

Strong persuades Therne to stand for Parliament for Dunchester as a Radical. It is essential in this context that he appears wholeheartedly to support the cause of anti-vaccination, so he decides not have his own daughter vaccinated. He is elected. Strong dies of a heart attack. Thereafter Therne is supported financially by Mrs Strong and, when she dies, he inherits her wealth. Under pressure from the Radicals the government make concessions to the ant-vaccionationists.

Therne's daughter Jane falls in love with Merchison, a poor doctor and a convinced vaccionationist. Smallpox strikes Dunchester and Jane comes into contact with the disease, Merchison wants to vaccinate her but she refuses out of respect for her father. She contracts smallpox. Therne vaccinates himself and is seen doing so by Jane. She reproaches him but eventually forgives him. She dies. Merchison publicly exposes Therne as a hypocrite.

Stella Fregelius (1904)

Morris Monk is an inventor. His father, whose financial ventures are unsuccessful, is keen that Morris should marry his cousin Mary, whose own father, a rich businessman, is also in favour of the match. Morris, who is fond of Mary, whom he has known since childhood, proposes to her and she accepts.

Morris learns that Stella Fregelius, daughter of the local pastor, is missing after a shipwreck, and he sails out to rescue her. She and her father, who was injured in the shipwreck, move into Morris's home to recuperate. Morris and Stella grow spiritually close, but their relationship has no sexual content. Mary is meanwhile in France looking after her sick father. Morris thinks of going to see her but, under the influence of Stella, he changes his mind.

Morris's father observes his son's close relationship with Stella and upbraids him, reminding him that his uncle's will connects his marriage to Mary and the remitting of his father's debts. Mindful of his duty to his family, Morris resolves to marry Mary despite his feelings for Stella.

Stella decides to go away to avoid complications, and she and Morris meet in a ruined church to say goodbye. She encourages him to draw comfort from the eternal life they will share after death. After Morris has left, Stella remains and falls asleep near the altar. A fierce storm blows up, and the church, with Stella in it, is swept out to sea.

Morris confesses to Mary his close relationship with Stella. But he cannot prevent himself from using every available means to attempt to speak to her spirit. Finally, she appears to him. Thereafter his obsession becomes worse and he eventually dies in the process of trying once more to communicate with her.

The Way of the Spirit (1906)

The youthful Rupert Ullershaw, cousin and heir of Lord Devine, is having an affair with Devine's wife, Clara. Devine discovers the affair and urges Clara to commit suicide. Rupert, devastated by the experience, confides in his mother. She advises sexual renunciation.

Eleven years later, in Egypt as an army colonel, Rupert is asked to return home by his sick mother. Devine is keen that Rupert should marry his cousin Edith, and he advises her to encourage Rupert. Eventually Rupert falls in love with her, but she has no feelings for him, loving their cousin Dick, who is dissolute and calculating. Rupert and Edith get married, but three hours later Rupert goes off to Egypt on a secret and dangerous mission for which his candidacy has been advanced by the scheming Dick.

Rupert encounters the witch-like mystic Bakhita and the beautiful Mea. He allows them to join his party to protect them from Ibrahim, Sheik of the Sweet Wells, who wants Mea for his harem, and in doing so compromises the success of his mission. In a fight with Ibrahim's soldiers, Rupert is captured and mutilated after refusing to acknowledge Islam, but he is saved from death and nursed by Mea, who loves him and wants to marry him. He declines on the grounds that he is already married.

Rupert returns to England intending to be reunited with Edith, having promised Mea that should his hopes and love come to nothing he will return to her. He arrives home to find that he is disgraced and presumed dead. Edith rejects him because he is mutilated. He contemplates suicide, but a vision of Mea makes him recollect his promise to her. He returns to her but once more insists, although he now hates Edith, that his marriage vows prevent them from having a sexual relationship.

Edith is prevented from marrying Dick because she now knows that Rupert is alive and begins to wonder whether she might not be well advised to return to him. She goes to Egypt accompanied by Dick, and presses Rupert to return to her. Rupert asks Mea what he should do, and she advises him to agree. Dick, who remains jealous of Rupert, arranges for him to catch the plague. Rupert dies, and Mea elects to do the same so that they can be reunited in death.

Love Eternal (1918)

The independent-minded Isobel Blake is born to rich parents of a loveless marriage. Godfrey Knight is the son of the rector of the living owned by John Blake, Isobel's businessman father. Isobel and Godfrey are close.

Godfrey is sent to Switzerland by his father to learn French and to get him away from the free-thinking Isobel. On the journey to Switzerland, where he is to lodge with Pasteur Boiset, his wife and their pretty daughter Juliette, he meets the middle-aged but still attractive Edith Ogilvy. He subsequently attends seances with a group of Edith's associates, led by the malevolent Madame Riennes, and it is discovered that he is a medium. Madame Riennes attempts to establish a hold over him, but she is defeated by the intervention of Pasteur Boiset. Edith dies of consumption, leaving Godfrey a significant amount of money.

Isobel writes to Godfrey but her letter is intercepted and retained by his father. Meanwhile, Juliette is encouraged by her mother to try to appeal to Godfrey, but they soon realize they do not love each other.

Godfrey returns to England and resumes his close relationship with Isobel. They intend to marry, but their fathers collude in opposition, and they decide on a separation until they come of age.

Godfrey joins the army, is subsequently wounded in the Great War and by chance is nursed by Isobel. Both of their fathers are now dead, and they marry. Godfrey is posted to East Africa and badly injured again. He learns that Isobel has been killed in England during a Zeppelin raid, and he dies to join her in eternal love in an afterlife.

Mary of Marion Isle (1929)

Andrew West, a socialist with progressive views, is the nephew of the rich Lord Atterton. He works in Whitechapel for the Radical Dr Watson and is in love with Watson's daughter Rose, who is weak and materialistic. He proposes but she puts him off, and they agree to wait a year before considering marriage. Dr Somerville Black, a rich widower and an associate of Dr Watson, is also attracted by Rose.

Andrew goes to Egypt, accompanying his sick cousin Algernon, who dies there. He returns to England to find his uncle has died and he has inherited the title. However, his uncle, disliking him and blaming him for Algernon's death, has left most of his fortune to Clara, Andrew's cousin. She offers Andrew half, but he declines. He discovers that Rose has married Black, and Black discovers that Rose does not love him but married only for his money and position. He offers Andrew the chance to elope with her, but he declines. Andrew confronts Rose with her betrayal; she is remorseful and mortified since he has inherited a title.

Clara determines to marry Andrew and, almost by default, they become engaged and marry, but get on indifferently. They have a daughter, Janet, who dies of diphtheria.

Andrew enters the House of Lords, eventually becoming undersecretary for the colonies, and Clara persuades him to accept the post of governor general of Oceania. On the voyage, their ship strikes an iceberg and sinks. Andrew is thought lost but in fact survives, and he eventually lands on the remote Marion Isle, where he encounters Mary, herself shipwrecked a long time ago and now half native. They become close, eventually consummate their relationship, and Mary gives birth to a daughter. They send off an albatross with a message strapped to its leg in the hope of rescue, but later regret having done so because they are loath to be rescued from their happy life.

A ship arrives, with a rescue party led by Clara, and Mary decides to kill herself rather than ruin Andrew's reputation. Before she can do so, however, a small boat carrying Clara ashore is caught in a storm and Mary abandons her suicidal intentions in an unsuccessful attempt to rescue her. Clara drowns, and Andrew and Mary resolve to lead the rest of their lives together on the island.

NOTES

Introduction

1. Wendy Katz, *Rider Haggard and the Fiction of Empire: A Critical Study of British Imperial Fiction* (Cambridge: Cambridge University Press, 1987), 33.
2. H. Rider Haggard, *The Days of My Life: An Autobiography*, 2 vols. (London: Longman, Green, 1926), 2: 85–86.
3. H. Rider Haggard, *She* (London: Longmans, Green, 1887), 186. After the initial reference in each chapter, subsequent references to Haggard's novels and romances will be given in parentheses.
4. Lilias Rider Haggard, *The Cloak That I Left* (London: Hodder and Stoughton, 1951), 31–32.
5. Ibid., 21.
6. Sir John Kotze, *Biographical Memoirs and Reminiscences* (Capetown: Maskew Miller, 1940), vol. 1: 487–88. Quoted by D. S. Higgins, *Rider Haggard: The Great Storyteller* (London: Cassell, 1981), 33.
7. Morton Cohen, *Rider Haggard: His Life and Works* (London: Hutchinson, 1960), 82.
8. D. S. Higgins, *Rider Haggard: The Great Storyteller* (London: Cassell, 1981).
9. Lindy Stiebel, *Imagining Africa: Landscape in H. Rider Haggard's African Romances* (Westport: Greenwood, 2001), 86.
10. Norman Etherington, *Rider Haggard* (Boston: Twayne, 1984), 27, 119.
11. Norman Etherington, 'Rider Haggard, Imperialism and the Layered Personality', *Victorian Studies*, 22 (1978): 71–87 (83).
12. Etherington, *Rider Haggard*, 56, 54.

Chapter One The Sexual Imperative

1. D. S. Higgins, *Rider Haggard: The Great Storyteller* (London: Cassell, 1981), 70.
2. H. Rider Haggard, *King Solomon's Mines* (1885; London: Cassell, 1887), 9.
3. H. Rider Haggard, 'My First Book: Dawn', *The Idler* 3 (1893): 279–91 (283).
4. Ibid., 284.
5. Elaine Showalter, *Sexual Anarchy: Gender and Culture at the Fin de Siecle* (London: Bloomsbury, 1991), 7.
6. Peter Gay, *The Bourgeois Experience: Victoria to Freud* (New York: Oxford University Press, 1984), 1: 175.
7. Michael Mason, *The Making of Victorian Sexuality* (Oxford: Oxford University Press, 1995), 178.
8. Sally Ledger, *The New Woman: Fiction and Feminism at the Fin de Siecle* (Manchester: Manchester University Press, 1997), 1.
9. Mason, *The Making of Victorian Sexuality*, 7.
10. Roy Porter and Leslie Hall, *The Facts of Life: The Creation of Sexual Knowledge in Britain 1650–1950* (New Haven and London: Yale University Press, 1995), 153, 133, 132.
11. John Holmes, *Dante Gabriel Rossetti and the Late Victorian Sonnet Sequence: Sexuality, Belief and the Self* (Aldershot: Ashgate, 2005), 83, 85.
12. Shannon Young, 'Myths of Castration: Freud's *Eternal Feminine* and Rider Haggard's *She*', *The Victorian Newsletter* 108 (2005): 21–30 (22).
13. Showalter, *Sexual Anarchy*, 6, 10.

14 Ledger, *The New Woman*, 6.
15 Carolyn Dever, 'Everywhere and Nowhere: Sexuality in Victorian Fiction', in *A Concise Companion to the Victorian Novel*, edited by Francis O'Gorman (Oxford: Blackwell, 2005), 156–79 (171).
16 Peter Keating, *The Haunted Study: A Social History of the English Novel 1875–1914* (London: Secker & Warburg, 1989), 121.
17 Norman Etherington, *Rider Haggard* (Boston: Twayne, 1984), 37.
18 Sigmund Freud, *The Interpretation of Dreams* (1899; London: Penguin, 1991), 586–87.
19 Young, 'Myths of Castration', 22.
20 Etherington, *Rider Haggard*, 38.
21 H. Rider Haggard, *Allan Quatermain* (1887; London: Longmans, Green, 1893), 6.
22 Keating, *The Haunted Study*, 22.
23 Etherington, *Rider Haggard*, 54.
24 Dever, 'Everywhere and Nowhere', 157.
25 Keating, *The Haunted Study*, 244, 252.
26 George Gissing, 'The New Censorship of Literature', *Pall Mall Gazette* 40 (1884): 2.
27 Keating, *The Haunted Study*, 270, 281.
28 Dever, 'Everywhere and Nowhere', 157.
29 Max Saunders, *Self Impression: Life Writing, Autobiografiction, and the Forms of Modern Literature* (New York: Oxford University Press, 2010), 1.
30 H. Rider Haggard, *The Days of My Life: An Autobiography*, 2 vols. (London: Longman, Green, 1926), 2: 256–57.
31 H. Rider Haggard, 'About Fiction', *Contemporary Review* 51 (1887): 172–80 (176).

Chapter Two The Origins of Haggard's Fictional Writing

1 Thomas Hardy, 'General Preface to the Novels and Poems' in *The Works of Thomas Hardy in Prose and Verse*, Wessex Edition, Prose (London: Macmillan, 1912), 1: vii.
2 Simon Gatrell, 'The Collected Editions of Hardy, James and Meredith, with Some Concluding Thoughts on the Desirability of a Taxonomy of the Book' in *The Culture of Collected Editions*, edited by Andrew Nash (Basingstoke: Palgrave Macmillan, 2003), 87.
3 Kenneth Graham, *English Criticism of the Novel 1865–1900* (Oxford: Oxford University Press, 1965), 66.
4 Peter Keating, *The Haunted Study: A Social History of the English Novel 1875–1914* (London: Secker & Warburg, 1989), 345.
5 Graham, *English Criticism of the Novel*, 61.
6 R. L. Stevenson, 'A Gossip on Romance', *Longman's Magazine* 1 (1882): 69–79 (73).
7 Ibid., 72.
8 H. Rider Haggard, 'About Fiction', *Contemporary Review* 51 (1887): 172–80 (173).
9 Wendy Katz, *Rider Haggard and the Fiction of Empire: A Critical Study of British Imperial Fiction* (Cambridge: Cambridge University Press, 1987), 30.
10 Elaine Showalter, *Sexual Anarchy: Gender and Culture at the Fin de Siecle* (London: Bloomsbury, 1991), 79.
11 Stephen Arata, *Fictions of Loss in the Victorian Fin de Siecle* (Cambridge: Cambridge University Press, 1996), 80, 89.
12 Haggard, 'About Fiction', 177.
13 Ibid., 178.
14 Robert Fraser, *Victorian Quest Romance: Stevenson, Haggard, Kipling and Conan Doyle* (Plymouth: Northcote House, 1998), 14, 77.
15 Walter Besant, *The Art of Fiction* (London: Chatto & Windus, 1884), 10.
16 Henry James, 'The Art of Fiction', *Longman's Magazine* 4 (1884): 502–31 (503).
17 R. L. Stevenson, 'A Humble Remonstrance', *Longman's Magazine* 5 (1884–85): 139–47 (143).

18 Haggard, 'About Fiction', 175, 176, 179.
19 'The Modern Novel', *Saturday Review* 54 (1882): 633–34 (634).
20 George Saintsbury, 'The Present State of the Novel', *Fortnightly Review* 48 (1887): 410–17 (415).
21 Andrew Lang, 'Realism and Romance', *Contemporary Review* 52 (1887): 683–93 (688, 692).
22 H. Rider Haggard, *The Days of My Life: An Autobiography*, 2 vols. (London: Longman, Green, 1926), 1: 219–20.
23 Lilias Rider Haggard, *The Cloak That I Left* (London: Hodder and Stoughton, 1951), 115.
24 Haggard, *The Days of My Life*, 1: 220.
25 D. E. Whatmore, *H. Rider Haggard: A Bibliography* (London: Mansell, 1987), 8, 12, 14.
26 Haggard, *The Days of My Life*, 2: 84–85.
27 Charles Longman. Letter to H. Rider Haggard, 6 January 1907, Huntington Collection, MS HM 43641.
28 Katz, *Rider Haggard and the Fiction of Empire*, 44.
29 Haggard, *The Days of My Life*, 1: 265.
30 Ibid., 1: 13.
31 Morton Cohen, *Rider Haggard: His Life and Works* (London: Hutchinson, 1960), 256.
32 Ibid., 268–69.
33 Haggard, *The Days of My Life*, 2: 84.
34 H. Rider Haggard, *Stella Fregelius* (London: Longmans, Green, 1904).
35 H. Rider Haggard, *The Way of the Spirit* (London: Hutchinson, 1906).
36 H. Rider Haggard, *Love Eternal* (London: Cassell, 1918).
37 D. S. Higgins, ed., *The Private Diaries of Sir Henry Rider Haggard* (London: Cassell, 1980), 178–79.
38 Haggard, *The Days of My Life*, 1: 279.
39 H. Rider Haggard. Letter to A. P. Watt, 5 December 1899, Huntington Collection, MS HM 43578.
40 H. Rider Haggard. Letter to A. P. Watt, 10 August 1900, Huntington Collection, MS HM 43581.
41 H. Rider Haggard, *Doctor Therne* (London: Longmans, Green, 1898), vii–viii.
42 Richard Reeve, 'Henry Rider Haggard's Debt to Anthony Trollope: *Dr Therne* and *Dr Thorne*', *Notes and Queries*, 261, no. 2 (2016): 274–78.
43 H. Rider Haggard, 'My First Book: Dawn', *The Idler* 3 (1893): 279–91 (285).
44 H. Rider Haggard, 'Books Which Have Influenced Me', *The British Weekly* 2 (1887): 53.
45 Haggard, 'About Fiction', 172.
46 Ibid., 173.
47 Ibid., 172.
48 Haggard, *The Days of My Life*, 1: 264–65.
49 Cohen, *Rider Haggard*, 125.
50 'The Culture of the Horrible: Mr Haggard's Stories', *Church Quarterly Review* 25 (1888): 389–411 (390).
51 Ibid., 396.
52 William Watson, 'The Fall of Fiction, *Fortnightly Review* 50 (1888): 324–36 (325, 329, 336).
53 Cohen, *Rider Haggard*, 136.
54 Lilias Haggard, *The Cloak That I Left*, 130.
55 Haggard, *The Days of My Life*, 2: 85.
56 Ibid., 1: xxii.
57 Ibid., 2: 92–93.
58 Cohen, *Rider Haggard*, 256.
59 Haggard, *The Days of My Life*, 1: xxiii.
60 Lang, 'Realism and Romance', 691–92.
61 Higgins, *The Private Diaries of Sir Henry Rider Haggard*, 152.
62 Cohen, *Rider Haggard*, 180.

63 Ibid.
64 Cohen, *Rider Haggard*, 204.
65 Haggard, *The Days of My Life*, 2: 132.
66 Ibid., 2: 140.
67 Ibid., 2: 131.
68 Ibid., 1: xxiv.
69 Cohen, *Rider Haggard*, 246.
70 Haggard, *The Days of My Life*, 2: 216.
71 H. Rider Haggard. Letter to Andrew C. P. Haggard, 22 June 1903, Columbia Collection, MS #0532.
72 Haggard, *The Days of My Life*, 1: xxii.
73 Ibid., 2: 13.
74 Lilias Haggard, *The Cloak That I Left*, 29.
75 Haggard, *The Days of My Life*, 1: 5, 28–29, 31.
76 Ibid., 1: 20–21.
77 Lilias Haggard, *The Cloak That I Left*, 70.
78 Ibid., 69.
79 Haggard, *The Days of My Life*, 1: 21, 22.
80 *Mr Meeson's Will, Nada the Lily, The People of the Mist, Montezuma's Daughter, Heart of the World, Lysbeth, The Ghost Kings, The Yellow God, The Lady of Blossholme, Morning Star, Red Eve, Marie, Child of Storm, When the World Shook, Queen of the Dawn, Moon of Israel.*
81 Victoria Manthorpe, *Children of the Empire: The Victorian Haggards* (London: Victor Gollanz, 1996), 20.
82 Ella Doveton, Journal 1841, Rhodes House Library Oxford, MSS.Brit.Emp.s465 (11).
83 Ella Haggard, *Myra or The Rose of the East* (London: Longman, Brown, Green, Longmans and Roberts, 1857).
84 Ella Doveton, Journals 1837–1839, Rhodes House Library Oxford, MSS.Brit.Emp.s465 (11).
85 Ella Haggard, *Life and Its Author: An Essay in Verse* (London and Norwich: E. H. Jarrold, 1890).
86 H. Rider Haggard, *Cleopatra* (London: Longmans, Green, 1889).
87 Haggard, *The Days of My Life*, 1: 271.
88 Lilias Haggard, *The Cloak That I Left*, 135.
89 Rider Haggard, *In Memoriam*, Foreword to Ella Haggard, *Life and Its Author*.
90 Haggard, *The Days of My Life*, 1: 24.
91 Lilias Haggard, *The Cloak That I Left*, 148.
92 Manthorpe, *Children of the Empire*, 41.
93 Ibid., 21.
94 H. Rider Haggard, *The Brethren* (London: Cassell, 1904).
95 H. Rider Haggard. Letter to Ella Maddison Green, 22 June 1875, Columbia Collection, MS #0532.
96 Higgins, *The Private Diaries of Sir Henry Rider Haggard*, 218.
97 D. S. Higgins, *Rider Haggard: The Great Storyteller* (London: Cassell, 1981), 14.
98 Haggard, *The Days of My Life*, 1: 42.
99 Manthorpe, *Children of the Empire*, 82.
100 H. Rider Haggard. Letter to Ella Maddison Green, 22 June 1875, Columbia Collection, MS #0532.
101 Higgins, *Rider Haggard*, 15.
102 Lilias Haggard, *The Cloak That I Left*, 69.
103 Haggard, *The Days of My Life*, 1: 116.
104 Ibid., 1: 21.
105 Lilias Haggard, *The Cloak That I Left*, 72.
106 Higgins, *Rider Haggard*, 34.

107 Ibid., 62.
108 Manthorpe, *Children of the Empire*, 149.
109 Higgins, *Rider Haggard*, 165.
110 Lilias Haggard, *The Cloak That I Left*, 191.
111 Higgins, *Rider Haggard*, 188.
112 Lilias Haggard, *The Cloak That I Left*, 202.
113 Haggard, *The Days of My Life*, 1: 43.
114 Lilias Rider Haggard, *The Cloak That I Left*, 73.
115 Haggard, *The Days of My Life*, 1: 116.
116 Manthorpe, *Children of the Empire*, 89.
117 Stephen Coan, ed., *H.Rider Haggard: The Diary of an African Journey, 1914* (London: C. Hurst, 2001), 8, 38.
118 Manthorpe, *Children of the Empire*, 89.
119 Lilias Haggard, *The Cloak That I Left*, 85.
120 Haggard, *The Days of My Life*, 1: 141.
121 Manthorpe, *Children of the Empire*, 91, 92, 92–93.
122 H. Rider Haggard. Letter to his brother William, 21 December 1879, British Library, MSS Sur/RP/2804. Permission to quote from this source has kindly been granted by Mrs N. Cheyne, the copyright holder.
123 Manthorpe, *Children of the Empire*, 100.
124 Ibid., 229.
125 Lilias Haggard, *The Cloak That I Left*, 156.
126 Haggard, *The Days of My Life*, 2: 47, 43.
127 Ibid., 2: 251, 256.
128 Coan, ed., *Rider Haggard: The Diary of an African Journey*, 131.
129 Henry Rider Haggard. Rough Diary February – May 1914, Norfolk Records Office, MC 32/51 478X7. Permission to quote from this source has kindly been granted by Mrs N. Cheyne, the copyright holder.
130 Coan, ed., *Rider Haggard: The Diary of an African Journey*, 131.
131 Lilias Haggard, *The Cloak That I Left*, 89.
132 Ibid., 90.
133 Higgins, *Rider Haggard*, 41.
134 Cohen, *Rider Haggard*, 53.
135 Haggard, *The Days of My Life*, 1: 164.
136 Lilias Haggard, *The Cloak That I Left*, 90.
137 Cohen, *Rider Haggard*, 55.
138 H. Rider Haggard. Letter to his brother William, 21 December 1879, British Library, MSS Sur/RP/2804.
139 Manthorpe, *Children of the Empire*, 93.
140 Lilias Haggard, *The Cloak That I Left*, 91.
141 Manthorpe, *Children of the Empire*, 170.
142 Lilias Haggard, *The Cloak That I Left*, 15.
143 Ibid., 157, 155.
144 Higgins, *Rider Haggard*, 146, 90, 150.
145 Lilias Haggard, *The Cloak That I Left*, 157.
146 H. Rider Haggard. Letters to Agnes Barber, 10 December 1892, Columbia Collection, MS #0532.
147 Lilias Haggard, *The Cloak That I Left*, 190, 202.
148 Ibid., 194.
149 Higgins, *Rider Haggard*, 232.
150 Haggard, *The Days of My Life*, 1: 163.

151 Manthorpe, *Children of the Empire*, 133.
152 Higgins, *Rider Haggard*, 40.
153 H. Rider Haggard. Letters to Agnes Barber, 16 September 1879, Columbia Collection, MS #0532.
154 Ibid., 6 September 1882.
155 Ibid., 10 September 1883.
156 Higgins, *Rider Haggard*, 56–57.
157 Ibid., 89–90.
158 Agnes Barber. Letter to Ella M. Green, 28 December 1885, Rhodes House Library, MSS. Brit.Emp.s.465(2).

Chapter Three The Early Novels (1884–95): Youthful Anger

1 Lyn Pykett, *The Improper Feminine: The Women's Sensation Novel and The New Woman Writing* (London: Routledge, 1992), 5.
2 Morton Cohen, *Rider Haggard: His Life and Works* (London: Hutchinson, 1960), 79.
3 H. Rider Haggard, 'My First Book: *Dawn*', *The Idler* 3 (1893): 279–91 (282).
4 Ibid.
5 Lilias Rider Haggard, *The Cloak That I Left* (London: Hodder and Stoughton, 1951), 119.
6 H. Rider Haggard, *Dawn* (1884: London: Longmans, Green, 1914), 10.
7 H. Rider Haggard. Letter to his brother William, 21 December 1879, British Library, MSS Sur/RP/2804. Permission to quote from this source has kindly been granted by Mrs N. Cheyne, the copyright holder.
8 H. Rider Haggard, *The Days of My Life: An Autobiography*, 2 vols. (London: Longman, Green, 1926), 2: 259, 255.
9 Henry Rider Haggard. The Original Draft of 'Dawn' under the title of 'There Remaineth a Rest', which was never published, Norfolk Records Office, MS 4692/4.
10 D. S. Higgins, *Rider Haggard: The Great Storyteller* (London: Cassell, 1981), 60.
11 Lilias Haggard, *The Cloak That I Left*, 72.
12 Ibid., 120.
13 Haggard, *The Days of My Life*, 1: 42.
14 H. Rider Haggard, *The Witch's Head* (1884; London: Longmans, Green, 1894), 45.
15 H. Rider Haggard, *Beatrice* (1890; London: Longmans, Green, 1903), iv.
16 Lilias Haggard, *The Cloak That I Left*, 156.
17 Pykett, *The Improper Feminine*, 9.
18 Simon Dentith, *Epic and Empire in Nineteenth Century Britain* (Cambridge: Cambridge University Press, 2006), 185.
19 Robin Gilmour, *The Idea of the Gentleman in the Victorian Novel* (London: Allen & Unwin, 1981), 3, 8.
20 Peter Keating, *The Haunted Study: A Social History of the English Novel 1875–1914* (London: Secker & Warburg, 1989), 166–67.
21 Elaine Showalter, *Sexual Anarchy: Gender and Culture at the Fin de Siecle* (London: Bloomsbury, 1991), 19, 21, 38, 145.
22 H. Rider Haggard, *King Solomon's Mines* (1885; London: Cassell, 1887), 123.
23 H. Rider Haggard, *She* (London: Longmans, Green & Co, 1887), 155, 154.
24 Showalter, *Sexual Anarchy*, 149, 145.
25 H. Rider Haggard and Andrew Lang, *The World's Desire* (Longmans, Green, 1890), 191.
26 Showalter, *Sexual Anarchy*, 149.
27 H. Rider Haggard, 'Who Is She?' *Pall Mall Gazette* 45 (1887): 13–14 (13).
28 H. Rider Haggard, *Allan Quatermain* (1887; London: Longmans, Green, 1893), 218.
29 H. Rider Haggard, *Cleopatra* (London: Longmans, Green, 1889), 188.

30 H. Rider Haggard, *Joan Haste* (1895; London: Longmans, Green, 1897), 129–30.
31 Thomas Hardy, *The Return of the Native* (1878; London: Macmillan, 1968), 74.
32 Keating, *The Haunted Study*, 251.
33 Bradley Deane, 'Mummy Fiction and the Occupation of Egypt', *English Literature in Transition 1880–1920* 51, no. 4 (2008): 381–410 (384).
34 H. Rider Haggard, *Colonel Quaritch V. C.* (1888; London: Longmans, Green, 1896), 55.
35 H. Rider Haggard, *Lysbeth* (London: Longmans, Green, 1901), 112.
36 Thomas Hardy, *Desperate Remedies* (London: Macmillan, 1978), 250.
37 Haggard, 'Who Is She?' 14.
38 Shannon Young, 'Myths of Castration: Freud's *Eternal Feminine* and Rider Haggard's *She*, *The Victorian Newsletter* 108 (2005): 21–30 (25).
39 Norman Etherington, *Rider Haggard* (Boston: Twayne, 1984), 89.
40 H. Rider Haggard. Letters to Agnes Barber, 5 August 1883, Columbia Collection, MS #0532.
41 Max Saunders, *'Self Impression: Life Writing, Autobiografiction, and the Forms of Modern Literature* (New York: Oxford University Press, 2010), 175.
42 Lilias Haggard, *The Cloak That I Left*, 73.
43 Authorized Version, John, 19. 2.
44 Haggard, 'Who Is She?' 14.
45 Etherington, *Rider Haggard*, 80.
46 Joseph Kestner, *Masculinity in British Adventure Fiction 1880–1915* (Farnham: Ashgate, 2010), 86.
47 Mary Braddon, *Aurora Floyd* (London: Tinsley Brothers, 1863), 2: 59.
48 Richard Pearson, 'Archaeology and Gothic Desire: Vitality Beyond the Grave in H. Rider Haggard's Ancient Egypt', in *Victorian Gothic*, edited by Ruth Robbins and Julian Wolfreys (London: Palgrave, 2000), 218–44 (236).
49 Ibid., 242.
50 Higgins, *Rider Haggard*, 99.
51 Victoria Manthorpe, *Children of the Empire: The Victorian Haggards* (London: Victor Gollanz, 1996), 92.
52 Gerald Parsons in *Religion in Victorian Britain*, ed. Gerald Parsons (Manchester: Manchester University Press, 1988), 3: 192.
53 Roy Porter and Leslie Hall, *The Facts of Life: The Creation of Sexual Knowledge in Britain 1650–1950* (New Haven and London: Yale University Press, 1995), 153.
54 Parsons, *Religion in Victorian Britain*, 3: 199.
55 Haggard, *The Days of My Life*, 2: 236.
56 H. Rider Haggard, *Red Eve* (London: Hodder & Stoughton, 1911), 89.
57 H. Rider Haggard, *The Ghost Kings* (1908; London: Cassell, 1926), 75, 198.
58 Lilias Haggard, *The Cloak That I Left*, 72.
59 Manthorpe, *Children of the Empire*, 92–93.
60 Pykett, *The Improper Feminine*, 89.
61 H. Rider Haggard, *Montezuma's Daughter* (1893; London: Longmans, Green, 1894), 307.
62 H. Rider Haggard, *Stella Fregelius* (London: Longmans, Green, 1904), 282.
63 Talia Schaffer, *Romance's Rival: Familiar Marriage in Victorian Fiction* (New York: Oxford University Press, 2016), 131.
64 Carolyn Dever, 'Everywhere and Nowhere: Sexuality in Victorian Fiction' in *A Concise Companion to the Victorian Novel*, edited by Francis O'Gorman (Oxford: Blackwell, 2005), 157.
65 Nicola Beauman, *A Very Great Profession: The Woman's Novel 1914–39* (London: Virago, 1983), 94.
66 Etherington, *Rider Haggard*, 85.
67 Higgins, *Rider Haggard*, 146.
68 Manthorpe, *Children of the Empire*, 229.
69 H. Rider Haggard, *Heart of the World* (London: Longmans, Green, 1896), 342.

70 Patrick Brantlinger, 'What is Sensational about the Sensation Novel?' *Nineteenth Century Fiction* 37 (1982): 1–28 (1).
71 Pykett, *The Improper Feminine*, 49, 56, 87.
72 Ellen Wood, *East Lynne* (Ormskirk: Broadview, 2002), 335.
73 Haggard, *The Days of My Life*, 2: 256.

Chapter Four The New Woman, Female Self-Sacrifice and Spirituality (1887–1901)

1 'Mr Rider Haggard's New Story', *Pall Mall Gazette* 45 (15 March 1887): 5.
2 'Novels of the Week', *Athenaeum* 3099 (1887): 375–76 (375).
3 D. S. Higgins, *Rider Haggard: The Great Storyteller* (London: Cassell, 1981), 86.
4 H. Rider Haggard, *The Days of My Life: An Autobiography*, 2 vols. (London: Longman, Green, 1926), 1: 245.
5 Lilias Rider Haggard, *The Cloak That I Left* (London: Hodder and Stoughton, 1951), 128.
6 Haggard, *The Days of My Life*, 1: 265.
7 Higgins, *Rider Haggard*, 88.
8 H. Rider Haggard, *Jess* (Smith, Elder, 1887), 9.
9 H. Rider Haggard. Portrait of Agnes Barber, 16 September 1879, Columbia Collection, MS # 0532.
10 Letters of Agnes Marion Haggard, Rhodes House Library, MSS.Brit.Emp.s.465(8).
11 H. Rider Haggard. Letter to Agnes Barber, 7 July 1882, Columbia Collection, MS # 0532.
12 Ibid., 6 September 1882.
13 Michael Mason, *The Making of Victorian Sexuality* (Oxford: Oxford University Press, 1995), 114, 115.
14 Jane Eldridge Miller, *Rebel Women: Feminism, Modernism and the Edwardian Novel* (London: Virago, 1994), 70.
15 Barbara Leckie, *Culture and Adultery: The Novel, the Newspaper and the Law 1857–1914* (Philadelphia: University of Pennsylvania Press, 1999), 18.
16 Leckie, *Culture and Adultery*, 62, 64.
17 'Novels of the Week', *Athenaeum* 3265 (1890): 669–70 (670).
18 Haggard, *The Days of My Life*, 1: 279, 2: 9–10.
19 Ibid., 2: 13–14.
20 Lilias Haggard, *The Cloak That I Left*, 157.
21 Ibid., 72.
22 Angelique Richardson, *Love and Eugenics in the Late Nineteenth Century* (Oxford: Oxford University Press, 2003), 1, 2, 4.
23 Lyn Pykett, *The Improper Feminine: The Women's Sensation Novel and The New Woman Writing* (London: Routledge, 1992), 153.
24 Peter Keating, *The Haunted Study: A Social History of the English Novel 1875–1914* (London: Secker & Warburg, 1989), 188, 190.
25 Pykett, *The Improper Feminine*, 200.
26 Elaine Showalter, *Sexual Anarchy* (London: Bloomsbury, 1990), 38.
27 Carolyn Christensen Nelson, *A New Woman Reader: Fiction, Articles, Drama of the 1890s* (Letchworth: Broadview, 2001), 184, 195–96, 197.
28 Sally Ledger, *The New Woman: Fiction and Feminism at the Fin de Siecle* (Manchester: Manchester University Press, 1997), 11.
29 Keating, *The Haunted Study*, 189.
30 Richardson, *Love and Eugenics in the Late Nineteenth Century*, 4–5.
31 Ibid.
32 Keating, *The Haunted Study*, 190.

33 H. Rider Haggard, *Dawn* (1884: Longmans, Green, 1914), 87.
34 H. Rider Haggard, *Beatrice* (1890; London: Longmans, Green, 1903), 2.
35 George Egerton, *Keynotes and Discords*, edited by Sally Ledger (London: Continuum, 2006), 92.
36 Richardson, *Love and Eugenics in the Late Nineteenth Century*, 40.
37 Norman Etherington, *Rider Haggard* (Boston: Twayne, 1984), 27.
38 H. Rider Haggard. Letter to his brother Jack, 17 February 1885, British Library, MSS Sur/RP/2804. Permission to quote from this source has kindly been granted by Mrs N. Cheyne, the copyright holder.
39 Showalter, *Sexual Anarchy*, 40.
40 Pykett, *The Improper Feminine*, 137.
41 Gail Cunningham, 'He-Notes: Reconstructing Masculinity' in *The New Woman in Fiction and Fact*, edited by Angelique Richardson and Chris Willis (Basingstoke: Palgrave, 2001), 94–106 (95).
42 H. Rider Haggard, *Heart of the World* (Longmans, Green, 1896), 158.
43 Pykett, *The Improper Feminine*, 158.
44 *The Book of Common Prayer* (Oxford: Oxford University Press, 1900), 258.
45 Carolyn Dever, 'Everywhere and Nowhere: Sexuality in Victorian Fiction' in *A Concise Companion to the Victorian Novel*, edited by Francis O'Gorman (Oxford: Blackwell, 2005), 164–65.
46 Showalter, *Sexual Anarchy*, 180.
47 H. Rider Haggard, *Ayesha* (1905; London: Ward, Lock, 1911), 222.
48 H. Rider Haggard, *The Yellow God* (London: Cassell, 1909), 243.
49 H. Rider Haggard, *Love Eternal* (London: Cassell, 1918), 181.
50 H. Rider Haggard, *She* (London: Longmans, Green, 1887), 201.
51 H. Rider Haggard, *Joan Haste* (1895; London: Longmans, Green, 1897), 129.
52 John Milton, *Paradise Lost*, 1: 1–2 in *The Poetical Works*, ed. Helen Darbishire (Oxford: Oxford University Press, 1967), 1: 5.
53 Diana Wallace, *Sisters and Rivals in British Woman's Fiction 1914–39* (Basingstoke: Macmillan Press, 2000), 183.
54 Sarah Annes Brown, *Devoted Sisters: Representations of the Sister Relationship in Nineteenth British and American Literature* (Aldershot: Aldgate, 2003), 109, 107.
55 Thomas Hardy, *Tess of the D'Urbervilles* (1891; London: Osgood, McIlvaine, 1892), 3: 269.
56 Etherington, *Rider Haggard*, 13–14.
57 Lilias Haggard, *The Cloak That I Left*, 157.
58 Jenny Bourne Taylor and Sally Shuttleworth, *Embodied Selves: An Anthology of Psychological Texts 1830–1890* (Oxford: Clarendon, 1998), 167, 166.
59 Lilias Haggard, *The Cloak That I Left*, 185.
60 'Mr Rider Haggard's New Story', 5.
61 Haggard, *The Days of My Life*, 2: 256.
62 Pykett, *The Improper Feminine*, 7, 8.
63 William Barry, 'The Strike of a Sex', *Quarterly Review* 179 (1894): 289–318.
64 Haggard, *The Days of My Life*, 2: 15.
65 H. Rider Haggard, 'About Fiction', *Contemporary Review* 51 (1887): 172–80 (178).
66 Ledger, *The New Woman*, 11.
67 *The Book of Common Prayer*, 272.
68 Rhoda Broughton, *Cometh Up As A Flower* (London: Richard Bentley, 1867), 2: 291.

Chapter Five Spiritual Love and Sexual Renunciation (1899–1908)

1 Lilias Rider Haggard, *The Cloak That I Left* (London: Hodder and Stoughton, 1951), 136.
2 H. Rider Haggard, *The Days of My Life: An Autobiography*, 2 vols. (London: Longman, Green, 1926), 1: 24.

3 Lilias Haggard, *The Cloak That I Left*, 153.
4 Haggard, *The Days of My Life*, 2: 43.
5 Ibid., 2: 44.
6 H. Rider Haggard, *Stella Fregelius* (London: Longmans, Green, 1904), 282.
7 Lilias Haggard, *The Cloak That I Left*, 190.
8 Ibid.
9 D. S. Higgins, *Rider Haggard: The Great Storyteller* (London: Cassell, 1981), 169.
10 Ibid., 198.
11 Ibid., 3, 146.
12 Arthur Conan Doyle, *The History of Spiritualism* (London: Cassell, 1926), 1:1.
13 Joseph McCabe, *Spiritualism: A Popular History from 1847* (London: T. Fisher Unwin, 1920), 9.
14 McCabe, *Spiritualism*, 11–12.
15 Alex Owen, *The Darkened Room: Women, Power, and Spiritualism in Late Victorian England* (Chicago: University of Chicago Press, 2004), 1.
16 Ibid., 23.
17 Michael Wheeler, *Heaven, Hell and the Victorians* (Cambridge: Cambridge University Press, 1994), 121.
18 Frank Podmore, *Modern Spiritualism: A History and A Criticism*, (London: Methuen, 1902), 1: 15.
19 Owen, *The Darkened Room*, 21.
20 McCabe, *Spiritualism*, 148.
21 Podmore, *Modern Spiritualism*, 2: 163.
22 McCabe, *Spiritualism*, 172.
23 Haggard, *The Days of My Life*, 1: 38–39.
24 Ibid., 1: 41.
25 Ibid., 2: 250.
26 Wendy Katz, *Rider Haggard and the Fiction of Empire: A Critical Study of British Imperial Fiction* (Cambridge: Cambridge University Press, 1987), 118.
27 Christine Ferguson, *Determined Spirits: Eugenics, Heredity and Racial Regeneration in Anglo-American Spiritualist Writing 1848–1930* (Edinburgh: Edinburgh University Press, 2012), 183.
28 Haggard, *The Days of My Life*, 2: 250.
29 Ibid., 1: 41.
30 Morton Cohen, *Rider Haggard: His Life and Works* (London: Hutchinson, 1960), 111.
31 Haggard, *The Days of My Life*, 1: 254.
32 H. Rider Haggard. Letter to W. T. Horton, 14 February 1899, Reading University Special Collections. MS 289. Permission to quote from this source has kindly been granted by Mrs N. Cheyne, the copyright holder.
33 Haggard, *The Days of My Life*, 2: 259.
34 H. Rider Haggard. Letter to A. P. Watt, 5 December 1899, Huntington Library, HM 43578.
35 'Stella Fregelius', *Times Literary Supplement* 108 (1904): 36.
36 Norman Etherington, *Rider Haggard* (Boston: Twayne, 1984), 35.
37 Lilias Haggard, *The Cloak That I Left*, 190.
38 Higgins, *Rider Haggard*, 183.
39 H. Rider Haggard, *Allan's Wife* (1889; London: Spencer Blackett, 1895), 160.
40 Haggard, *The Days of My Life*, 2: 85–86.
41 H. Rider Haggard, *The Way of the Spirit* (London: Hutchinson, 1906), 10.
42 Haggard, *The Days of My Life*, 2: 159.
43 Morton Cohen, ed., *Rudyard Kipling to Rider Haggard: The Record of a Friendship* (London: Hutchinson, 1965), 56.
44 Ecclesiastes, 2. 9–10.
45 H. Rider Haggard, 'Books Which Have Influenced Me', *British Weekly* 2, no. 3 (1887): 53.
46 Lilias Haggard, *The Cloak That I Left*, 184.

47 Charles Longman. Letter to H. Rider Haggard, 30 January 1905, Huntington Library, HM 43640.
48 Lilias Haggard, *The Cloak That I Left*, 184–85.
49 'The Way of the Spirit', *Times Literary Supplement* 217 (1906): 84.
50 'The Way of the Spirit', *Saturday Review* 101 (1906): 432–33 (433).
51 Higgins, *Rider Haggard*, 187–88.
52 Sally Ledger, *The New Woman: Fiction and Feminism at the Fin de Siecle* (Manchester: Manchester University Press, 1997), 186.
53 Elaine Showalter, *Sexual Anarchy* (London: Bloomsbury, 1990), 19.
54 William R. Greg, 'Why are Women Redundant?' *National Review* 14 (1862): 434–60 (436).
55 Showalter, *Sexual Anarchy*, 20, 27–31.
56 Ibid, 21.
57 Lilias Haggard, *The Cloak That I Left*, 93.
58 H. Rider Haggard, *Ayesha* (1905; London: Ward, Lock, 1911), 370.
59 Lilias Haggard, *The Cloak That I Left*, 24.
60 H. Rider Haggard, *Swallow* (1899; London: Longmans, Green, 1916), 320.
61 Haggard, *The Days of My Life*, 2: 256.
62 Emanuel Swedenborg, *Conjugial Love* (1768; London: The Swedenborg Society, 1910), 39.
63 H. Rider Haggard, *Pearl Maiden* (London: Longmans, Green, 1903), 121.
64 H. Rider Haggard, *The Ghost Kings* (1908; London: Cassell, 1926), 197.
65 H. Rider Haggard, *The Brethren* (London: Cassell, 1904), 117.
66 Higgins, *Rider Haggard*, 3.
67 Janet Oppenheim, *The Other World: Spiritualism and Psychical Research in England 1850–1914* (Cambridge: Cambridge University Press, 1985), 162.
68 H. Rider Haggard, *Benita* (1906, London: Cassell, 1926), 205.
69 G. Barlow, *The Gospel of Humanity; or, the Connection between Spirituality and Modern Thought* (London: James Burns, 1876), 11.
70 G. Barlow, *The Higher Love: A Plea for a Nobler Conception of Human Love* (London: Roxburghe Press, 1895), 5.
71 Laurie Garrison, *Science, Sexuality and Sensation Novels: Pleasures of the Senses* (Basingstoke: Palgrave Macmillan, 2011), 105.
72 D. G. Rossetti, *Collected Poetry and Prose*, edited by Jerome McGann (New Haven and London: Yale University Press, 2003), 130.
73 L. Oliphant, *Scientific Religion* (Edinburgh: Blackwood, 1888), 336.
74 Barlow, *The Higher Love*, 58–59.
75 Anne Stiles, *Popular Fiction and Brain Science in the Late Nineteenth Century* (Cambridge: Cambridge University Press, 2012), 162.
76 P. B. Shelley, *The Major Works*, edited by Zachary Leader and Michael O'Neil (Oxford: Oxford University Press, 2003), 573–74.
77 Marie Corelli, *The Life Everlasting: A Reality of Romance* (London: Methuen, 1911), 268.
78 Oliphant, *Scientific Religion*, 327.
79 Florence Marryat, *There Is No Death* (London: Kegan, Paul, Trench, Trubner, 1891), 364.
80 Wheeler, *Heaven, Hell and the Victorians*, 5.
81 Robert Buchanan, *The Moment After* (London: William Heinemann, 1890), 212.
82 G. Barlow, *The Marriage Before Death and Other Poems* (London: Remington, 1878), 164.
83 Rhoda Broughton, *Cometh Up As A Flower* (London: Richard Bentley, 1867), 2: 291.
84 Barlow, *The Higher Love*, 38.
85 Swedenborg, *Conjugial Love*, 66.
86 R. Pearsall, *The Worm in the Bud: The World of Victorian Sexuality* (London: Weidenfeld and Nicholson, 1969), 187.
87 Theodore Watts-Dunton, *Alywin* (London: Hurst and Blackett, 1898), 265–66.

88 Catherine Maxwell, *Second Sight: The Visionary Imagination in Late Victorian Literature* (Manchester: Manchester University Press, 2006), 178.
89 John Holmes, *Dante Gabriel Rossetti and the Late Victorian Sonnet Sequence* (Aldershot: Ashgate, 2005), 82.
90 Etherington, *Rider Haggard*, 35.
91 Haggard, *The Days of My Life*, 1: 41.
92 Barlow, *The Higher Love*, 35.

Chapter Six The Final Fiction: Spiritual Consolation and the Dictates of the Sexual Imperative (1909–30)

1 Lilias Rider Haggard, *The Cloak That I Left* (London: Hodder and Stoughton, 1951), 202.
2 H. Rider Haggard, *The Witch's Head* (1884; London: Longmans, Green, 1894), 299.
3 H. Rider Haggard, *The Days of My Life: An Autobiography*, 2 vols. (London: Longman, Green, 1926), 2: 80.
4 D. S. Higgins, *Rider Haggard: The Great Storyteller* (London: Cassell, 1981), 206.
5 Haggard, *The Days of My Life*, 1: xxii.
6 Andrew Lang, 'Realism and Romance', *Contemporary Review* 52 (1887), 683–93 (691–92).
7 Higgins, *Rider Haggard*, 207.
8 Haggard, *The Days of My Life*, 1: xvii.
9 D. S. Higgins, ed., *The Private Diaries of Sir Henry Rider Haggard* (London: Cassell, 1980), 67.
10 Lilias Haggard, *The Cloak That I Left*, 258.
11 Morton Cohen, *Rider Haggard: His Life and Works* (London: Hutchinson, 1960), 268.
12 Higgins, *Rider Haggard*, 218.
13 Lilias Haggard, *The Cloak That I Left*, 267.
14 'Love Eternal', *Times Literary Supplement* 846 (1918), 160.
15 Higgins, ed., *The Private Diaries of Sir Henry Rider Haggard*, 132.
16 H. Rider Haggard, *Love Eternal* (Cassell, 1918), 33.
17 Haggard, *The Days of My Life*, 1: 28.
18 Lilias Haggard, *The Cloak That I Left*, 27.
19 Higgins, *Rider Haggard*, 15.
20 Haggard, *The Days of My Life*, 1: 42.
21 Ibid., 1: 35.
22 Ibid., 2: 250.
23 Ibid., 1: 36.
24 Lilias Haggard, *The Cloak That I Left*, 70.
25 H. Rider Haggard, *Mary of Marion Isle* (Hutchinson, 1929), 39.
26 Lilias Haggard, *The Cloak That I Left*, 69.
27 Ibid., 72.
28 Haggard, *The Days of My Life*, 1: 116.
29 Lilias Haggard, *The Cloak That I Left*, 156.
30 Haggard, *The Days of My Life*, 2: 44.
31 H. Rider Haggard, *Montezuma's Daughter* (1893; Longmans, Green, 1894), 304.
32 H. Rider Haggard, *The Yellow God* (London: Cassell, 1909), 348.
33 H. Rider Haggard, *Child of Storm* (London: Cassell, 1913), 88.
34 H. Rider Haggard, *Allan and the Ice-Gods* (London: Hutchinson, 1927), 163.
35 H. Rider Haggard, *Wisdom's Daughter* (London: Hutchinson, 1923), 227, 259.
36 Higgins, ed., *The Private Diaries of Sir Henry Rider Haggard*, 255.
37 Arthur Conan Doyle, *The History of Spiritualism* (London: Cassell, 1926), 2: 225.
38 Joseph McCabe, *Spiritualism: A Popular History from 1847* (London: T. Fisher Unwin, 1920), 234.

39 Randall Stevenson, *Literature and The Great War* (Oxford: , 2013), 204, 221.
40 H. Rider Haggard, *When the World Shook* (London: Cassell, 1919), 328.
41 Philip Waller, *Writers, Readers and Reputations: Literary Life in Britain 1870–1918* (Oxford: Oxford University Press, 2006), 927.
42 Higgins, *Rider Haggard*, 219.
43 Jane Potter, *Boys in Khaki, Girls in Print: Woman's Literary Responses to the Great War 1914–1918* (Oxford: Clarendon, 2005), 89.
44 Waller, *Writers, Readers and Reputations*, 973.
45 Higgins, ed., *The Private Diaries of Sir Henry Rider Haggard*, 10.
46 Ibid., 27.
47 Ibid., 33.
48 Ibid., 49.
49 Ibid., 32.
50 Potter, *Boys in Khaki, Girls in Print*, 9.
51 McCabe, *Spiritualism*, 234.
52 G. Barlow, *The Higher Love: A Plea for a Nobler Conception of Human Love* (London: Roxburghe Press, 1895), 11, 24.
53 Charles Dickens, *The Old Curiosity Shop* (1841; London: Everyman, 1928), 524.
54 D. G. Rossetti, *Collected Poetry and Prose*, edited by Jerome McGann (New Haven and London: Yale University Press, 2003), 22.
55 H. Rider Haggard, *Stella Fregelius* (London: Longmans, Green, 1904), 234.
56 H. Rider Haggard, *The Ghost Kings* (London: Cassell, 1908), 22.
57 H. Rider Haggard, *Moon of Israel* (London: John Murray, 1918), 325.
58 H. Rider Haggard. Letter to Ella Maddison Green, 9 June 1918, Columbia Collection. # 0532.
59 Waller, *Writers, Readers and Reputations*, 935.
60 H. Rider Haggard, *Finished* (London: Ward, Lock, 1917), 212.
61 Janet Laing, *Before the Wind* (London: J. M. Dent, 1918), 8, 21.
62 H. Rider Haggard, *Dawn* (1884: London: Longmans, Green, 1914), 143.
63 H. Rider Haggard, *Jess* (Smith, Elder, 1887), 169.
64 *The Book of Common Prayer* (Oxford: Oxford University Press, 1900), 258.
65 H. Rider Haggard, *Beatrice* (1890: London: Longmans, Green, 1903), 216.
66 Haggard, *The Days of My Life*, 2: 259.
67 Mrs Humphry Ward, *Missing* (London: W. Collins, 1917), 203.
68 Haggard, *The Days of My Life*, 2: 259.
69 Ibid., 1: 37.
70 Cohen, *Rider Haggard*, 27.
71 Haggard, *The Days of My Life*, 1: 41.
72 H. Rider Haggard, *She and Allan* (London: Hutchinson, 1921), 14, 256.
73 Haggard, *The Days of My Life*, 2: 237.
74 H. Rider Haggard, *The Wanderer's Necklace* (London: Cassell, 1914), 133.
75 H. Rider Haggard, *The Virgin of the Sun* (London: Cassell, 1922), 87, 102, 49.
76 Higgins, *Rider Haggard*, 215.
77 H. Rider Haggard, *Belshazzar* (London: Stanley Paul, 1930), 56.
78 Lilias Haggard, *The Cloak That I Left*, 98.
79 Gertrude Himmelfarb, *Marriage and Morals Among the Victorians* (London: Faber & Faber, 1986), 78.
80 Haggard, *The Days of My Life*, 2: 236–38.
81 Ibid., 2: 85.
82 Chris Baldick, 'The Modern Movement', in *The Oxford English Literary History 1910–1940* (Oxford: Oxford University Press, 2004), 10: 8, 365.
83 Peter Keating, *The Haunted Study: A Social History of the English Novel 1875–1914* (London: Secker & Warburg, 1989), 166–67.

84 Higgins, *Rider Haggard*, 237.
85 Lindy Stiebel, *Imagining Africa: Landscape in H. Rider Haggard's African Romances* (Westport: Greenwood, 2001), 87.
86 Diana Wallace, *Sisters and Rivals in British Woman's Fiction 1914–39* (Basingstoke: Macmillan Press, 2000), 10.
87 Baldick, *The Modern Movement*, 363, 374.
88 Celia Marshik, *British Modernism and Censorship* (Cambridge: Cambridge University Press, 2006), 206, 203–4.
89 Keating, *The Haunted Study*, 262–63.
90 Ibid., 210.
91 Nicola Beauman, *A Very Great Profession: The Woman's Novel 1914–39* (London: Virago, 1983), 124.
92 Keating, *The Haunted Study*, 275.
93 Higgins, *Rider Haggard*, 237–38.
94 Baldick, *The Modern Movement*, 371.
95 Martin Hipsky, *Modernism and the Woman's Popular Romance in Britain 1885–1925* (Athens: Ohio University Press, 2011), 16.
96 H. De Vere Stacpoole, *The Blue Lagoon* (London: T. Fisher Unwin, 1908), 229.
97 Nicola Wilson, 'Circulating Morals 1900–1915' in *Prudes on the Prowl: Fiction and Obscenity in England 1850 to the Present Day*, edited by David Bradshaw and Rachel Potter (Oxford: Oxford University Press, 2013), 57, 52–53, 55, 63–64.
98 D. H. Lawrence, *The Rainbow* (1915; London: Penguin, 1969), 238.
99 Haggard, *The Days of My Life*, 2: 245.
100 Ibid., 1: 99–100.

Chapter Seven   Summation: A Personal Odyssey

1 Carolyn Dever, 'Everywhere and Nowhere: Sexuality in Victorian Fiction' in *A Concise Companion to the Victorian Novel*, edited by Francis O'Gorman (Oxford: Blackwell, 2005), 171.
2 Talia Schaffer, *Romance's Rival: Familiar Marriage in Victorian Fiction* (New York: Oxford University Press, 2016), 134.
3 Max Saunders, *Self Impression: Life Writing, Autobiografiction, and the Forms of Modern Literature* (New York: Oxford University Press, 2010), 113, 161.
4 H. Rider Haggard, *The Days of My Life: An Autobiography*, 2 vols. (London: Longman, Green, 1926), 1: xviii.
5 H. Rider Haggard, *Cleopatra* (London: Longmans, Green, 1889), 50.
6 Norman Etherington, *Rider Haggard* (Boston: Twayne, 1984), 88.
7 Shannon Young, 'Myths of Castration: Freud's *Eternal Feminine* and Rider Haggard's *She*', *The Victorian Newsletter*, 108 (2005), 21–30 (25).
8 H. Rider Haggard, *When the World Shook* (Cassell, 1919), 345.
9 Wendy Katz, *Rider Haggard and the Fiction of Empire: A Critical Study of British Imperial Fiction* (Cambridge: Cambridge University Press, 1987), 4.
10 Bruce Mazlish, 'A Triptych: Freud's *Interpretation of Dreams*, Rider Haggard's *She* and Bulwer-Lytton's *The Coming Race*', *Comparative Studies in Society and History*, 35 (1994), 726–45 (733).
11 Thomas Hardy, 'General Preface to the Novels and Poems', *The Works of Thomas Hardy in Prose and Verse*, Prose (London: Macmillan, 1912), 1: viii–ix.
12 Linda Dryden, '*Heart of Darkness* and *Allan Quatermain*: Apocalypse and Utopia', *Conradiana: A Journal of Joseph Conrad Studies*, 31 (1999), 173–97 (181).
13 H. Rider Haggard, 'About Fiction', *Contemporary Review*, 51 (1887), 172–80 (176).
14 Haggard, *The Days of My Life*, 2: 256.

15 Etherington, *Rider Haggard*, 90.
16 Haggard, *The Days of My Life*, 1: xxiii.
17 Francis O'Gorman, 'Speculative Fictions and the Fortunes of H. Rider Haggard' in *Victorian Literature and Finance*, edited by Francis O'Gorman (Oxford: Oxford University Press, 2007), 157–72 (158).
18 Haggard, *The Days of My Life*, 1: 279.

BIBLIOGRAPHY

Letters and Journals

Barber, Agnes Marion. Letters. Rhodes House Library, Oxford, MSS.Brit.Emp.s.465.
Doveton, Ella. Journals 1837–1839, 1841. Rhodes House Library, Oxford, MSS. Brit.Emp.s.465.
Haggard, H. Rider. Rough Diary, February–May 1914. Norfolk Records Office, MC 32/51 478X7.
———. Letters to various correspondents. Longman archives. Reading University Special Collections, MS 289.
———. Letters to various correspondents. Columbia Collection, MS# 0532.
———. Letters to family. British Library, MSS Sur/RP/2804.
———. Letters to and from various correspondents. Huntington Library, HM 43578; HM 43581; HM 43640–1.

Primary Works and Editions Consulted

Allen, Grant. 2004 [1895]. *The Woman Who Did*. Plymouth: Broadview.
Barlow, George. 1876. *The Gospel of Humanity; or the Connection between Spirituality and Modern Thought*. London: James Burns.
———. 1878. *The Marriage before Death and Other Poems*. London: Remington.
———. 1895a. *The Higher Love: A Plea for a Nobler Conception of Human Love*. London: Roxburghe Press.
———. 1895b. *Woman Regained: A Novel of Artistic Life*. London: Roxburghe Press.
Barrie, J. M. 1890. *My Lady Nicotine*. London: Hodder & Stoughton.
———. 1928 [1918]. 'A Well-Remembered Voice'. In *The Plays of J. M. Barrie*. London: Hodder & Stoughton.
Barry, William. 1894. 'The Strike of a Sex'. *Quarterly Review* 179: 239–318.
Bennett, Arnold. 1906. *Sacred and Profane Love*. Leipzig: Bernhard Tauchnitz.
Berwick, John. 1897. *The Secret of Saint Florel*. London: Macmillan.
———. 1898. *A Philosopher's Romance*. London: Macmillan.
Besant, Walter. 1884. *The Art of Fiction*. London: Chatto & Windus.
Braddon, Mary. 1863. *Aurora Floyd*. 3 vols. London: Tinsley Brothers.
———. 2008 [1862]. *Lady Audley's Secret*. Oxford: Oxford University Press.
Broughton, Rhoda. 1867. *Cometh Up As A Flower*. 2 vols. London: Richard Bentley.
Buchanan, Robert. 1890. *The Moment After*. London: William Heinemann.
Bulwer-Lytton, Edward. 1871. *The Coming Race*. Edinburgh: William Blackwood.
Bunyan, John. 1926 [1678]. *The Pilgrim's Progress*. London: Society for Promoting Christian Knowledge.
Caine, Hall. 1913. *The Woman Thou Gavest Me*. London: Heinemann.
Conrad, Joseph. 1946 [1902]. *Youth; Heart of Darkness; The End of the Tether*. London: Dent.
Corelli, Marie. 1886. *A Romance of Two Worlds*. 2 vols. London: Richard Bentley.
———. 1911. *The Life Everlasting: A Reality of Romance*. London: Methuen.
Defoe, Daniel. 1864 [1719]. *The Life and Adventures of Robinson Crusoe*. London: Routledge, Warner and Routledge.
De La Brete, Jean. 1898. *The Cure of Buisson*. Translated by John Berwick. London: Dean.
Dickens, Charles. 1859. *A Tale of Two Cities*. London: Chapman & Hall.

———. 1928 [1841]. *The Old Curiosity Shop*. London: Everyman.
———. 1985 [1861]. *Great Expectations*. London: Penguin.
Doyle, Arthur Conan. 1926. *The History of Spiritualism*. 2 vols. London: Cassell.
Dumas, Alexandre. 1853 [1844]. *The Three Musketeers*. Translated by William Robson. London: George Routledge.
Du Maurier, George. 1998 [1894]. *Trilby*. Oxford: Oxford University Press.
Egerton, George. 2006. *Keynotes and Discords*, edited by Sally Ledger. London: Continuum.
Fairless, Michael. 1902. *The Roadmender*. London: Duckworth.
Forster, E. M. *Maurice*. 1975 [1971]. London: Penguin.
Freud, Sigmund. 1949 [1910]. *Three Essays on the Theory of Sexuality*. London: Imago.
———. 1991 [1899]. *The Interpretation of Dreams*. London: Penguin.
Gissing, George. 2000 [1893]. *The Odd Women*. Oxford: Oxford University Press.
Grand, Sarah. 1894 [1893]. *The Heavenly Twins*. London: Heinemann.
Greg, William. 1862. 'Why Are Women Redundant?' *National Review* 14: 434–60 (436).
Haggard, Ella. 1857. *Myra or the Rose of the East*. London: Longmans, Green.
———. 1890. *Life and Its Author: An Essay in Verse*. London and Norwich: E. H. Jarrold.
Haggard, H. Rider. 1877a. 'A Zulu War Dance', *Gentleman's Magazine* 19: 94–107.
———. 1877b. 'A Visit to the Chief Secocoeni', *Gentleman's Magazine* 19: 302–18.
———. 1882. *Cetewayo and His White Neighbours*. London: Trubner.
———. 1887a [1885]. *King Solomon's Mines*. London: Cassell.
———. 1887b. *Jess*. London: Smith, Elder.
———. 1887c. *She*. London: Longmans, Green.
———. 1887d. 'About Fiction', *Contemporary Review*, 51: 172–80.
———. 1887e. 'Books Which Have Influenced Me', *British Weekly* 2: 53.
———. 1887f. 'Who Is She?' *Pall Mall Gazette* 45: 13–14.
———. 1888a. *Maiwa's Revenge*. London: Longmans, Green.
———. 1888b. *Mr Meeson's Will*. London: Spencer Blackett.
———. 1889. *Cleopatra*. London: Longmans, Green.
———, and Andrew Lang. 1890. *The World's Desire*. London: Longmans, Green.
———. 1892. *Nada the Lily*. London: Longmans, Green.
———. 1893a [1887]. *Allan Quatermain*. London: Longmans, Green.
———. 1893b. 'My First Book: Dawn', *Idler* 3: 279–91.
———. 1894a [1893]. *Montezuma's Daughter*. London: Longmans, Green.
———. 1894b [1884]. *The Witch's Head*. London: Longmans.
———. 1895 [1889]. *Allan's Wife*. London: Longmans, Green.
———. 1896a [1888]. *Colonel Quaritch V. C.* London: Longmans, Green.
———. 1896b. *Heart of the World*. London: Longmans, Green.
———. 1897 [1895]. *Joan Haste*. London: Longmans, Green.
———. 1898. *Doctor Therne*. London: Longmans, Green.
———. 1899. *A Farmer's Year*. London: Longmans, Green.
———. 1901 *Lysbeth*. London: Longmans, Green.
———. 1902. *Rural England*. London: Longmans, Green.
———. 1903a [1890]. *Beatrice*. London: Longmans, Green.
———. 1903b. *Pearl-Maiden*. London: Longmans, Green.
———. 1904a. *Stella Fregelius*. London: Longmans, Green.
———. 1904b. *The Brethren*. London: Cassell.
———. 1905a. *A Gardener's Year*. London: Longmans, Green.
———. 1905b [1891]. *Eric Brighteyes*. London: Longmans, Green.
———. 1906. *The Way of the Spirit*. London: Hutchinson.
———. 1909a. *The Lady of Blossholme*. London: Hodder & Stoughton.
———. 1909b. *The Yellow God*. London: Cassell.
———. 1910. *Regeneration*. London: Longmans, Green.

———. 1911a [1905]. *Ayesha*. London: Longmans, Green.
———. 1911b. *The Mahatma and the Hare*. London: Longmans, Green.
———. 1911c. *Red Eve*. London: Hodder & Stoughton.
———. 1911d. *Rural Denmark*. London: Longmans, Green.
———. 1912. *Marie*. London: Cassell.
———. 1913. *Child of Storm*. London: Cassell.
———. 1914a [1884]. *Dawn*. London: Longmans, Green.
———. 1914b. *The Wanderer's Necklace*. London: Cassell.
———. 1915 [1910]. *Morning Star*. London: Cassell.
———. 1916 [1899]. *Swallow*. London: Longmans, Green.
———. 1917. *Finished*. London: Ward, Lock.
———. 1918a. *Love Eternal*. London: Cassell.
———. 1918b. *Moon of Israel*. London: John Murray.
———. 1919. *When the World Shook*. London: Cassell.
———. 1921. *She and Allan*. London: Hutchinson.
———. 1923. *Wisdom's Daughter*. London: Hutchinson.
———. 1925. *Queen of the Dawn*. London: Hutchinson.
———. 1926a. *Benita*. 1906; London: Cassell.
———. 1926b. *The Days of My Life*. 2 vols. London: Longmans, Green.
———. 1926c. *The Ghost Kings*. 1908; London: Cassell.
———. 1927. *Allan and the Ice-Gods*. London: Hutchinson.
———. 1929. *Mary of Marion Isle*. London: Hutchinson.
———. 1930. *Belshazzar*. London: Stanley Paul.
———. 1935 [1922] *The Virgin of the Sun*. London: Cassell.
———. 1937 [1894]. *The People of the Mist*. London: Longmans, Green.
Hall, Radclyffe. 1983 [1928]. *The Well of Loneliness*. London: Virago.
Hardy, Thomas. 1891. *Tess of the D'Urbervilles*. 3 vols. London: Osgood, McIlvaine.
———. 1924 [1895]. *Jude the Obscure*. London: Macmillan.
———. 1966 [1886]. *The Mayor of Casterbridge*. London: Macmillan.
———. 1968 [1878]. *The Return of the Native*. London: Macmillan.
———. 1978 [1871]. *Desperate Remedies*. London: Macmillan.
Iron, Ralph. 1883. *The Story of An African Farm*. 2 vols. London: Chapman & Hall.
James, Henry. 1884, 'The Art of Fiction'. *Longman's Magazine*, 4: 502–31.
Jerome, K. 1889. *Three Men in a Boat*. London: Dent.
Kipling, Rudyard. 1901. *Kim*. London: Macmillan.
Lane, E. W. 1850 [1706]. *The Arabian Nights' Entertainment or the Thousand and One Nights*. 3 vols. London: John Murray.
Lang, Andrew. 1887. 'Realism and Romance'. *Contemporary Review*, 52: 683–93.
Laing, Janet. 1918. *Before the Wind*. London: J. M. Dent.
Lawrence, D. H. 1966 [1913]. *Sons and Lovers*. London: Penguin.
———. 1969 [1915]. *The Rainbow*. London: Penguin.
———. 2010 [1928]. *Lady Chatterley's Lover*. London: Penguin.
Marryat, Florence. 1891. *There Is No Death*. London: Kegan, Paul, Trench, Trubner.
McCabe, Joseph. 1920. *Spiritualism: A Popular History From 1847*. London: T. Fisher Unwin.
Milton, John. 1967. *The Poetical Works*, edited by Helen Darbishire. Oxford: Oxford University Press.
Moore, George. 1991 [1894]. *Esther Waters*. Oxford: Oxford University Press.
Meredith, George. 1908 [1891]. *One of Our Conquerors*. London: Constable.
Oliphant, Lawrence. 1888. *Scientific Religion*. Edinburgh: Blackwood.
Phelps, Arthur. 1901. *Lord Dunchester or The End of Dr Therne*. London: Swan, Sonnenschein.
Podmore, Frank. 1902. *Modern Spiritualism: A History and a Criticism*. 2 vols. London: Methuen.
Rossetti, D. G. 2003. *Collected Poetry and Prose*, edited by Jerome McGann. New Haven and London: Yale University Press.

Saintsbury, George. 1887. 'The Present State of the Novel'. *Fortnightly Review*, 48: 410–17.
Shelley, P. B. 2003. *The Major Works*, edited by Zachary Leader and Michael O'Neil. Oxford: Oxford University Press.
Stacpoole, H. De Vere. 1908. *The Blue Lagoon*. London: T. Fisher Unwin.
Stevenson, R. L. 1882. 'A Gossip on Romance'. *Longman's Magazine*, 1: 69–79.
——— . 1884. 'A Humble Remonstrance', *Longman's Magazine*, 5: 139–47.
——— . 1998 [1883]. *Treasure Island*. Oxford: Oxford University Press.
——— . 2000 [1886]. *Strange Case of Dr Jekyll and Mr Hyde*. Oxford: Oxford University Press.
Stoker, Bram. 1993 [1897]. *Dracula*. London: Dent.
Swedenborg, Emanuel. 1910 [1768]. *Conjugial Love*. London: The Swedenborg Society.
Tennyson, Alfred Lord. 1967. *Poems and Plays*. London: Oxford University Press.
Thackeray, William Makepeace. 1985 [1847–48]. *Vanity Fair*. London: Penguin.
Trollope, Anthony. 1923 [1883]. *An Autobiography*. London: Oxford University Press.
———. 1983 [1872]. *The Eustace Diamonds*. Oxford: Oxford University Press.
———. 1984 [1858]. *Dr Thorne*. London: Chatto and Windus.
Wales, Hubert. 1907. *The Yoke*. London: John Long.
Ward, Mrs Humphry. 1917. *Missing*. London: W. Collins.
Watson, William. 1888. 'The Fall of Fiction', *Fortnightly Review*, 50: 324–36.
Watts-Dunton, Theodore. 1898. *Aylwin*. London, Hurst and Blackett.
Wells, H. G. 1943 [1910]. *Ann Veronica*. London: J. M. Dent.
Wood, Ellen. 2002 [1861]. *East Lynne*. Ormskirk: Broadview.
Woolf, Virginia. 1996 [1925]. *Mrs Dalloway*. London: Penguin.
———. 2002 [1927]. *To the Lighthouse*. Ware: Wordsworth.

Secondary Works

Arata, Stephen. 1996. *Fictions of Loss in the Victorian Fin de Siecle*. Cambridge: Cambridge University Press.
Baldick, Chris. 2004. *The Oxford English Literary History, Volume 10. 1910–1940: The Modern Movement*. Oxford: Oxford University Press.
Beauman, Nicola. 1983. *A Very Great Profession: The Woman's Novel 1914–39*. London: Virago.
Bourne Taylor, Jenny and Sally Shuttleworth. 1998. *Embodied Selves: An Anthology of Psychological Texts 1830–1890*. Oxford: Clarendon.
Brantlinger, Patrick. 1982. 'What Is Sensational about the Sensation Novel?' *Nineteenth Century Fiction*, 37: 1–28.
Brown, Sarah Annes. 2003. *Devoted Sisters: Representations of the Sister Relationship in Nineteenth-Century British and American Literature*. Aldershot: Ashgate.
Chrisman, Laura. 2000. *Rereading the Imperial Romance: British Imperialism and South African Resistance in Haggard, Schreiner and Plaatje*. Oxford: Clarendon.
Coan, Stephen, ed. 2001. *H. Rider Haggard: Diary of an African Journey 1914*. London: C. Hurst.
Cohen, Morton. 1960. *Rider Haggard: His Life and Works*. London: Hutchinson.
———, ed. 1965. *Rudyard Kipling to Rider Haggard: The Record of a Friendship*. London: Hutchinson.
Cunningham, Gail. 2001. 'He-Notes: Reconstructing Masculinity'. In *The New Woman Fiction and Fact*, edited by Angelique Richardson and Chris Willis, 94–106. Basingstoke: Palgrave.
Deane, Bradley. 2008. 'Mummy Fiction and the Occupation of Egypt', *English Literature in Transition 1880–1920*, 51: 381–410.
Dentith, Simon. 2006. *Epic and Empire in Nineteenth-Century Britain*. Cambridge: Cambridge University Press.
Dever, Carolyn. 2005. 'Everywhere and Nowhere: Sexuality in Victorian Fiction'. In *A Concise Companion to the Victorian Novel*, edited by Francis O'Gorman, 156–79. Oxford: Blackwell.

Dryden, Linda. 1999. '*Heart of Darkness* and *Allan Quatermain*: Apocalypse and Utopia', *Conradia: A Journal of Joseph Conrad Studies*, 31: 173–97.
Etherington, Norman. 1978. 'Rider Haggard, Imperialism, and the Layered Personality', *Victorian Studies: A Journal of the Humanities, Arts and Sciences*, 22: 71–87.
———. 1984. *Rider Haggard*. Boston: Twayne.
Fraser, Robert. 1998. *Victorian Quest Romance: Stevenson, Haggard, Kipling and Conan Doyle*. Plymouth: Northcote House.
Garrison, Laurie. 2011. *Science, Sexuality and Sensation Novels: Pleasures of the Senses*. Basingstoke: Palgrave Macmillan.
Gatrell, Simon. 2003. 'The Collected Editions of Hardy, James and Meredith, with Some Concluding Thoughts on the Desirability of a Taxonomy of the Book', In *The Culture of Collected Editions*, edited by Andrew Nash, 80–94. Basingstoke: Palgrave Macmillan.
Gilmour, Robin. 1981. *The Idea of the Gentleman in the Victorian Novel*. London: Allen and Unwin.
Graham, Kenneth. 1965. *English Criticism of the Novel 1865–1900*. Oxford: Oxford University Press.
Haggard, Lilias Rider. 1951. *The Cloak That I Left: A Biography of the Author Henry Rider Haggard K. B. E.* London: Hodder & Stoughton.
Higgins, D. S., ed. 1980. *The Private Diaries of Sir Henry Rider Haggard*. London: Cassell.
———. 1981. *Rider Haggard: The Great Storyteller* London: Cassell.
Himmelfarb, Gertrude. 1986. *Marriage and Morals Among the Victorians*. London: Faber and Faber.
Hipsky, Martin. 2011. *Modernism and the Woman's Popular Romance in Britain 1885–1925*. Athens: Ohio University Press.
Holmes, John. 2005. *Dante Gabriel Rossetti and the Late Victorian Sonnet Sequence*. Aldershot: Ashgate.
Katz, Wendy. 1987. *Rider Haggard and the Fiction of Empire: A Critical Study of British Imperial Fiction*. Cambridge: Cambridge University Press.
Keating, Peter. 1989. *The Haunted Study: A Social History of the English Novel, 1875–1914*. London: Secker & Warburg.
Kennedy, Meegan. 2010. *Revising the Clinic: Vision and Representation in Victorian Medical Narrative and the Novel*. Columbus: Ohio State University Press.
Kestner, Joseph. 2010. *Masculinities in British Adventure Fiction 1880–1915*. Farnham: Ashgate.
Leckie, Barbara. 1999. *Culture and Adultery: The Novel, the Newspaper and the Law 1857–1914*. Philadelphia: University of Pennsylvania Press.
Ledger, Sally. 1997. *The New Woman: Fiction and Feminism at the Fin de Siecle*. Manchester: Manchester University Press.
Manthorpe, Victoria. 1996. *Children of the Empire: The Victorian Haggards*. London: Gollancz.
Marshik, Celia. 2006. *British Modernism and Censorship*. Cambridge: Cambridge University Press.
Mason, Michael. 1995. *The Making of Victorian Sexuality*. Oxford: Oxford University Press.
Maxwell, Catherine. 2008. *Second Sight: The Visionary Imagination in Late Victorian Literature*. Manchester: Manchester University Press.
Mazlish, Bruce. 1993. 'A Triptych: Freud's 'The Interpretation of Dreams', Rider Haggard's *She*, and Bulwer-Lytton's *The Coming Race*', *Comparative Studies in Society and History*, 35: 726–45.
Miller, Jane Eldridge. 1994. *Rebel Women: Feminism, Modernism and the Edwardian Novel*. London: Virago.
Monsman, Gerald. 2006. *H. Rider Haggard on the Imperial Frontier: The Political and Literary Contexts of his African Romances*. University of North Carolina at Greensboro: ELT Press.
Nelson, Carolyn Christensen. 2001. *A New Woman Reader: Fiction, Articles, Drama of the 1890s*. Letchworth: Broadview.
O'Gorman, Francis. 2007. 'Speculative Fictions and the Fortunes of H. Rider Haggard'. In *Victorian Literature and Finance*, edited by Francis O'Gorman, 157–72. Oxford: Oxford University Press.
Oppenheim, Janet. 1985. *The Other World: Spiritualism and Psychical Research in England 1850–1914*. Cambridge: Cambridge University Press.
Owen, Alex. 2004. *The Darkened Room: Women, Power, and Spiritualism in Late Victorian England*. Chicago: University of Chicago Press.

Parsons, Gerald, ed. 1988. *Religion in Victorian Britain*. Manchester: Manchester University Press.
Pearsall, Ronald. 1969. *The Worm in the Bud: The World of Victorian Sexuality*. London: Weidenfeld and Nicholson.
Pearson, Richard. 2000. 'Archaeology and Gothic Desire: Vitality beyond the Grave in H. Rider Haggard's Ancient Egypt'. In *Victorian Gothic: Literary and Cultural Manifestations in the Nineteenth Century*, edited by Ruth Robbins and Julian Wolfreys. 218–44. Basingstoke: Palgrave.
Porter, Roy and Lesley Hall. 1995. *The Facts of Life: The Creation of Sexual Knowledge in Britain 1650–1950*. New Haven and London: Yale University Press.
Potter, Jane. 2005. *Boys in Khaki, Girls in Print: Women's Literary Responses to The Great War 1914–1918*. Oxford: Clarendon.
Pykett, Lyn. 1992. *The Improper Feminine: The Women's Sensation Novel and New Woman Writing*. London: Routledge.
Richardson, Angelique. 2003. *Love and Eugenics in the Late Nineteenth Century: Rational Reproduction and the New Woman*. Oxford: Oxford University Press.
Saunders, Max. 2010. *Self Impression: Life Writing, Autobiografiction, and the Forms of Modern Literature*. New York: Oxford University Press.
Schaffer, Talia. 2016. *Romance's Rival: Familiar Marriage in Victorian Fiction*. New York: Oxford University Press.
Sedgwick, Eve Kosofsky. 1985. *Between Men: English Literature and Male Homosocial Desire*. New York: Columbia University Press.
———. 2008. *Epistemology of the Closet*. Berkeley: University of California Press.
Showalter, Elaine. 1991. *Sexual Anarchy: Gender and Culture at the Fin de Siecle*. London: Bloomsbury.
Stevenson, Randall. 2013. *Literature and The Great War*. Oxford: Oxford University Press.
Stiebel, Lindy. 2001. *Imagining Africa: Landscape in H Rider Haggard's African Romances*. Westport: Greenwood.
Stiles, Anne. 2012. *Popular Fiction and Brain Science in the Late Nineteenth Century*. Cambridge: Cambridge University Press.
Waller, Philip. 2006. *Writers, Readers, and Reputations: Literary Life in Britain 1870–1918*. Oxford: Oxford University Press.
Wallace, Diana. 2000. *Sisters and Rivals in British Woman's Fiction 1914–39*. Basingstoke: Macmillan Press.
Whatmore, D. E. 1987. *H. Rider Haggard: A Bibliography*. London: Mansell.
Wheeler, Michael. 1994. *Heaven, Hell and the Victorians*. Cambridge: Cambridge University Press.
Wilson, Nicola. 2013. 'Circulating Morals 1900–1915'. In *Prudes on the Prowl: Fiction and Obscenity in England 1850 to the Present Day*, edited by David Bradshaw and Rachel Potter. Oxford: Oxford University Press.
Young, Shannon. 2005. 'Myths of Castration: Freud's 'Eternal Feminine' and Rider Haggard's *She*'. *Victorian Newsletter*, 108: 21–30.

INDEX

'About Fiction' (Haggard) 9, 13, 20, 21
adultery, in Haggard's novels 79–80, 89
afterlife, love and, in Haggard's fiction 28, 71–73, 119, 138–39
agriculture, Haggard's concern about 23
Allan and the Ice Gods (Haggard) 131, 147, 154, 156, 159, 162
Allan Quatermain (Haggard)
   consequences of sexual imperative in 68
   criticism of 20–21
   emotionally disruptive power of women in 59, 62, 74
   female power and divinity in 116
   gender stereotypes in 47
   sibling rivalry in 89
   success of 15–16
   woman's sexual potency in 50–51, 52, 156
Allan's Wife (Haggard) 104, 105
Allen, Grant 82, 95
Ann Veronica (Wells) 152
Arata, Stephen 13
Archer, Francis Bradley 30, 100
Aurora Floyd (Braddon) 6, 47, 55, 59
'Autobiografiction' (Reynolds) 57
autobiography, elision of fiction and 8
Ayesha (Haggard) 22, 86, 113, 114, 133, 143, 156, 158
Aylwin (Watts-Dunton) 7, 103, 116, 120

Bainbrigge, Philip (Rev.) 17
Baldick, Chris 148, 150–51, 152
Ballantyne, R. M. 15
Barber, Agnes. *See* Haggard, Agnes (Barber)
Barber, Marjorie 36
Barlow, George 7, 103, 116, 117, 119, 120, 121, 135
Barrie, J. M. 133, 141, 157
Barry, William 94
Beatrice (Haggard) 3, 17
   biographical overtones in 79–81, 160
   communication of lovers in 138–39
   criticism of established church in 145
   emotionally disruptive power of women in 86–87, 122, 123
   father figure in 25
   female self-sacrifice in 132
   marital relationships in 147
   New Woman fiction and 82–84
   public reaction to 46
   sexual imperative in 67, 94–95, 150
   sexual potency and passion in 84–85, 129
   spirituality in 96–97, 112, 118, 122–23, 138–39
Before the Wind (Laing) 138
Belshazzar (Haggard) 144–45, 152
Benita (Haggard) 67
Bennett, Arnold 133, 152
Berwick, John (pseud). *See* Haggard, Agnes (Barber)
Besant, Walter 14
Between Men (Sedgwick) 157
Blake, Frederick J. 34
The Blue Lagoon (Stacpoole) 151, 152
Blunt, Wilfred 6
Book of Ecclesiastes, Haggard's references to 105
The Bostonians (James) 106
Bourne-Taylor, Jenny 89
Braddon, Mary 6, 59
Brantlinger, Patrick 73
The Brethren (Haggard) 11, 28, 113, 114, 120, 123, 156, 162
Bridges, Robert 137
Broughton, Rhoda 6, 42, 97, 117, 119
Brown, Sarah Annes 89
Buchanan, Robert 103, 119
Bulwer, Henry 29
Bulwer Lytton, Charles 27
Bunyan, John 58

Caine, Hall 133, 152
Cassell & Co. 11
celibacy, in Haggard's fiction 106–10, 121–22
Cetewayo and His White Neighbours (Haggard) 20, 37, 78
Chance (Conrad) 110
Child of Storm (Haggard) 130, 143, 156
Christianity
    Haggard's belief in 8–9, 119
    in *Jess* and *Beatrice* 85
    reunion with loved ones in the afterlife and 119
Church Quarterly Review 21
Cleopatra (Haggard)
    biographical resonances in 158, 160
    male responsibility for sexual sin in 61–62, 64, 65, 74, 143, 162
    marriage in 45
    non-marital sexual relations in 34
    spiritual love and afterlife in 28, 72
    woman's sexual potency in 51, 53, 156
Coan, Stephen 33–34
Cochrane, Arthur 31, 64, 68, 128
Cohen, Morton
    on autobiographical references in Haggard's work 2, 105
    on criticism of Haggard 20–21
    on *Dawn* 42
    on Haggard's marriage 34
    on spiritualism in Haggard's fiction 103, 140
Collins, Wilkie 73, 85
Colonel Quaritch V. C. (Haggard) 3
    biographical resonances in 45–46, 158, 159, 161
    consequences of sexual imperative in 65, 67, 155
    father figure in 25
    male responsibility for sexual sin in 64, 74, 87
    marital relationships in 147
    non-marital sexual relations in 34
    punishment of disruptive women in 54, 56
    sexual imperative in 156
    sexual vulnerability of women in 53
    spiritual love and afterlife in 72
    woman's sexual potency in 52
Cometh Up As A Flower (Broughton) 6, 42, 97, 117, 119
The Coming Race (Bulwer-Lytton) 20, 27
'Commonplace Book' (Haggard) 32

communication with the dead, in Haggard's fiction 120–21, 141–42
Conan Doyle, Arthur 101, 132, 157
Conjugial Love (Swedenborg) 112
Conrad, Joseph 110, 162
The Contemporary Review 13
Corelli, Marie 7, 80, 103, 118
'The Culture of the Horrible' 21
Cunningham, Gail 83

Dawn (Haggard) 2, 3, 20
    biographical resonances in 42–43, 158, 159
    consequences of sexual imperative in 65, 66
    consolatory and redemptive women in 69
    emotionally disruptive power of women in 59–60, 74, 87, 143, 155
    father figure in 25, 115
    first love in 60
    Haggard's comments on 5
    marital relationships in 146, 147
    negative depictions of marriage in 70
    punishment of disruptive women in 56
    sexual imperative in 156
    sexual vulnerability of women in 53
    spiritual love and afterlife in 71–72, 115, 127, 138–40
    woman's sexual potency and vulnerability in 48–53
The Days of My Life (Haggard) 22
Deceased Wife's Sister Marriage Act of 1835 88
Dentith, Simon 47
Desperate Remedies (Hardy) 45, 55
Dever, Carolyn 6–7, 8, 70, 85, 157
Dickens, Charles 6, 89, 135
Divorce Law of 1857 6
Doctor Therne (Haggard) 17–19, 159
Doctor Thorne (Trollope) 18
Dracula (Stoker) 7, 85, 157
Dryden, Linda 162
Du Maurier, George 157

East Lynne (Wood) 6, 45, 47, 55, 73–74, 155
    woman's sexual potency in 49
Egerton, George 82
'Epipsychidion' (Shelley) 118
Epistemology of the Closet (Sedgwick) 157
Eric Brighteyes (Haggard) 34, 46

INDEX

consequences of sexual imperative in 68, 156
gender stereotypes in 47
male responsibility for sexual sin in 61, 64, 74, 162
spiritual love and afterlife in 72
woman's sexual passion in 86
eroticism, in Victorian fiction 8
Esther Waters (Moore) 46
Etherington, Norman 2, 7, 55
   on adultery in Haggard's work 89
   on biographical elements in Haggard's fiction 1560
   on *Stella Fregelius* 104
   on women in Haggard's work 59, 82–83
The Eustace Diamonds (Trollope) 6, 55
Eveleigh Nash 11

'The Fall of Fiction' (Watson) 21
The Farmer's Year (Haggard) 23
father, sins of, in Haggard's fiction 68–69
father figures in Haggard's fiction
   in *Beatrice* 25
   in *Colonel Quaritch V. C.* 25
   in *Dawn* 25, 115
   in *Joan Haste* 25, 155
   in *Love Eternal* 25
   in *Stella Fregelius* 25
   in *The Way of the Spirit* 25
   in *The Witch's Head* 25
feminism
   celibacy and 106–7
   Ella Haggard's interest in 26
   Haggard's fiction in context of 5, 6
   New Women writers and 6
   women in Haggard's work and 82–83
femme fatale, Haggard's preoccupation with 55, 94, 122
Ferguson, Christine 102
Finished (Haggard) 121, 133, 137 138, 141, 156
fire imagery, Haggard's use of 86
first love, in Haggard's work 60, 61, 158, 159
Ford, Johanna Catherine (Lehmkuhl) 158
   death of Haggard's child with 68–69
   Haggard's feeling of responsibility toward 64, 108
   Haggard's relationship with 31–34, 38, 141–42
   influence in Haggard's fiction of 45, 128, 158

Ford, Josephine 31
Ford, Peter Lewis 31, 45
Forster, E. M. 153
Fortnightly Review 14, 21
Fragments of Inner Life (Myers) 120
Fraser, Robert 13
French Naturalist school of fiction 14, 95
Freud, Sigmund 1, 7

Galsworthy, John 133
A Gardener's Year (Haggard) 23
Garrison, Laurie 117
Gatrell, Simon 12
Gay, Peter 5
gender stereotypes in Haggard's fiction 47–48
Gentleman's Magazine 19
The Ghost Kings (Haggard)
   communication between lovers in 118, 138
   communication with the dead in 121, 141
   female power and divinity in 125
   sexual imperative in 67
   spiritual love in 99, 127, 156
Gissing, George 8, 95, 106
'A Gossip on Romance' (Stevenson) 14
Graham, Kenneth 12
Grand, Sarah 81, 83, 107
Great Expectations (Dickens) 6
Great War
   authorial restrictions imposed by 133
   Haggard and 127, 132, 133–35
   sexuality in fiction after 152
Greg, William 106
Guest, W. 65

Haggard, Agnes (nee Barber) 36–38, 56, 100, 128, 159–60
   influence on *Jess* 78–79
   influence on *Stella Fregelius* 104–5
Haggard, Andrew 15, 23, 42
Haggard, Ella (Doveton) (mother) 24, 25–28, 29, 99–100
Haggard, Ella (sister) 28, 38
Haggard, Godfrey 2, 32–33
Haggard, Henry Rider (Sir)
   anger in early novels of 41
   attitude toward writing of 19–24
   attraction of Romance writing for 15–16, 161–62
   autobiography of 8, 15, 16, 21–22
   biographical elements in fiction of 1–3, 19, 41, 42–44, 45–46, 157–61

Haggard, Henry Rider (Sir) (*cont.*)
  celibacy in fiction of 106–10, 121–22
  criticism of his books 1, 20–21, 77–80
  death of son Jock 33, 35, 62, 68, 99–100
  division of fiction into novels and romances of 11–15, 161–62
  early life of 24–29
  early writing of 19–20
  family crises and bereavements of 99–100, 126–27
  final novels of 125
  gender stereotypes in work of 47–48
  Great War and 133–35
  literary criticism by 20
  literary influences on 20
  literary reputation of 127
  marriage to Louisa Margitson 32, 34–36, 38, 107
  Modernism and fiction of 9, 150–54
  novels of 11, 16, 161–62
  position on realism and romance in fiction 12
  reading of fiction by 3
  relationship with Johanna Ford 31–34
  relationship with Lilly Jackson 2, 25, 29–31, 36, 38–39, 100
  relations with Agnes Barber 36–38, 56, 100
  relations with father 25, 128–29
  relations with mother 25–29, 99–100
  spiritualism and fiction of 5, 7, 17, 71–73, 96–97, 101–3, 121–23, 135–36, 140–41
  women's sexual passion in romances of 86
Haggard, Jack 37, 38, 79
Haggard, Jock 33, 35–36, 62, 68, 99–100
Haggard, Lilias
  on biographical elements in Haggard's fiction 1–3, 42, 43
  on death of Haggard's son Jock 33, 46
  on Haggard and Johanna Ford 31
  on Haggard and Lilly Jackson 29–31, 126, 127, 129
  on Haggard's early life 24, 25, 28
  on Haggard's marriage 34–36, 81
  on Haggard's non-fiction writing 21
  on *Way of the Spirit* 105
Haggard, Louisa (Margitson) (wife) 32, 34–36, 100, 107
Haggard, William (father) 24, 25, 128–29
Hall, Leslie 6, 65
Hall, Radclyffe 153
Hardy, Thomas 7, 12, 44, 51

Heart of Darkness (Conrad) 162
The Heart of the World (Haggard) 7, 34, 68, 73, 83, 86, 87
The Heavenly Twins (Grand) 83, 94, 106, 107, 110, 121
Henty, G. A. 15
Higgins, D. S. 2, 30, 35, 36, 78, 100, 105, 126, 128
The Higher Love (Barlow) 117, 120, 121, 135
Himmelfarb, Gertrude 146
Hipsky, Martin 152
Hodder & Stoughton 11
Hogarth, Georgina 89
Holmes, John 6, 120
Hope, Anthony 133
Horton, William T. 103
'The House of Life' (Rossetti) 117, 135
Hurst and Blackett 11
Hutchinson & Co. 11

The Idler 5
The Interpretation of Dreams (Freud) 7

Jackson, Frederick 30
Jackson, John 29
Jackson, Mary Elizabeth (Lilly)
  death of 30–31, 126
  Ella Haggard and 28
  Haggard's relationship with 2, 25, 29–31, 36, 38–39, 100
  influence on Haggard's women characters of 56–58, 104, 128, 129, 141, 143
  marriage to Archer 30
James, Henry 14
Jerome, Jerome K. 157
Jess (Haggard) 3, 38
  biographical resonances in 77–79, 158, 159, 161
  communication of lovers in 138–39
  criticism of 77–79
  emotionally disruptive power of women in 86–87
  female self-sacrifice in 132
  marital relationships in 147
  New Woman fiction and 82–84, 97–98
  romance aspects of 161
  sexual imperative in 95, 150
  sexual potency and passion in 84–85
  spirituality in 96–97, 111, 112, 118, 122–23
Joan Haste (Haggard) 1, 3

biographical resonances in 46–47, 158, 159, 161
consolatory and redemptive women in 69
father figure in 25
female self-sacrifice in 132
male responsibility for sexual sin in 63, 74, 88
marital relationships in 147
mother figure in 28–29
non-marital sexual relations in 70, 94
sexual imperative in 67, 155
sexual vulnerability of women in 53
sins of the father in 68–69
spiritual love and afterlife in 72
woman's sexual potency in 51
John Murray and Stanley Paul & Co. 11
Jude the Obscure (Hardy) 7, 82, 95, 106, 121
J. W. Arrowsmith 11

Katz, Wendy 1, 13, 16, 102, 161
Keating, Peter 52
  on *Blue Lagoon* 151
  on Freud 7
  on Hardy 151
  on literary representations of sexuality 8
  on New Woman novelists 81
  on realism and romance in fiction 12
  on Victorian non-marital relations 148
Keats, John 72
Kegan, Paul, Trench, Trubner 11
Kestner, Joseph 59
Kim (Kipling) 109
King Solomon's Mines (Haggard)
  criticism of 1, 20–21
  juvenile market for 15
  Stevenson's influence on 20
  success of 15
  threats to the male in 58–59, 74
  woman's sexual potency in 5, 49, 156
Kipling, Rudyard 22, 59, 105, 127, 131–32
Kotze, John (Sir) 2

Lady Audley's Secret (Braddon) 6, 47, 55, 73
Lady Chatterley's Lover (Lawrence) 153
Laing, Janet 138
Lang, Andrew 12, 14, 22, 80, 126
Lawrence, D. H. 152–53
Leckie, Barbara 80
Ledger, Sally 6, 81, 95, 106

'Life and Its Author' (E. Haggard) 27
The Life Everlasting (Corelli) 7, 103, 118
The Light That Failed (Kipling) 59
literary criticism
  by Haggard 20
  of Haggard 20–21
Long, John 152
Longman, Charles 15, 80, 105, 127
Longmans, Green & Co. 11
Longman's Magazine 12
Lord Dunchester or The End of Dr Therne: An Autobiography (Phelps) 18
Love Eternal (Haggard) 3, 17
  biographical resonances in 127–29, 154, 158, 161
  communication with the dead in 141–42
  criticism of established church in 145, 146
  dangers of spiritualism in 140–41
  divine and eternal aspects of spiritual love in 138–39
  father figure in 25
  female self-sacrifice in 132–33
  Great War and 133–35
  marital relationships in 147
  mutual spirituality in 138–39
  non-marital sexual relations in 148
  reunion in an afterlife in 139–40
  sexual imperative in 136–38, 142, 148, 153, 154, 155
  spirituality and spiritual union in 103, 125, 131, 135–36
  threat to the male in 142–43
Lysbeth (Haggard) 67, 68, 73, 87, 158

Macmillan's Magazine 38
Maiwa's Revenge (Haggard) 15
Manthorpe, Victoria 25–26, 28, 31, 32, 35, 36
Margitson, Louisa. *See* Haggard, Louisa (Margitson)
marriage
  celibacy as alternative to 106–7
  Haggard's scrutiny of 77, 89, 146–48, 159
  negative depictions of 70–71
  in New Woman fiction 81
  union outside of 5, 8
Marryat, Florence 119
Marryat, Frederick 15
Marshik, Celia 151

Mary of Marion Isle (Haggard) 3
  biographical resonances in 129–30, 154, 158, 159, 160, 161
  criticism of established church in 145
  emotionally disruptive power of women in 143, 155
  father figure in 25
  female self-sacrifice in 132
  marital relationships in 147
  Modernist elements in 125, 150, 151, 152–53, 154
  non-marital relations in 149, 150
  romance aspects of 161–62
  sexual imperative in 94, 131, 149, 150
  spirituality in 136
  union outside marriage in 8
masculinity
  in Haggard's fiction 157
  sexual imperative and 6, 61–65, 74
  in Victorian era 6
  women as threat to 61, 74, 85, 142–45
Mason, Michael 5–6
Masterman, Charles 133
Maurice (Forster) 153
Maxwell, Catherine 120
The Mayor of Casterbridge (Hardy) 19
Mazlish, Bruce 161
McCabe, Joseph 101, 132, 135
Meredith, George 84
Miller, Jane Eldridge 80
Missing (Ward) 139–40
Modernism, Haggard's fiction and 9, 125, 150–54
The Moment After (Buchanan) 103, 119
Montezuma's Daughter (Haggard)
  biographical elements in 33, 46, 62, 130, 158
  first love in 61
  marital relationships in 146
  masculinity in 143
  non-marital sexual relations in 34
  sexual imperative in 65, 67
  sins of the father in 68–69
  spiritual love in 72, 99–100
Moon of Israel (Haggard) 121, 133, 137, 140, 141, 156
Moore, George 46
Morning Star (Haggard) 130, 156
mothers in Haggard's fiction 28–29, 160
Mrs Dalloway (Woolf) 153
Myers, F. W. H. 120

My Lady Nicotine (Barrie) 157
'Myra or The Rose of the East' (E. Haggard) 26

Nada the Lily (Haggard) 47, 51, 53, 59, 141–42
National Anti-Vaccination League 18
National Vigilance Society 152
Nelson, Carolyn 81
New Woman novels
  celibacy in 106, 107, 110
  death and despair in 83
  feminism in 6
  Haggard's novels and 77, 81–84, 97–98
  as threat to marriage 95
non-fiction, Haggard's works of 23
non-marital sexual relations
  in Haggard's novels 79–80, 89–95
  sexual imperative and 148–50
'A Note on Religion' (Haggard) 8, 33, 43, 103

Obscene Publications Act of 1857 8
The Odd Women (Gissing) 95, 106, 110, 121
'Ode on a Grecian Urn' (Keats) 72
O'Gorman, Francis 163
The Old Curiosity Shop (Dickens) 135
Oliphant, Laurence 7, 103, 117
One of Our Conquerors (Meredith) 84, 95
'On Women' (Maeterlinck) 116
otherness, in Haggard's novels 52
Owen, Alex 101

Parsons, Gerald 65
Pearl Maiden (Haggard) 106, 112, 120, 156
Pearson, Richard 61–62
The People of the Mist (Haggard) 62, 71, 73, 147, 158, 159, 161
Phelps, Arthur 18
A Philosopher's Romance (Berwick) 38
The Pickwick Papers (Dickens) 27
The Pilgrim's Progress (Bunyan) 58
Podmore, Frank 101
Porter, Roy 6, 65
Portman, Charlotte Fanny (Lady Poulett) 140
Potter, Jane 133, 135
The Progress of Romance (Reeve) 12
A Psychological Moment (Egerton) 82
psychosexual analysis
  of Haggard's works 1, 7
  in Victorian fiction 7
Pykett, Lyn 41, 68, 73, 81, 83, 84, 94

The Rainbow (Lawrence) 152, 153
'Realism and Romance' (Lang) 14, 22
Realist fiction, definitions of 12
Red Eve (Haggard) 67
Reeve, Clara 12
Regeneration (Haggard) 23
religion
    Haggard and 8–9
    Haggard's criticism of established church 145–46
The Return of the Native (Hardy) 51
reunion in an afterlife, in Haggard's fiction 118–20, 139–40
Reynolds, Stephen 57
Richardson, Angelique 81, 82
Rider, Ethel 31, 32, 33, 34, 68
The Roadmender (Fairless/ Barber) 36
Robinson Crusoe (Defoe) 20
A Romance of Two Worlds (Corelli) 118
Romance fiction
    definitions of 12–15
    Haggard and 15–16, 21–22
Rossetti, Dante Gabriel 6, 103, 117, 135
Rough Diary (Haggard) 33
Rural Denmark (Haggard) 23
Rural England (Haggard) 23

Sacred and Profane Love (Bennett) 152
Saintsbury, George 12, 14
Salvation Army 23
Saturday Review 12, 14, 105
Saunders, Max 8, 57, 159
Schaffer, Talia 70, 159
Schreiner, Olive 81, 82–83
Scientific Religion 118
The Secret of Saint Florel (Berwick) 38
Sedgwick, Eve Kosofsky 157
self-sacrificial women, in Haggard's fiction 132–133
sensation fiction 9
    Haggard's use of the genre 43–44, 45, 73–74
sexual imperative
    in *Colonel Quaritch V.C.* 46
    consequences in Haggard's fiction of 65–68
    in *Dawn* 43
    in final fiction 125
    limitations of spiritual love and 110–16
    in *Love Eternal* 136–38
    masculinity and 61–65, 155–56

    non-marital sexual relations and 148–50
    spirituality and spiritual love and 121–23
    Victorian sexuality and 8
    in *The Witch's Head* 43–44
    women's sexual potency in Haggard's fiction and 48–53, 84–85, 130–32
sexual renunciation
    celibacy and 106–10
    in Haggard's fiction 121–23
Shaw, George Bernard 133
She (Haggard)
    biographical elements in 1, 158, 160
    consequences of sexual imperative in 65
    female sexual potency and vulnerability in 48–53, 156
    focus on women in 6
    gender stereotypes in 47
    Jess in context of 77
    masculinity threatened in 59, 60, 61, 74
    punishment of disruptive women in 58
    realism and romanticism in 161–62
    spiritual love and afterlife in 73
    success of 15–16
She and Allan (Haggard) 133, 141, 142
Shelley, Percy Bysshe 118
Showalter, Elaine 5, 6, 13, 81, 106, 107
Shuttleworth, Sally 89
Smith, Elder & Co. 11
Sons and Lovers (Lawrence) 152, 153
Spiritual Athenaeum 140
spiritualism and spiritual love. *See also* specific works
    capacities and limitations in Haggard's novels of 110–16
    communication between lovers and 118
    communication with the dead and 120–21, 141–42
    contemporary interest in 100–1
    dangers of 140–41
    divine and eternal aspects of 138–39
    female power and divinity and 116–18
    Great War and 132–33
    in Haggard's fiction 3, 5, 7, 17, 71–73, 96–98, 121–23, 135–36
    mutual spirituality and 138–39
    reunion in an afterlife and 118–20, 139–40
    sexual imperative and 121–23
Stacpoole, H. De Vere 151
Stella Fregelius (Haggard) 3, 17
    biographical resonances in 103–5, 158, 159, 161

Stella Fregelius (Haggard) *(cont.)*
   capacities and limitations of spirituality in
      110, 111, 112, 114
   celibacy in 106, 107, 110
   communication with the dead in
      120–21, 141–42
   criticism of established church in 145
   dangers of spiritualism in 140–41
   father figure in 25
   female power and divinity in 118, 125
   religion in 27
   reunion in an afterlife and 120
   sexual imperative in 137–38, 155
   spiritual intimacy in 118, 138–39
   spiritual love in 96, 99, 100, 102, 103,
      121–23, 136
Stevenson, Randall 132
Stevenson, Robert Louis 12, 14, 157
   Haggard and 15, 19, 22
Stiebel, Lindy 2, 150
Stiles, Anne 118
Stoker, Bram 7, 85, 157
storms, imagery in Haggard's
   novels of 92
The Story of An African Farm (Schreiner) 81,
   83, 106
Strange Case of Doctor Jekyll and Mr. Hyde
   (Stevenson) 19, 157
Swallow (Haggard)
   communication between lovers in 138
   spiritual love in 99, 156
Swedenborg, Emanuel 7, 101, 103, 112, 120

A Tale of Two Cities (Dickens) 20
Tess of the D'Urbervilles (Hardy) 44, 46, 89
Thackeray, William Makepeace 55
There Is No Death (Marryat) 119
There Remaineth a Rest (Haggard draft) 43
Three Essays on the Theory of Sexuality
   (Freud) 7
Three Men in a Boat (Jerome) 157
The Three Musketeers (Dumas) 20
Times Literary Supplement 104, 105, 127
'To Gertrude in the Spirit World' (Barlow)
   119, 120
To the Lighthouse (Woolf) 153
Treasure Island (Stevenson) 14, 15, 20
The Treasure of the Humble (Barlow) 116
Trilby (Du Maurier) 157
Trollope, Anthony 6, 18, 55
Trubner & Co. 11, 20

Vaccination Act of 1898 18
Vanity Fair (Thackeray) 55
Victorian era
   eroticism in fiction of 8
   reunion in an afterlife and 119
   revival of romance fiction in 12
   sensation novels of 41
   sexual relations in 6
   spiritualism in 101
   'Woman Question' in 5
The Virgin of the Sun (Haggard) 143, 146, 154,
   156, 158
'A Visit to the Chief Secocoeni' (Haggard) 20

Wales, Hubert 152
Wallace, Diana 88, 150
Waller, Philip 133, 137
The Wanderer's Necklace (Haggard) 130, 143, 156
Ward, Humphry (Mrs.) 139–40
Ward Lock & Co. 11
Watson, William 21
Watt, A. P. 17, 104, 105
Watts-Dunton, Theodore 7, 103, 116, 120
The Way of the Spirit (Haggard) 3, 17, 22, 100
   biographical resonances in 105–6, 129, 158,
      159, 160, 161
   capacities and limitations of spirituality in
      110, 112, 113, 114
   celibacy in 106, 107, 108, 110, 121–22
   father figure in 25
   marital relationships in 147
   mother figure in 28–29
   non-marital sexual relations in 34
   romance aspects of 161–62
   sexual imperative in 156
   spiritual love in 99, 103, 118, 142, 155
A Well-Remembered Voice (Barrie) 141
Wells, H. G. 133, 152
The Well of Loneliness (Hall) 153
Wheeler, Michael 101, 119
When the World Shook (Haggard)
   biographical resonances in 158, 160, 161
   communication with the dead in 141
   criticism of established Church in 146
   dangers of spiritualism in 141
   Great War and 132, 133, 134
   sexual imperative in 135–36, 137–38, 156
Wilson, Nicola 152
Wisdom's Daughter (Haggard) 131–32, 148, 149,
   150, 153–54, 156, 162
The Witch's Head (Haggard) 2, 3

biographical resonances in 43–44, 126, 158, 159, 161
consequences of sexual imperative in 67
consolatory and redemptive women in 69
criticism of established church in 145
emotionally disruptive power of women in 59, 60, 61, 74, 143, 144, 155, 157
father figure in 25
marriage in 73, 147
negative depictions of marriage in 70
punishment of disruptive women in 56, 57
sexual vulnerability in 54, 129, 130, 131
spiritual love and afterlife in 72, 119–20, 140, 141–42
woman's sexual potency in 49, 131
Woman Regained (Barlow) 7
The Woman in White (Collins) 73, 155
The Woman Thou Gavest Me (Caine) 152
The Woman Who Did (Allen) 82, 83, 95
women
  consolatory and redemptive women, Haggard's presentation of 69–70
  destructive impact on men of 58–61
  disruptive women, punishment in Haggard's fiction of 54–58
  in Haggard's fiction 5–7, 9, 77, 156–57, 160–61
  self-sacrifice by, in Haggard's fiction 132–33
  sexual potency and vulnerability of 48–54, 84–85, 86, 125, 130–32
  stereotypes in Haggard's fiction of 47–48
Wood, Ellen 6, 45
Woolf, Virginia 153
The World's Desire (Lang & Haggard) 22, 34, 46, 47, 126
  biographical elements in 158
  consequences of sexual imperative in 67–68, 156
  femme fatale in 55
  gender stereotypes in 47
  masculinity threatened in 59, 60, 61, 62, 63, 64, 74, 162
  negative depictions of marriage in 70, 89
  sexual vulnerability of women in 53
  spiritual love and afterlife in 72, 96
  woman's sexual potency in 50, 51, 53, 86, 156

The Yellow God (Haggard) 86, 130, 143, 156
The Yoke (Wales) 152
Young, Shannon 6, 7, 55, 160

'A Zulu War Dance' (Haggard) 19

www.ingramcontent.com/pod-product-compliance
Lightning Source LLC
Chambersburg PA
CBHW021828300426
44114CB00009BA/362